THE STRUGGLE FOR HUMAN RIGHTS IN LATIN AMERICA

Edward L. Cleary

Westport, Connecticut
London

Library of Congress Cataloging-in-Publication Data

Cleary, Edward L.
The struggle for human rights in Latin America / Edward L. Cleary.
p. cm.
Includes bibliographical references and index.
ISBN 0–275–95980–5 (alk. paper).—ISBN 0–275–95981–3 (pbk. : alk. paper)
1. Human rights—Latin America. I. Title.
JC599.L3C58 1997
323'.098—dc21 97–5580

British Library Cataloguing in Publication Data is available.

Library of Congress Catalog Card Number: 97–5580
ISBN: 0–275–95980–5
0–275–95981–3 (pbk.)

First published in 1997

Praeger Publishers, 88 Post Road West, Westport, CT 06881
An imprint of Greenwood Publishing Group, Inc.

Printed in the United States of America

The paper used in this book complies with the Permanent Paper Standard issued by the National Information Standards Organization (Z39.48–1984).

10 9 8 7 6 5 4 3 2 1

Contents

Preface

A few years ago the president of Mexico was spending the end of the year at Huatulco. Carlos Salinas de Gotari, his wife, and three children spent the day before New Year's at the presidential resort on Mexico's Pacific coast. They swam and sunbathed, languishing on a day when privileged Mexicans did as little as possible. In the evening they were joined by Donaldo Colosio and family. Colosio, named presidential candidate by Salinas, enjoyed the president's deepest confidences.

The families ate turkey done in high-Aztec style and seafood delicacies, traditional for the end-of-the-year meal. Bottles of Dom Perignon champagne were opened. By 2:00 A.M., not very late by Mexican standards, a military attaché asked the president to come aside.[1] An unknown paramilitary group had opened hostilities in Chiapas, to the far south. Mexico would never be the same.

In Boston and Minneapolis computer printers were delivering messages *simultaneously* as the uprising was taking place. Within hours, some 1,300 e-mail messages had passed back and forth between Mexico and the United States. Remembering how the Mexican security forces had wiped out more than 300 demonstrators in 1968, Mexicans and their friends in the United States were desperately working to avert wholesale massacre. Human rights organizing had gone high-tech.

At 12:30 A.M. in the high-mountain cold, armed men and women, faces hidden by bandanas and ski masks, had begun occupying the central plaza of San Cristóbal de Las Casas. At the head of the group, Subcomandante Marcos began with a ceremonial and loud ''Feliz Año Nuevo'' and delivered the rebels' central message: They were protesting NAFTA (the North American Free Trade Agreement), which President Salinas made effective at midnight. They were also mounting a protest about the heightened social inequities that doomed millions of Mexicans to lives of poverty and social exclusion.

Perhaps some 150 soldiers, police, and civilians were killed in the ensuing violence. Hundreds of Mexicans and Americans hurried to the area. Others set to work in New York, Washington, D.C., and Mexico City. A shield of human rights defenders averted a further bloodbath. Human rights advocates placed themselves between two violent forces. Nonviolent themselves, they understood well that repressive control is embedded in a context of broad economic inequalities and a system of profoundly asymmetrical social relations. Human rights violations are not new; what Latin Americans are doing about them is new.

Chiapas brought prominence to surface events. Quietly, Mexicans had been creating a human rights movement for ten years. From three groups in 1984 the Mexican human rights movement had grown to some 300 groups in 1994. These groups, large and small, regional and national, wanted a different Mexico. Why now, after centuries of human rights violations, are Mexicans, Brazilians, and Central Americans defending human rights? This volume attempts to address the reasons why they have joined in an often dangerous enterprise. Why this matters to Latin Americans and to citizens of the United States is also considered.

This book began in 1969 when, returning to Latin America after four years absence, the author found violence against ordinary citizens becoming systematic. Torture and beatings by police and security forces had been episodic, a way to control the worst criminals. Now high school and university student demonstrators in Santa Cruz and Cochabamba were not sent home after a short detention. Families found they were beaten and sent away to remote camps. Worse, parents sometimes could not locate their children.

When asked, police and army officers, who were social friends from such occasions as baseball games, would say only: "The Brazilians have been here." Unravelling the mystery of large-scale military repression began my journey, which went on for years. After 1989, many observers put their books on the Latin American military in the basement. General Augusto Pinochet was packing up his goods from the presidential palace in Chile. President Ronald Reagan moved on, reducing the U.S. military pressures on Central America.

In New England, snow days are welcomed, bringing a free agenda. During three snow days at Yale in 1992, time was available to look again at what was supposed to be a moribund topic: What was going on in the human rights groups that had been active in Latin America? I expected to find little, and set aside only four pages to cover the topic within a chapter focusing on Latin American politics after the military.

Within hours, a wide, technologically sophisticated universe opened up. An explosion of human rights organizing was taking place in Latin America. Few Americans were paying attention. Those who were devoting time to the issue represented a new generation of human rights advocates in the United States. The center of human rights activity in New Haven had shifted from the grassroots organizing for the Nicaragua Sister City project to the emphasis on law and technology through the Yale Law School and the Diana computer net.

Rather than being limited to account after account of torture and killing, the story which unfolded became one of hope. Thousands of Latin Americans and their allies felt that something substantial, beyond defense of individuals, was being accomplished by taking a stand about human rights.

The accounts which follow are fundamentally political, dealing with contests of power and policymaking. People organize with their friends and acquaintances to mount protests against governmentally sponsored or permitted violence. Movement members struggle with press and television about how to frame the meaning of what they are doing. Clashes occur over ways and means, laws, and appropriations of money.

The motivations which drive human rights leaders and workers often can only be surmised. Many persons clearly have entered the contest because they learned about social Christianity in small Christian communities. Others would only say that for them the step from inertia to action was huge; they likened it to a step on the moon. The step from passivity to helping foreigners is even greater. When asked, the Argentine activist Emilio Mignone said: ''The defense of human dignity knows no boundaries.'' That provides the major thread of this work.

NOTE

1. This account is found in Mexican published sources and is reported by John Ross in *Rebellion from the Roots: Indian Uprising in Chiapas* (Monroe, Me.: Common Courage Press, 1995), pp. 1–14.

Acknowledgments

Resources and encouragement from Providence College's administration and political science department and the Yale University Center for International and Area Studies sustained my efforts at various stages. Administrators who fostered this scholarship include Carol Hartley, Thomas McGonigle, Thomas Canavan, Nancy Ruther, and James Carlson. A grant from Providence College through its Committee to Aid Faculty Research made research in Argentina and Brazil possible.

Robert Trudeau and John Gitlitz, co-chairs of the Latin American Studies Association's Task Force on Human Rights, offered valuable comments. Alexander Wilde, Virginia Bouvier, and others at the Washington Office on Latin America, Human Rights Watch, and Amnesty International aided in the chronology of events. So, too, did Lawrence Hall, Steven Fought, and Thomas Bruneau, who were familiar with the U.S. and Latin American militaries.

A network of social researchers led me through the puzzle of social movements, beginning with Carol Lee. Then Sidney Tarrow, Margaret Keck, Margaret Crahan, Alison Brysk, Thomas Greaves, Kay Warren, LaVonne Poteet, Phillip Berryman, and Michelle Mood added their valuable comments. Rodolfo Stavenhagen (Mexico), Roberto Cuéllar (Central America), Kevin Goonan (Peru), Geraldo Whelan (Chile), and Paulo Sergio Pinheiro, Richard Pelczar, and Jack Hammond (Brazil) helped immeasurably in the interpretation of events.

Shaping the work editorially benefitted greatly from comments by John Harney, James Sabin, and editors at Praeger Publishers. Unusually competent and creative research assistance came from Michelle Schrieber and Erica Morse.

Travels of four years took me to Chile, Argentina, Brazil, Peru, Guatemala, Costa Rica, and Mexico. Centers of human rights, national and regional movement headquarters, grassroots workers, and newspaper editors there and in Washington and London generously aided research. I am deeply grateful to them and to the Dominican and other communities in North and Latin America for their hospitality and support.

1

Beginning of the Human Rights Era: Military Repression

When the human rights era began in Latin America, it came with explosive force.[1] In Chile, Hawker Hunter planes, tanks with heavy automatic weapons, and soldiers with small arms directed rockets and bullets at the presidential palace. On September 11, 1973, military commanders wanted to do away with President Salvador Allende Gossens and his elected government. Allende brought his own end, turning a carbine on himself. Fidel Castro gave him the weapon.

A cloud of military governance now covered Chile. This was not supposed to happen. Civilian rule and civic tradition had been the norms in Chile. Since 1932, the military had restrained itself within barracks walls.[2] No longer. Military and civilian collaborators installed authoritarian control of the country.

Military rule now covered all but two South American countries and all but one Central American country. Brazil, the largest Latin American country, and Bolivia, among the smallest, suffered military takeovers in 1964. Other countries followed in the 1960s and 1970s. The regimes of the 1960s were considered soft dictatorships (*dictablandas*). Later regimes became brutally harsh. Chile offers a clear example not only of what human rights violations occurred in many countries, but also shows the tortuous path and resolute response to human rights violations, as seen in the history which follows.

MILITARY TAKEOVER: REPRESSION

In terms of fighting, the dramatic storming of the presidential palace did not signal wide-scale conflict. Resistance to military takeover by armed leftists was sporadic and generally terminated within a brief period. Some military planners anticipated a generalized internal war with many casualties. Instead, persons killed in the initial conflicts numbered more than a hundred civilians and less than a hundred military and police. Small opposition *focos* hid out and continued hit-and-run tactics for some months, but they formed nothing like a unified force.

Chileans had little notion of a military takeover. The military and police turning on civilians, picking them up and detaining them without warrant, was unknown to most Chileans.[3] Arbitrary state repression touched many families. Further, to be detained or to have a relative detained in a law-abiding country caused social isolation.[4]

Uniformed men snatched Chileans and foreigners from streets, offices, and classrooms. Security forces typically showed no warrant nor offered explanations for arrests. Military men and police gave commands and did not answer questions. Security forces herded thousands into vans and cars. They drove many prisoners to unknown destinations. (Relatives and friends would spend years looking for, often not finding, many detainees.)

The National Stadium became a symbol for change in politics and for conflict over popular culture. Security forces took 7,000 Chileans and foreigners from vehicles, led or dragged them up stairs of the stadium, and placed them at intervals on spectator benches. Four years earlier, in the basketball stadium, Víctor Jara won the first festival of "Nueva Canción," music associated with Allende's government.[5] Now, in the large National Stadium, military men broke his fingers and wrists, riddled his body with bullets.[6]

Other thousands picked up in the first days of the takeover were briefly held in city jails or barracks. Then the army moved many of them to harsh imprisonment in military camps. The navy alternated between penning its share of prisoners below decks or displaying them on open decks.

Security forces searched widely, seized property, and snatched persons from the streets or their homes throughout metropolitan Santiago, the national center of political activity. (The congress has since moved to Valparaíso.) Military and police forces also rounded up many civilians in Chile's south. In cities like Concepción and rural areas like Paine, support for Allende's Unidad Popular was strong.

As time passed, observers watched as military leaders targeted leftist politicians and their supporters. The force of their blows fell heavily on the lower classes. In Paine, peasants and low-level leaders were taken to a remote area, shot, and buried in a common grave. Military authorities accorded the political class better treatment. Fifty national leaders—senators, ministers of government, and others of the socialist *gente decente*—were transported in stages to Dawson Island's wasteland. Most of them managed to stay alive, although scarred in one fashion or other.

More than 7,000 of those pursued by the government escaped the country in the early days of the coup. Other hundreds sought asylum in embassies. They were fleeing not only arbitrary imprisonment but death. The military shot 200 leftist militants in military camps. Foreigners who came to Chile as a haven from repression in their own countries or who had been attracted by the promise of Allende's democratic socialism became especially vulnerable. Security forces detained many of them, summarily executing a sufficient number to increase widespread panic.

ORGANIZING: FIRST WAVE

Chileans matched the scale of repression with exceptional response. No country generated a human rights movement more quickly or more appropriately than Chile. Within days, Chileans began pulling together. Military strategists in late-twentieth-century Latin America designed takeovers to atomize society. The strength of Chile's civil society began quickly to work in counter trend.

A social movement was developing.[7] Its membership was never large and its existence was precarious. The following sections describe several waves of expansion.[8] A perspective from social movement theory guides the discussion; thus we look for seizing political opportunities, mobilizing resources, mounting challenges to the government, and the interplay of political forces and institutions.

In contrast, citizens of other countries under military repression mounted only scattered initial responses. In Argentina and elsewhere, individuals and families reacted as best they could. In Chile citizens formed organizations rapidly through churches, which were the one institution left standing with their civil rights largely intact. Within days Catholics and some Protestants organized themselves into two groups. Committee One looked after foreigners who had come to the country to work for the Frei or Allende governments. Committee Two worked for the protection and care of Chileans. Both committees sought as their priority safe passage to exile of persons threatened with incarceration, rather than detention or death.

A larger organizational force emerged from these efforts. Within three weeks of the takeover, Chileans created the pivotal organization, the Committee for Cooperation for Peace in Chile (COPACHI). The Catholic, Methodist, Evangelical Lutheran, and Methodist Pentecostal churches, Rabbinical college, and World Council of Churches were the founding members. Catholic Bishop Fernando Ariztía and Lutheran Bishop Helmut Frenz stood as the strong copresidents.[9] Brian Smith and others have ably traced the human rights efforts of churches as institutions.[10] Here I examine the organizations directly dealing with human rights concerns and the movement which grew from their efforts.

The largest number of persons detained by the military were members of Allende's party or other groups on the left. Many civilian judges had little sympathy for the accused and their ideological leanings. Further, to bypass the normal Chilean judicial processes, military courts were set up in cities and villages throughout the country. Authorities brought some 3,000 Chileans to judgment before these military tribunals.

Lawyers associated with COPACHI often were Christian Democrats. They had to defend many persons who had been their political enemies. About ten full-time lawyers, with some 40 associate lawyers, assumed the heavy load of cases. These counselors investigated charges made against the accused, assessed allegations, and prepared defenses, often under great stress. Sometimes they had only hours for preparation before hearings. Often military judges had no legal experience and were hostile to civilian attorneys. Working long hours, COPACHI staff looked into thousands of cases and, when possible, filed habeas corpus petitions.

From Organization to Movement

Like other social movements, the human rights movement in Chile was born not only out of need but out of opportunity. At first, movement members sought public shelter and space to organize. Then they felt impelled to mount a challenge to government repression. The military government severely curtailed public activity, imposing a state of siege. This condition reinforced the government's ability to withhold information and to suppress, if possible, denunciations of its massive violations of civil procedures. However, the military dared not systematically attack religious institutions, which enjoyed high social prestige in Chile. Catholics and non-Catholics, believers, agnostics, and a few atheists were drawn to the one protected political space available, COPACHI. "When it is raining, everybody can stand under the same large umbrella," many informants later recalled.[11] The COPACHI thus offered the only systematic source of protest against arbitrary governmental actions in Chilean society.

The military did not directly attack COPACHI in the first year. Instead, it conducted full-scale defamatory campaigns, detentions, torture, and threats against its members. Prominence was no guarantee of untouchability. Security forces detained and sent to exile lawyer José Zalaquett; Bishop Frenz became a target of government repression. Fifty employees or associates of COPACHI in Santiago or the provinces were detained, some remaining in prison for months. Two hundred priests and sisters, many of them collaborators with COPACHI, were exiled.

COPACHI opened offices throughout the country. As much as possible, it reinforced work of local groups, as small communities within parishes. Committee members enlarged their work beyond denunciation and legal defense to social work. By December 1975, COPACHI aided 40,000 persons with legal and other assistance, provided basic medical care for 70,000 persons, and helped to feed 35,000 children daily.

While many persons made their way openly to the central office at Santa Mónica 2424, in a nondescript section of Santiago, and to provincial offices, an informal underground also functioned. As leftist-opposition leaders fled from government searchers they were sometimes passed from one private home to another in poor neighborhoods. Movement members cautiously moved them from house to house to asylum at the Papal Nuncio's or other foreign embassy residences in Santiago and then to safe passage out of the country. Movement activists believed detection was sure death for many of those fleeing.

The initial period of mobilizing legal challenges and caring for victims continued through the first two years of military dictatorship. The last months of the second year, 1975, brought the celebrated case of Sheila Cassidy. Dr. Cassidy, an English Catholic volunteer, was working at Emergency Care Post 3 on the western edge of Santiago. Friends asked her to go to a private residence to care for a leftist leader, wounded in a confrontation with security forces. Later, when government forces closed in on the hunted man, Cassidy was swept in as part of the conspiracy. Security forces placed her in solitary confinement, brutally treated, and raped her.

In the interrogations she identified two priests, including Father Gerald Whelan, director of renowned St. George's College, as having offered overnight room and board to the injured man or associates. Security men picked up Whelan and another priest and placed them in solitary confinement.[12] In the confrontation between church and state which followed, Cardinal Silva said he would hide fugitives under his own bed if necessary.[13] Officials of the Vatican, Father William Lewers of the Congregation of the Holy Cross, the British government, and others obtained the release of the prisoners.

This form of transnational support for the human rights movement was effective but episodic. Foreign agencies typically played a more systematic role in the human rights movement in Chile and Latin America. Their help took many forms and helped to shape the movement. From the first days of the military takeover, the World Council of Churches played a prominent part in the work of Committee One and Two and COPACHI. But many other transnational agencies brought millions of Austrian and German marks and American dollars to back Chilean efforts to defend citizens and to mount protest.

At the time (1975), the military's economic model was not yet fully in place. The Chilean military did not then see itself as fully fitting into the world economic system, nor had the political views of the generals moved beyond control. Manuel Antonio Garretón, Chile's leading political scientist, remarked: ''Prior to 1978 . . . [there was] neither innovation nor new rules of the game, but only repression, dismantling, and immobility.''[14]

In sum, churches formed the ''early risers'' in the human rights movement. They were virtually the only political actors sharing a space in the public arena dominated by the military. As Garretón says: ''Almost total silence [existed] within Chilean society, the exceptions being the voices of the church and those sectors under its protection.''[15] The human rights movement became the small and limited but singular and organized voice of protest. It mounted a systematic challenge to arbitrary exercise of power.

Governmental Counterattack

The intensity of Pinochet's and the military's fury over this opposition intensified. Government leaders probed for weakness in the movement. Some Chilean Lutherans, socialized in the ''government knows best'' ideology, became increasingly restive with Bishop Frenz's leadership as co-chair of COPACHI.[16] The government observed (and may have fostered) church divisions and Frenz's vulnerability. In October 1975 it attacked. When Frenz left the country to seek international support for COPACHI and other works, he found his reentry to the country blocked.

Pinochet next attacked COPACHI directly. In a letter to Cardinal Raúl Silva Henríquez, Pinochet called it "an instrument used by Marxists-Leninists to create problems directed at altering the tranquillity of the citizenry."[17] Silva replied that the dissolution of COPACHI would bring greater harm to the country.

Nimbly, in November and December 1975, the churches acted to reorganize. As movement leaders, church officials divided human rights activities among church groups. In Santiago, Cardinal Silva quickly took the main thrust of the human rights work under direct Catholic Church protection. He and clever associates created the Vicariate of Solidarity (Vicariate). They made the Vicariate a formally organized church office like none else in the world. Further, Silva established the central office in the most prominent place imaginable in Santiago, the Plaza de Armas, next to the cathedral. This was January 1, 1976, just weeks after Pinochet's letter.

Protestant churches, those who wished to continue, gradually formed the Foundation for Social Help of the Christian Churches (FASIC). The Foundation had a more traditional caste and appealed to conservative church members in Chile and their counterparts in international funding agencies, especially European ones. But, in the bundle of FASIC's activities were ones implicitly critical of the regime: help to political prisoners and psychological treatment to victims of torture.

Resource Mobilization

The division of labor did not imply that most Catholics were progressive and most Protestants conservative. The leadership judged that the Catholic Church, given its size and social standing in Chile, could play a more conflictive role. Individual Chileans, whatever their political or social proclivities, joined its protest and stood under its protective, sometimes leaky, umbrella.

Movement groups especially mobilized many persons previously active in lay Catholic movements. During the 1950s and 1960s the Chilean Catholic Church organized and trained many lay persons "for action in the world," especially through Catholic Action. By the late 1950s experienced Catholic Action members numbered almost 50,000.[18] Thus priests and lay persons formed long-term bonds through Chile's lay movements. More broadly, church officials and Christian Democrat and other party leaders had formed bonds through friendship, family, and school associations. Human rights organizers used these ties to recruit new members.

By many accounts, Christian Precht was the ideal priest to act as a main liaison for the Catholic Church in this work.[19] He attended St. George's College, where he gained a wide circle of friends who became leaders at universities and later in the professions and party politics. His family was well connected in these circles. Precht also honed his motivational skills, acting as mentor in Catholic lay movements.[20]

The legal and social service workloads at the Vicariate brought increased demands for lawyers and staff personnel in central offices. The church began expanding its efforts to inform parish and neighborhood groups about human rights. Salaries for core members were low; associates often worked as unpaid volunteers. A number of lawyers and professionals from middle-and upper-middle-class backgrounds responded to the mobilization.

So, too, did lawyers and human rights workers from differing backgrounds join in. Gloria Torres, a 22-year-old lawyer, had become a law-abiding Marxist at a state university in the pre-coup days. She was drawn to COPACHI because "the suffering and the injustices visited upon hundreds of those detained was so great I felt compelled to join the Committee for Peace."[21] She eventually became part of a Vicariate group working out of a branch office in the eastern section of Santiago. Her small group included a Dutch priest, Nicolás Cumen; an older nun, Mercedes Chaín; and a social worker, Gloria Cruz.

The small team went out to meetings in parishes to explain their work. But Torres noted that "people were so terrified by the events after the coup and so isolated from one another that they did not know what was happening."[22] Mothers or wives of the disappeared, unable to engage lawyers, began trickling into the COPACHI offices. Neighbors who had been at the parish meetings advised them to seek out its services. Hearsay became the principal vehicle for drawing people to human rights assistance.

A larger corps of part-time volunteers joined in the work after daytime jobs. Priests, sisters, and lay persons worked doggedly to bring victims of repression and their families to Vicariate professionals. Gerald Whelan, as teacher and parish priest, heard of hundreds of former students and current parishioners harmed by the repression. He referred a constant stream of those needing assistance to Torres and other Vicariate lawyers and social workers. "He was our No. 1 bridge-builder," recalled Torres.[23]

Torres herself grew to understand profoundly the plight of persons seeking legal help for freeing their relatives or obtaining information about their death or disappearance. In the seventeen years Torres worked for COPACHI and the Vicariate, she lost two husbands who were "disappeared." Neither her employment as a church worker nor her status as daughter of a Carabinero official ensured protection from government repression.

The Vicariate appeared to be speaking for the Chilean national church. Many observers thus depicted the organization. But the Vicariate represented the church of Santiago. Churches in other regions created offices with similar names. However, the 4,000 kilometers of Chile's geography contained other dioceses, with bishops whose political proclivities differed with Cardinal Silva's. Some, as the archbishop of Chile's second city, did not establish a vicariate nor look favorably on special care for leftists. However, FASIC, as an ecumenical and not a specifically Catholic institution, established an office in Valparaíso.[24]

The Vicariate and Silva achieved national symbolic leadership. Vicariate publications, such as *Solidaridad*, reinforced this status. Precht and other collaborators brought circulation of the magazine to 20,000; for some years *Solidaridad* was the largest printed source of opposition to regime tactics. Writing, printing, and distributing required courageous staff. Precht helped to anchor the organization as its first vicar.

The budding human rights movement increasingly centered its challenge to Pinochet's government in Santiago. The church of Santiago offered protection for intellectuals who created a program in human rights at Academia de Humanismo Cristiano[25] and its journal, *Revista Chilena de Derechos Humanos*. This magazine became an expression of the growing maturity of the movement.[26] Centered, too, in Santiago, leaders of FASIC, the ecumenical church group, formed and reformed committees and structures to meet needs of families and detainees, foreign and national.[27] They formalized their organizations by legal conventions to respond to attacks on individual Protestant activists.[28]

SECOND WAVE

Within these church organizations movement members began to foster new organizations. Patricio Orellana has called these groups the second generation of human rights organizations. Family affinity served as the basis for recruitment and resource mobilization against military repression. These groups projected images of grieving widows and mothers, of being victims. At first glance, government leaders assessed them as weak, with little possible impact in oppositional politics.[29] Their challenge to military rule would develop only slowly.

Family members of persons disappeared or imprisoned made up the first two groups of this generation. ''Disappeared'' was a new and despicable violation of human rights in Chile and Latin America. Under the old rules of the political game, exile or imprisonment were the typical punishments. Under Chilean repression, disappearance meant that family or friends could never put to rest their fears or hopes for the lost person. Disappearance was like a wound that never healed, and it altered the lives of thousands of relatives and friends and the victims.

Families of other types of victims, especially of exile or internal banishment, also sought the assistance of COPACHI. Families of victims made daily trips to COPACHI. Lawyers assigned to their cases and family members went through the bureaucratic steps thought necessary to obtain information about the lost or detained. In previous eras of Chilean history bureaucratic procedures might have seemed endless but typically yielded some results; this time the military and police attempted to maintain a wall of silence and noncooperation.

To aid the families of victims, a priest and a sister began small group meetings with family members. These became groups of Christian reflection on the grief they were suffering. Group members at first offered support to one another; little by little, group members turned outward. Members of these small groups created the first formal organization as the Association of Family Members of the Detained-Disappeared (AFDD).[30] In 1974 this group began to take shape forcefully. Another set of members of the reflection groups organized a little later as the Association of Family Members of Political Prisoners.[31] Then four other groups emerged, representing the exiled, the executed, the banished, and the children of adult victims.[32] The groups addressed specific legal and psychological needs of victims, and went on to press pointed political demands against the government. Chileans thus achieved a level of specialization of human rights groups, as did few other countries.

Central to these human rights groups was the conflict over language and discourse they waged with the government. They forged a battle over the words ''detained-disappeared.'' The government would only allow public use of ''presumed,'' denying that detentions had taken place. Further, government officials accused relatives of causing problems for the government for mischievous political motives. Family members who persisted—and most of them did—often found themselves victims of whispering campaigns in their neighborhoods and falsehoods in newspapers. Police and other security forces periodically harassed them, throwing some members in jail more than fifteen times.

Despite harassment, the groups held steady. Membership grew as the government-declared status of many victims shifted from the detained to ''disappeared.'' Although many relatives joined initially for family reasons, many soon engaged fully in political challenge. Some wives and mothers shared the socialist or Communist convictions of their husbands or children (thereby being diminished in the eyes of many Chileans), but the majority were women with no political experience. They learned quickly.

Members of the groups typically followed the political repertoire common to protest movements in other countries. They borrowed heavily from the repertoire of nonviolence. The groups of family members did not choose active nonviolence as a doctrinaire position; rather, the theme migrated to Chile through the regional ecumenical group, Service for Peace and Justice (SERPAJ). This group, founded by Nobel prizewinner Adolfo Pérez Esquivel, established chapters widely in Latin America. Their tactics, such as peaceful demonstrations and passive resistance to arrest, crossed easily across national boundaries.

The Association of Relatives of the Detained-Disappeared (AFDD) became the core group for several prominent acts, unusual for the time. In 1977, AFDD members and other human rights activists chained themselves to the gates of the Economic Commission for Latin America building. They carried on an extensive hunger strike. Later they chained themselves to the gates of the Ministry of Justice. They went on pilgrimage to Lonquén, the site of a presumed massacre of prisoners in 1978. AFDD members thus began a long series of public and confrontational events. Some challenges to governmental cover-ups brought sad revelations. Tracing sites of mass graves uncovered remains of relatives and other victims of military slaughter. Nonetheless, AFDD members made Lonquén, Laja, and Yumbel stinging denunciations of the government.

Church pastors continued to offer support for AFDD and similar family member groups. In turn, the family groups extended their outreach, opening branches in various parts of the country. They affiliated internationally with FEDEFAM, a Latin American group claiming to represent family members of 90,000 disappeared in Latin America.

THIRD WAVE

The human rights movement continued to fit like a hand into the glove of opportunity. Prominent Chileans began forming three new, influential groups as early as 1978. The government severely limited political parties after the takeover; Pinochet's administration formally outlawed the parties in 1977. In many Latin American countries, personalities such as Alberto Fuijimori in Peru or Carlos Menem in Argentina dominated politics. In Chile, organized political parties were the principal players. Their legal removal from the political scene had been unthinkable to Chileans and, most of all, to the political party leaders.

Members of rightist parties mostly disbanded their organizations and often joined in the military government. Party members from the center and left went underground. National leaders managed to maintain structures of the parties and contacts with local bosses. The parties would emerge, in time, from the long period of military government with virtually the same cadres intact, but their faces in newspaper photos would be aged seventeen years. This story has not been fully told, but part of party members' survival is owed to spaces found for communication within church structures, national and local.

Party leaders needed greater political independence than church affiliation would allow them. The Chilean church had debated within itself for decades about remaining "above politics."[33] In short, church organizations were too religious to satisfy the political ambitions of the center and left parties. Party leaders wished to probe how far they could go in mounting challenges to Pinochet. The military government was vulnerable on the question of illegality; opponents could realistically challenge the constitutionality of its regime. They could protest the nonobservance of law and civil rights. The churches had shown political parties for some time that this challenge could be mounted, although at a cost.

The newest human rights organizations responded to a widely accepted Chilean tradition: Challenges to the government are best mounted when not religious. The churches had protected individuals and sponsored human rights activities in the first years of the movement (1973–1978). The new groups had impulses which were lay and secular in character, not anticlerical. Indeed, many members were priests, now engaged as citizens.

The most important new group was the Chilean Commission for Human Rights (CCHDH). By 1985 it grew to 1,500 members with branch offices in 30 cities and many local committees. Of all the Latin American human rights organizations of the period, the CCHDH may have become the one with the greatest scope. Membership was highly diverse. Lawyers furnished the initial and eventually dominant impulse. But Hugo Frühling found three principal groups among the members: a showcase directorate[34] with a wide range of prominent persons from the arts, academic, labor, and other spheres; "distinguished" ex-cabinet members from the Frei Christian Democrat government (1964–1970); and largely unknown leaders from smaller parties. The organization opened a very wide umbrella to embrace "all ideologies, except those antagonistic to human rights."[35]

Mixing of law and politics as professions is especially common in Chile. The CCHDH presented itself as primarily lawyers working in defense of human rights. Its scope was broader than that of the Vicariate and FASIC; it handled many legal aspects of human rights cases, as did the church groups. It also added its weight to the denunciation of rights violations. The CCHDH was especially suited for the *denuncia*, whereas the Vicariate did not emphasize this as a systematic practice.[36] The Latin American practice of making denunciations, although too often used, can be a solemn event, similar to the medieval practice of posting theses. *Denuncia* points to grave nonobservance of public trust. A challenge to the government was thus issued.

Pinochet's government responded adroitly to this impressive array of lawyers. The government had finished its first era of indiscriminate repression and its second stage of selective repression and spectacular deeds (the Letelier bombing in Washington and the Leighton attempted assassination in Rome).[37] Pinochet's regime now adjusted more directly to the human rights challenge being mounted. Faced with legal challenges, the government attempted to influence public discourse about what was legitimate, what was just in Chilean society. The government also changed the basic rules of the game.

This it did by submitting a new constitution to a plebiscite in 1980, promulgating and making it effective as of March 1981. Pinochet thus gained legal basis to employ repression of various kinds without judicial control. For the time being, too, conventional forms of legal defense were done away with. Pinochet also reduced the grounds for challenge through constitutional law.

If lawyers' human rights groups could not challenge the political system imposed by the military, they could attempt a challenge about military behavior and raise questions of justice. Human rights law was an undeveloped area of law in Chile, both in theory and practice. However, Chilean law professionals did not take long to establish theoretical underpinnings needed for human rights practice. Their own legal traditions were strong and pointed clearly in the direction of protection of human rights.

Chilean legal theorists also drew from international sources. They centered many of their arguments on international instruments and conventions. The 1948

Universal Declaration of Human Rights served them well, as did other international human rights covenants and treaties. Further, as Chile's technocrats began setting the country's economic trajectory solidly within the international economic system, Chile would be subject to pressures to conform to the rules and legal expectations of the international regime.

The new CCHDH members were uncertain if Pinochet's wrath would descend on them without the umbrella of the church. Emboldened by their first steps, its members began to publish monthly, semiannual, and yearly statements about the situation of human rights in Chile. Taken together these publications became a comprehensive register of violations of fundamental rights. They reached national and international readers. Shifting to a secular basis also enhanced commission access to secular foreign assistance and to the United Nations, and it became associated with the International Commission of Jurists and other professional law groups.

Key to understanding the contribution of the CCHDH is the tie members made of human rights to democracy. This theme became central to human rights organizers in Latin America, in intensity and clarity; its members exploited democracy. The theme touched meanings deeply felt within many Chilean psyches: a future without Pinochet, a perfectible world to be achieved when political parties were restored to rightful place in Chilean society. Military government paradoxically created a hunger for democracy which may have been waning in Chile before Pinochet.

Three years after the founding of the CCHDH, a coalition of parties on the left, the Popular Democratic Movement, created its own human rights organization. Angry communists and socialists on the extreme left could not push their own political agenda within the CCHDH or within church groups. They started the Committee for the Defense of the Rights of the People (CODEPU). Members of the Committee added a further force for mobilization in defense of human rights; other groups both feared and welcomed it. Professionals from CODEPU were often the first to assist tortured political prisoners; its members also concentrated to a much greater extent than other groups on helping to organize grassroots groups to oppose repression.

The confrontational style and, most of all, the far-leftist character of the leaders of CODEPU brought death to Patricio Sobarzo, prison for many leaders, assaults on headquarters, and internal banishment for eleven leaders. Other human rights organizations resented the group. The association of far leftists with human rights work gave military rulers additional opportunity for surveillance and control of all human rights groups.

A third group of Chileans organized for human rights protection in this era grew from university politics. Politics within many Latin American universities resembles college athletics in the United States: a recruitment, selection, and training ground for urban and national politics. In the 1960s, Chilean university campuses became what Pamela Constable and Arturo Valenzuela called "nerve centers of debate and conflict" over the "political tide" sweeping Chile.[38] Just before the military took over, enrollment at the tuition-free state universities skyrocketed, tripling in seven years to 146,450 in 1973. The military intervened in universities almost immediately after the coup. Pinochet's government moved to control the university environment, to keep it free of politics, especially leftist politics. They expelled some 18,000–20,000 students, professors, and staff by 1975.[39] Military tutors had begun the long process of restructuring schools.[40]

Two years after the coup, student leaders in Valparaíso began to respond informally to government repression with a new theme for students, human rights. In 1977 student leaders began organizing the National Commission for the Rights of Young People in Valparaíso. They moved its central office to Santiago and extended the organization to other cities.

University students represented an intellectual challenge to the regime's legitimacy.[41] Further, university and high school–age persons, with greater free time, mobilized more easily than other groups. They were, according to Orellana, "in the front lines of campaigns for human rights."[42] Because of their activism and threat to the government, many leaders and members were arbitrarily detained, expelled from universities, tortured, and banished.

During this period Pinochet's government also moved indirectly against the Catholic Church and human rights groups under its protection. Pinochet sought to undercut the dominant position of the Catholic Church in Chilean society. He began moving toward the conservative segment of the Pentecostal churches. These churches held the largest Protestant populations. Their church leaders were happy (1) with Pinochet's recognition that they mattered in Chilean society (having long been on the fringes of acceptance) and (2) with the prospect that their marginal legal status might be increased to that of the Catholic Church.[43]

Pinochet happily received delegations of Pentecostal leaders at the presidential palace. He arranged for ceremonial affairs, previously held at the Catholic cathedral, to be transferred to the large Pentecostal "cathedral" in the Central Terminal neighborhood. Sycophant television reporters followed along, noting for the nation a new order of things.

FOURTH WAVE

Chilean human rights activists began another wave of human rights organizing in the early 1980s. They addressed the specific questions of women's issues, indigenous peoples' rights, or torture. Women had been in the forefront of human rights organizing since the 1973 coup. They were disproportionately active in groups such as COPACHI, FASIC, the Vicariate, and relatives' associations. The time had come for women at the grassroots level to call attention to the double oppression (as women and lower class) within the country. The first groups dealing specifically with women began in 1980.[44] The first of these groups, the Committee for the Defense of Women's Rights, grew from grassroots groups in *poblaciones*, slum or squatter neighborhoods.

Professional women working within the CCHDH proposed a separate commission on the rights of women. While women lawyers and other women professionals served as the instigators of this organization, they organized especially to serve peasant and working-class women. Women here bridged the wide valleys between classes which exist in Chile.

Persons from women's studies circles created another organization, the Center for Women's Studies. This group arose from studies circles within the Academia de Humanismo Cristiano, a group tied to the Catholic Church. Members attempted to document carefully the situation of inequality of women and the causes of it in Chile, and to help women organize effectively.

Indians and church leaders formed two human rights groups to confront the government. They were attempting to challenge the military government's decision to integrate Mapuche Indians into Chilean society by decrees in 1978. More than 1,350 Mapuche community representatives formed the largest group, the Guild Association of Mapuche Small Farmers and Artisans. Organization members attempted to fight the decrees believed by them to abolish their identity and to lead to the breaking up of their lands.

The following year the bishop of Temuco founded a similar organization, more broadly cultural, the Foundation for Indigenous Institutions. Bishop Sergio Contreras Navia and group members set out to defend the rights of Mapuche Indians to their culture and lands. Mapuche, some 600,000 strong in the south of Chile, resisted the government's depiction of them as a community. They insisted that they were a people, a distinct ethnic group, yet part of the nation.

On another theme, Chileans had grown acutely sensitive to the inhumane and untypically Chilean character of torture. Human rights activists accused Argentine, Brazilian, or Mexican police and security forces of rough treatment routinely administered to criminal suspects. By contrast, Chilean Carabineros (national) and other police forces had been renowned for their ''correct'' methods of policing. Torture, or at least the large-scale use of torture, had been unknown in Chile.

Under military rule, police and military forces introduced torture as a routine instrument of terror. They drew from an ample repertoire, including: beatings, near-drownings, submersion in filth, sleep-deprivation, and rape. Human rights activists could thus exploit torture as un-Chilean, inhumane, and associated only with the military regime.

The issue could have been exploited politically from the earliest days of military takeover. However, human rights activists could not exploit the issue until catalytic events took place ten years later. When members of the CCHDH were imprisoned and tortured in 1982, its leaders believed the time had come to establish a separate human rights group, the National Commission against Torture. The Vicariate of Solidarity, FASIC, and other groups lent their support.

In January 1983, human rights leaders organized a conference on torture in Chile and formed the new commission. Their efforts struck a nerve with the chief of security in Chile who responded publicly against their efforts. The group persisted. Although leaders had designed the organization to be secular, Chilean priests brought an important presence to its board of directors. The National Commission against Torture published *Así se tortura en Chile* (Here Is How They Torture in Chile) and similar publications.

Grassroots activists felt a similar impulse to counter torture. Members of a base Christian community in a poorer section of Santiago invited a psychiatrist, Dr. Fanny Pollarolo, to discuss with them the effects of torture. Dr. Pollarolo, working with FASIC, had experience through her counseling of victims. Religious reflections led group members to take nonviolent measures, as best they could, against the continuation of torture. From this was born the Movement against Torture "Sebastián Acevedo," named for a father distraught over the imprisonment and torture of his children.[45]

On September 14, 1983, they took their first activist step. Group members marched in front of a nondescript building where detention and torture were carried on. Members of other basic Christian communities enlarged organizational rolls within Santiago. The movement spread to other cities. Within two years, movement activists carried out 27 forbidden demonstrations. A Holy Cross seminarian recalls: "Communication was difficult across the city. So, small groups would decide ahead of time to meet, say, in front of a secret detention-torture house. At 3:00 P.M. we met and banded together, held up signs of protest against torture for a few minutes, and then exited separately, melding into passersby."[46]

Decisions to come forward nonviolently demanded courage by movement members to accept blows when they fell. The public campaign to reject violence had embarrassed the government. Carabineros sought out demonstrators and manhandled them. The government banished two movement members; exiled a foreign missionary, Denis O'Shea; and detained and tortured 39 members. Security forces first jailed Dr. Pollarolo and then subjected her to internal exile.

Members of the Movement against Torture were among the first grassroots groups to make a stand beyond the protective umbrella of the churches. They probed into new territory, mounting a challenge against the government's favored tactic of repression. The members of the Movement against Torture also learned about security forces' lack of respect for the lower classes. Repression of grassroots organizations—of the lower classes and priests and sisters who lived with them—fell on them with less restraint than on middle-class members of the older human rights groups. It was enough for a lower-class adolescent to sing "Yo te nombro libertad" (I Name You Liberty) to be clubbed and dragged away by a policeman.

Protests and Coordination

Anti-regime protesters organized large-scale demonstrations, unimaginable in previous years in 1983. At first protesters mounted small, tentative demonstrations. However, deeply felt economic hardships and political discontent drove demonstrators to the streets in larger numbers. Workers in the copper mines called a national strike for May 11, 1983. During the incident, many Chileans stayed home for a day. At 8:00 P.M. thousands began beating pots and pans or sounding car and truck horns, to the great annoyance of security forces. Observers called this the most important political event in ten years of military rule.[47] Workers and others took to the streets for several more demonstrations. Ordinary Chileans began criticizing the regime more openly than they had allowed themselves to do. The two-year period from 1983 to 1985 brought on other anti-government protests. Elements of democratic life were beginning to emerge.

The human rights groups had coordinated many activities among themselves. They did this informally, out of view of the military. They were working against the atomizing tendency of the military regime. However, inevitably, as in most social movements, formal coordination of the movement began. In 1980, leaders from three umbrella organizations engaged in loose, ad hoc coordination of some sectors of the movement. However, the main strength of the human rights movement remained its multifaceted base (church, family, political parties, grassroots groups).

The Plenary Assembly of Human Rights Organizations organized a unified front for human rights activities for core groups, especially the Vicariate, the CCHDH, COPEPU, and the Service for Peace and Justice. Establishing the Plenary Assembly showed the maturing of the movement. The Plenary Assembly, under the executive directorship of the Service for Peace and Justice, responded to government repression on short notice. They organized press conferences, denunciations, and interviews with church and political personalities. The Assembly also carried on campaigns of solidarity for those being intimidated or imprisoned, and helped mobilize opposition. Two other coordinating groups were created to care for families harmed by repression or for persons returning from exile.

Government Response and Movement Growth

In response to oppositional activities, security forces increased human rights violations. The government made it clear that Pinochet intended to continue as president through manipulation of the constitution and plebiscite rather than electoral freedom. In 1987, the CCHDH reported the highest level of violations in the country in seven years. Kidnappings, torture, and politically related killings were part of this; reported death threats grew to nearly 100 a month.

"Early in that period, just when we began to think things were changing for the better, we received the greatest shock," recalled Carmen Garretón, working for the Vicariate. "A sociologist, our colleague at the Vicaría, José Manuel Parada, was picked up in Santiago, as were two others. They were found the following day with their throats slit. I had been through exile in Argentina and now this."[48]

Table 1.1
Human Rights Groups in Latin America

Chile	52
Brazil	50
Argentina	24
Mexico	20
Various countries	(less than 20)
Total	241

Source: Fundación de Ayuda Social de las Iglesias Cristianas and Programa de Derechos Humanos de la Universidad Academia de Humanismo Cristiano, *Guía de las organizaciones de derechos humanos de América Latina y El Caribe* (Santiago: FASIC, 1989).

Responding to the intensified repression, more Chileans joined in human rights activities. Leaders and members of new groups perceived increasing political vulnerabilities of Pinochet's government. The year 1987 also marked the visit of Pope John Paul II to Chile and his support for human rights. Human rights organizing had been tightly grouped for twelve years, growing moderately from two groups to sixteen by 1985.[49] From 1985 to 1988, the movement expanded quickly to 52 groups.[50]

Organizations making up the human rights movement were only the core of groups in the larger Chilean human rights enterprise. Core groups were like the metal tip and central spine of a lance. Other groups and institutions were like the outer wooden handle improving the weight of the movement's thrust. Although not specifically directed to human rights work, dozens of other groups reinforced the impetus of the movement.[51] The Chilean Medical Association investigated Chilean medical professionals participating in human rights abuses, especially torture. (In response, the government jailed two officers of the association.) The Bishops' Commission for Justice and Peace published important statements against government repression. Similar groups added their weight.

By one accounting, Chile (a relatively small country) had more human rights groups than larger countries (Brazil) or ones with even greater human rights abuses (Argentina, Uruguay). FASIC surveyed the Latin American field in 1989 (see Table 1.1).

The number of members in Chilean human rights groups also grew. From 3,000 in 1985, core membership went to 6,500 in 1989. The CCHDH alone increased its membership from 1,000 to 3,500.

THE FUTURE: HUMAN RIGHTS AND PARTIES

After the first decade of dictatorship, both activists and theorists in the movement began expressing concern about human rights after Pinochet left power.

(Chileans may be unusual in their ability to plan and to organize for the future.) Commentators expressed concern that years had now passed since any one in Chile had experienced democracy. More, human rights as a concept was new, virtually unknown before Pinochet. Would concern about violations evaporate when the perpetrators of the worst violations were brought under control? Would the human rights movement disappear when democracy returned?

A major reason for Chileans' concerns came from watching as other Latin American countries moved toward electoral democracy. Neighboring Argentina's example both cheered and chilled Chileans. "Some great gains, some highly questionable losses," was a frequent Chilean judgment. Whatever political solution would be found to topple Pinochet, many Chilean analysts agreed that human rights should be a future institution, an established way of acting in Chilean society.

Further, in some fashion human rights had to be embedded in the national political system. For Chileans this meant tying human rights to political parties. Chileans had seen that Argentine political parties did not strongly support human rights; the Argentine human rights movement was declining. The beginning of this relation—between human rights agenda and political parties—can be seen as early as 1983. The CCHDH in that year issued: *Para que nunca más en Chile* (Never Again in Chile). Unusual for the time and place, this document against terror and repression bore the signatures of eminent political party representatives. Another milestone document, *Compromiso por la vida, los derechos humanos, y la democracia* (Commitment to Life, Human Rights, and Democracy) (in 1985), bore more signatures of party representatives. By 1987 the document *Declaración y compromiso con los derechos humanos* (Declaration and Commitment to Human Rights) had the signatures of the most important civic organizations and all the political parties of Chile, except the two parties supporting the continuation of military government.[52]

The Service for Peace and Justice played a key role in forging a link between political parties and a commitment to human rights observance in the future political system. As the seventeen parties created the Concertación (the political bloc opposing Pinochet), they also established the Justice and Human Rights Commission of the Concertación. They thus pledged themselves "to take up the political, legal, social and cultural initiatives proposed by the victims of gross human rights violations."[53]

Moving Against Pinochet's Continuation

Despite his advancing years, Pinochet expected to stay on as president indefinitely. However, Chileans in the political center and left were planning the strategy to move Pinochet out of the presidential palace. Fundamental agreements between major political parties are unusual in most Latin American countries. Chilean parties (except for some on the left) pulled together as a single coalition, the Concertación de Partidos por la Democracia (Alliance of Democractic Parties). Against the strength of entrenched government power, they succeeded in defeating Pinochet in the best way possible: in the electoral booths in 1988 and 1989.

The plebiscite of 1988 brought the famed "No" vote to Pinochet's continuation without electoral contest. Harrowing debate followed the "No" vote. The specter arose of political parties, released from virtual servitude, fielding a wide range of candidates with no chance to defeat candidates standing in for Pinochet. In the end, most parties on the center and left supported a single candidate, Patricio Aylwin.

The terms governing the 1989 election imposed limits on the new president, including only a four-year term of office (instead of six years). Aylwin, a centrist Christian Democrat, interpreted his presidency as transitional to full electoral democracy in 1994 when parties would field candidates in the typical manner.[54]

END OF LONG PHASE: SOFT LANDING

How much or how little Aylwin would or could do for human rights issues deeply concerned many Chileans, including persons responsible for violations, those affected directly by violations and their families, and many citizens who held profoundly felt views of justice. On March 12, 1990, the day after his inauguration, Aylwin took center stage at the National Stadium to celebrate his victory. He also wished to commemorate those who had suffered human rights atrocities in the sixteen and a half years of military rule. Prominent singers and performers from *Nueva Canción*, street theater, and other forms of popular culture which had grown up before and during the dictatorship joined in, to the great pleasure of 80,000 spectators. The mother of one of the disappeared danced the traditional *cueca* on the stadium field.[55]

Within a month, bodies of three disappeared persons were found by workers at the La Disputada mine north of Santiago. From time to time other grave sites of victims would be encountered. Pinochet supporters found it more difficult to deny the crimes of the regime. Sergio Diez, ambassador for Pinochet at the United Nations in New York, admitted: "No one had any idea of the extent of the abuses, and the truth must now be told about them."[56]

Many persons did have a long, clear view of the extent of abuses. These veteran members of human rights groups came forward to testify before the Rettig Commission. Aylwin formed this commission not long after his inauguration. The blue-ribbon group, headed by former high court justice Raúl Rettig, was charged with setting straight the human rights record of the Pinochet regime. This step might have brought the military from the barracks in insurrection; Aylwin counted on the strength of his electoral mandate to hold the military in check.

As top military commander, Pinochet retained a degree of influence to control the actions of others. This became apparent in the struggle over what part of the repression the Rettig Commission would investigate. It is important to note

Table 1.2
Killed or Disappeared

Total: 2,279

Victims of political violence: 164 (many killed in the coup)

Victims of violations of their human rights: 2,115

Of these:

a. Murdered by agents of the state or persons at their service: 1,068

b. Detained by agents of the state and disappeared: 957

c. Murdered in attacks by individuals under political pretext: 90

Inconclusive cases not included in total: 641

Source: *Síntesis del Informe de la Comisión Verdad y Reconciliacin para "Creer en Chile"* (Santiago: Comisión Chilena de Derechos Humanos, Centro Ideas, 1991), pp. 92–94.

that the Rettig Commission named the victims, not the perpetrators. It also decided not to investigate cases of torture which did not end in disppearance or death. In a sense, the Rettig Commission issued a partial report. The government did not risk regression to authoritarian rule.

Given the constraints, the Rettig Report was greeted as a major achievement. After almost seventeen years of imposed silence, a public record of violations was being written. For nine months the commission listened to testimony from individuals and organizations. The Vicariate of Solidarity had gone to great pains to record details (time, place, manner) of charges of torture, detention without charge, disappearance, and death. Similarly, the records of FASIC, with details of families of the affected, of the CCHDH and of other groups who aided victims or families were carried to Rettig offices.

How bad had repression been? Accounting for the worst, death or disappearance, was the most serious undertaking, the most awaited. The Rettig group accepted only what they felt was proven; a difficult task, since an adversarial regime was involved. The Rettig count (see Table 1.2) thus was conservative.

The Commission also noted important characteristics of the victims (see Table 1.3).

Aylwin's government addressed another issue. His administration arranged for compensation to victims and their families. A national corporation was set up to indemnify some of those affected by repression. For many recipients an initial payment of approximately $U.S. 3,000 was given, followed by monthly payments of about $U.S. 400. It was believed that about 2,000 relatives, mostly spouses, were granted indemnification by the end of 1994.[57]

Now that a good measure of democracy had returned to Chile, the Catholic Church judged that its direct work in human rights was finished. In November 1992, the Vicariate of Solidarity closed its offices; not the end of the movement, but the end of an easily identifiable phase was occurring. The Chilean human

Table 1.3
Characteristics of Killed or Disappeared (N=2,279)

Married	51%
Women	5.5%
Chilean	98%
Largest age group	21–35
Workers and farmers	686
Students	324
Religious	3
Carabineros	69

Source: See Table 1.2.

rights movement was extraordinary for its tenacity, constancy, and longevity. The movement was small in groups and strong in organizing for most of its sixteen and a half years under military rule. Only sixteen groups carried the weight of the movement for most of the period, from 1973 to 1985.

The number of cases handled, the sorrow borne, and the abuse and threats received marked the courage and convictions of rare groups of persons. When the Vicariate of Solidarity was closing, family members of the detained-disappeared expressed the sentiments of many others: "We relive that day when each of us, disoriented and anxious came to your house to save those in danger. . . . Your work will pass into the history of Chile."[58] These human rights workers were among the few in Chile who dared to break the crust of convention[59] and protested the social order dictated by the military.

The Rettig Report and the well-publicized trials of General Manuel Conteras and another general associated with secret police operations brought public recognition that grave wrongs had been committed. These symbolic acts brought closure in the minds of many Chileans to the major issues of human rights. The curtain began coming down on this era when the Vicaría closed its doors.

NOTES

1. Although Patricio Orellana (see below) notes the first effective human rights organization in Latin America began operating in Brazil a year previous to Chile, the impact of the Chilean (and Uruguayan) coups stimulated the great surge of international organizing that announced the beginning of an era. Margaret Keck and Kathryn Sikkink argue that the 1973 coup was a "watershed event." See their "Transnational Issue Networks in International Politics," paper for Latin American Studies Association International Congress, September 1995, pp. 11 and 18. Alison Brysk, "From Above and from Below: Social Movements, the International System, and Human Rights in Argentina," *Comparative Political Studies* 26, 3 (October 1993), p. 267, notes the international human rights regime emerging by 1975.

2. Chile did have two military seizures of government, in 1924 and 1931. Both were brief but showed an eroding of military subordination.

3. In the well-developed literature on the military in Latin America, see esp. Karen Remmer, *Military Rule in Latin America* (Boulder, Colo.: Westview, 1991), esp. pp. 113–150; Louis W. Goodman et al., *The Military and Democracy: The Future of Civil-Military Relations in Latin America* (Lexington, Mass.: Lexington Books, 1990); Gabriel Marcella, ''The Latin American Military, Low-Intensity Conflict, and Democracy,'' *Journal of Inter-American Studies and World Affairs* 32, 1 (1990), pp. 45–82; and Alfred Stepan, *Rethinking Military Politics: Brazil and the Southern Cone* (Princeton, N.J.: Princeton University Press, 1988).

4. A full history of the Pinochet years has yet to be written. Simon Collier and William F. Sater offer a short chapter, ''The Pinochet Years,'' in *A History of Chile, 1808–1994* (New York: Cambridge University Press, 1996), pp. 359–389. Pamela Constable, a correspondent for the *Boston Globe* and Arturo Valenzuela, a Chilean-born political scientist, provide a highly readable account in *A Nation of Enemies: Chile under Pinochet* (New York: Norton, 1991). Mary Helen Spooner has a more controversial version, especially of Pinochet's putative reluctant participation: *Soldiers in a Narrow Land: The Pinochet Regime in Chile* (Berkeley: University of California Press, 1994). Various authors provide political analysis in Paul W. Drake and Iván Jaksić, eds., *The Struggle for Democracy in Chile*, rev. ed. (Lincoln: University of Nebraska Press, 1995).

5. See enlightening description of *Nueva Canción* by Jan Fairley in Simon Broughton et al., *World Music: The Rough Guide* (London: The Rough Guides, 1994), pp. 569–577.

6. Details of Jara's life and death can be found in Joan Turner, *Victor Jara, un canto no truncado* (Concepción: Editorial LAR, 1988).

7. Four monographs about the history of the human rights movement are contained in Patricio Orellana and Elizabeth Quay Hutchinson, *El movimiento de derechos humanos en Chile, 1973–1990* (Santiago: Centro de Estudios Políticos Latinoamericanos Simón Bolívar, 1991). Both Orellana and Hutchinson incorporate material from earlier studies, such as those of Hugo Frühling. For the Vicariate of Solidarity, see also Americas Watch, *La Vicaría de la Solidaridad en Chile* (New York: Americas Watch, 1987) and Vicaría, *Vicaría de la Solidaridad: Historia de su trabajo social* (Santiago: Paulinas, 1991). A partial chronology is available: ''Cronología: Iglesia Católica y derechos humanos en Chile, período 1973–1993,'' in Aníbal Pastor et al., *''De Lonquén a Los Andes'': 20 Años de la Iglesia Católica Chilena* (Santiago: Ediciones Rehue, 1993), pp. 171–205. Interviews for this study were conducted in Chile, June–July 1989, March 1992, and March 1995.

8. In Chile, in contrast to other countries, periodization was unusually clear. New political opportunities encouraged distinct resource mobilization. Periods of a social movement, I believe, are better described by waves than ''generations,'' which Orellana and Hutchinson use.

9. Other church representatives who were members of the committee are noted in *Americas Watch, La Vicaría*, p. 43.

10. See esp. Brian Smith, *The Church and Politics in Chile: Challenges to Modern Catholicism* (Princeton, N.J.: Princeton University Press, 1982), and ''Churches and Human Rights: Recent Trends in the Subcontinent,'' *Journal of Interamerican Studies and World Affairs* 21 (February 1979), pp. 89–128.

11. Interviews, Santiago, March 1992 and March 1995.

12. Two lengthy volumes recount these events, with recollections of authors: Mario Terrazas Guzmán, *Quién Se Acuerda de Sheila Cassidy: Crónica de un conflicto religioso-político-diplomático* (Santiago: Ediciones Emete, 1992); and Sheila Cassidy, *Audacity to Believe* (Cleveland: Collins-World, 1978).

13. Constable and Valenzuela, *A Nation*, p. 120.

14. Manuel Antonio Garretón, *The Chilean Political Process* (Boston : Unwin Hyman, 1989), p. 120.

15. Ibid.

16. See Fernando Salas, ''Crisis en la Iglesia Luterana Chilena,'' *Mensaje* 24 (July 1975), pp. 312–315.

17. Americas Watch, *La Vicaría*, p. 14.

18. *Bilan du Monde: Encylopedie Catholique du Monde Chretien* (Paris: Eglise Vivante/Casterman, 1964), vol. 2, p. 221.

19. Interviews, University of Notre Dame, March 1989, and Santiago, March 1992.

20. Ibid.

21. Interview, Santiago, March 1992.

22. Ibid.

23. Ibid.

24. The ecumenical group, FASIC, was able to establish an office in Valparaíso. See Orellana, ''La lucha silenciosa por los derechos humanos: El caso de FASIC,'' in Orellana and Hutchinson, *El movimiento*, p. 179.

25. For establishment of the Academia see Jeffrey M. Puryear, *Thinking Politics: Intellectuals and Democracy in Chile, 1973–1988* (Baltimore: Johns Hopkins University Press, 1994), pp. 44–46.

26. Orellana in Orellana and Hutchinson, *El movimiento*, p. 26.

27. See esp. Orellana's general description of FASIC: ''La lucha silenciosa por los derechos humanos: El caso de FASIC,'' in Orellana and Hutchinson, *El movimiento*, pp. 143–198.

28. Georgina Ocararanza (Lutheran), Juan Polanco and Denis O'Shea (Presbyterian Church in Renewal), and others who were Protestants were detained by security forces.

29. Further consideration of the role of these groups will be made in the following chapter.

30. Agrupación de Familiares de Detenidos-Desaparecidos has a number of useful publications detailing its history, advocacy, and activities, including *Recuento de Actividades AFDD* (Santiago: Agrupación de Detenidos-Desaparecidos, various years).

31. Agrupación de Presos Políticos, AFDD.

32. Comité Pro-retorno de Exiliados, CPRE; Agrupación de Familiares de Ejecutados Políticos, AFEP; Agrupación de Familiares de Relegados y Ex-relegados, AFAREL; and Protección de la Infancia Dañada por los Estados de Emergencia, PIDEE.

33. See Hannah Stewart-Gambino, ''Redefining the Changes and Politics in Chile,'' in Edward L. Cleary and Stewart-Gambino, eds., *Conflict and Competition: The Latin American Church in a Changing Environment* (Boulder, Colo.: Lynne Rienner, 1992), esp. pp. 22–24.

34. The directorate held virtually no meetings. See Orellana and Hutchinson, *El movimiento*, p. 32.

35. Ibid.

36. Ibid., pp. 22–23.

37. See Paul E. Sigmund, *The United States and Democracy in Chile* (Baltimore: Johns Hopkins University Press, 1993), pp. 114–115. See also Taylor Branch and Eugene M. Popper, *Labyrinth* (New York: Penguin Books, 1983), among other works.

38. Constable and Valenzuela, *A Nation*, p. 247.

39. Ibid., p. 249.

40. Military tutelage of schools varied according to the personalities of commanders. See Constable and Valenzuela, *A Nation*, esp. pp. 254–256.

41. Ibid., p. 252.

42. Orellana and Hutchinson, *El movimiento*, p. 34.

43. Edward L. Cleary and Juan Sepúlveda, "Chilean Pentecostals: Coming of Age," in Cleary and Hannah Stewart-Gambino, eds., *Power, Politics, and Pentecostals in Latin America* (Boulder, Colo.: Westview, 1996), pp. 104–106.

44. A fuller discussion of women and human rights follows in Chapter 3 of this volume.

45. A lengthy ideological account of the movement is provided by Hernán Vidal, *El Movimiento Contra La Tortura "Sebastián Acevedo"* (Minneapolis: Institute for the Study of Ideologies and Literature, 1986).

46. Interview, Santiago, March 1992.

47. Pastor et al., *De Lonquén*, p. 188.

48. Interview, Santiago, March 15, 1995.

49. Orellana and Hutchinson, *El movimiento*, p. 207.

50. Ibid.

51. Ibid., esp. pp. 20–21, 65.

52. Ibid., p. 212.

53. Laurie S. Wiseburg et al., eds., *Directorio de organizaciones de derechos humanos: América Latína y El Caribe* (Cambridge, Mass.: Human Rights Internet, 1990), p. 199.

54. Garretón argues that Aylwin was mistaken in defining his government as transitional. See "Redemocratization in Chile," *Journal of Democracy* 6, 1 (January 1995), pp. 149-150.

55. For the use of the *cueca* as a symbol of protest against human rights violations, see the video "Dance of Hope" (New York: First Run Features, 1991).

56. Spooner, *Soldiers*, p. 257.

57. Estimate by Carmen Garretón, Santiago, March 15, 1995.

58. *Recuento de Actividades AFDD* (November 1992), pp. 162–163.

59. See Sidney Tarrow, *Power in Movement: Social Movements, Collective Action and Politics* (New York: Cambridge University Press, 1994), p. 186.

2

Human Rights Organizing Spreads: Mexico and the Theoretical Frame

Human rights organizations also began appearing in countries that had not experienced military rule.[1] In contrast to many Latin American countries, Mexico is a latecomer in human rights organizing. Human rights movements in most of Latin America began in the 1960s and 1970s and greatly expanded in the 1980s.[2] The term ''human rights'' was virtually unknown in Mexico until the mid-1980s, and came into common use from reports of military repression in South and Central America.[3]

The outlines of a new political epoch are becoming clearer. At the forefront of forging new relations between state and civil society have been human rights organizations. In twelve years, Mexican human rights groups have grown from three to over 300. Why now? After all, human rights violations have been commonplace for centuries in Mexico.

FRAMEWORK AND BACKGROUND

Social movements have enjoyed a resurgence internationally since the 1960s. Scholars have focused on civil rights, women's, and environmental movements in the United States and ''new'' social movements in Europe and Latin America. Many organizations making up these movements have ties to churches and nearly all movements have political implications.[4] Simultaneously, scholars have investigated these movements and pursued dense historical research of earlier ones. They have made theoretical gains in the process. Charles Tilly,[5] Doug McAdam,[6] and others[7] have stood in the forefront of this process.

Sidney Tarrow, benefitting from these advances, has provided a general framework for analyzing social movements.[8] This chapter uses main elements from his framework and additionally emphasizes transnational influences.[9] The chapter traces three lines of analysis: environmental, organizational, and transnational.[10] This model attempts to account for the environmental constraints or opportunities shaping the actions of mobilizing groups. It considers resources internal to the movement or organization. Further, it suggests transnational influences affecting both the national environment and organizations.

For Mexico, then, the outlines of the main argument can be described as follows. For most of the last 70 years, the Mexican state has controlled the political environment; it has done so vigorously.[11] Drastic economic downturns, massive earthquake destruction, governmental ineffectiveness and passivity in the face of disaster, and a changing world order brought new political discontent. Institutions, such as universities and the Catholic Church, provided structures in which political discontents about human rights were articulated. Movement leaders then mobilized these political discontents when opportunities became available, to make demands, to insist on human rights, as a challenge to the Partido Revolucionario Institutional (PRI) government to rule arbitrarily. Transnational pressures have influenced the Mexican political system, especially in the direction of democratization, free trade, and greater regard for human rights.

The focus of analysis will be on the interaction of these sectors. State and party control weakened at certain times, allowing for human rights initiatives, but the state also obstructed, co-opted, and repressed at other times. In elaborating this interaction, I am concerned with explaining how and why human rights groups have arisen, and especially, why now?

Human rights violations in Mexico went largely unchallenged until the mid-1980s. Abundant evidence existed of electoral irregularities, fraud, and corruption by the governing party. International organizations depicted police and security forces as committing widespread human rights crimes. Extrajudicial killings, disappearances, torture, and arbitrary detentions took place over most of the country. Among the victims were peasants in dispute with landowners, political militants, and many reporters.[12]

A consensus of interpretation about Mexico has grown up among that nations's political observers.[13] This provides a clearer view of Mexican politics than a previous era when opposing sides emphasized a romantic view of Mexican "democracy" or a pessimistic view of a single party's absolute control without regard for public opinion. The contemporary consensus allows one to say that a self-perpetuating elite within one party that controlled the government has ruled Mexico.[14] Thus, until the 1980s, Mexico had a party system on paper but not in reality. In a word, since 1929, PRI controlled the government and ruled with a strong hand. But economic hardship and a desire for modernization have brought notable changes to the Mexican political system, changes that engendered the human rights movement. The present analysis traces these changes in the political environment. Tarrow and others describe these changes as "structures of opportunity," as vulnerabilities of the state. The fissures within the ruling party[15] gave the human rights movement belief that now is the time to act because the movement could accomplish changes.

Human rights organizations are part of a larger phenomenon. In Mexico, as in Latin America, nongovernmental organizations (NGOs) have reached major proportions.[16] Many analysts presume these organizations contribute to establishing civil society as the basis for functioning Latin American democracies.[17] They further presume that movements emerge only when opportunities for their activities arise. Joe Foweraker more accurately characterizes their role in Mexico. He points out that popular movements create active political subjects in civil society, rather than the more idyllic depiction of "the birth of civil society."[18]

One can mark several notable occasions for changing the traditional political landscape. These are the structures of opportunity for mobilizing human rights activity. First, a drastic fall in oil prices in 1981 brought on a grave economic crisis after years of an economic "miracle." The crisis worsened into major economic depression in which real wages fell 10 percent. Mexico faltered in its debt payments and agreed to economic readjustment through the Baker plan. Most Mexicans suffered under the crisis and blame fell on the government.[19] In addition, social breakdowns brought increased crime rates and with that greater human rights violations through police violence.

Second, in its thrust toward becoming a modernizing First World country, the PRI government, especially in the mid-1980s, set up electoral reforms. However, as de Tocqueville remarks, "a state is never so vulnerable as when it begins to reform."[20] When the opposition won more votes than anticipated, the PRI government found itself having to obstruct the opposition's growth. A major cleavage developed in the party over aborted reform, and a splinter group, Democratic Current, resulted. This sector soon evolved into a center-left party, with Cuauhtémoc Cárdenas and key dissidents from PRI as leaders.

Third, a severe shock to the Mexican system occurred in September 1985 when a major earthquake struck Mexico City and other areas. In its response the Mexican government and PRI stood exposed as inept and sluggish. After waiting in vain for effective government response, hundreds of thousands of citizens threw themselves into organizing for survival and rebuilding. Major social analysts trace many social movements to this event. In effect, nongovernmental organizations mounted a successful challenge to the government.

These three vulnerabilities of the state and PRI helped bring human rights organizations into existence. A fourth vulnerability, the uprising in Chiapas, breathed new life into the human rights movement after January 1994.

It is important here to note the level of analysis being applied to a key player, the Catholic Church, and to the field of politics. In terms of high-level, institutional political activity, the church had its activity severely limited by law. The bishops also hoped to gradually regain the church's freedom by keeping silence. Church-state ties in Mexico have had a more tortured path than most Latin American countries.[21] The 1917 Constitution prohibited the church from political activity and denied its priests the right to vote.[22] After active persecution of the church extending into the 1930s, the church gained a measure of freedom for activity in the religious and educational fields. It still suffered severe restraints in the political field.[23] The church continued in what J. Lloyd Mecham describes as "a precarious position,"[24] relatively weak, without juridical personality and the right to own property in its name.

Further, major fields of political activity were virtually closed to all but the ruling party. Electoral politics did not exist until the mid- and late 1980s and legislative politics followed PRI dictates.[25] When the government promised legitimate presidential elections in 1988 and fraud was committed on a large scale, some bishops felt free to denounce fraud as a moral, if not a political, issue.

At the highest level the bishops, singly or as a conference, spoke episodically and infrequently in another arena of politics: public debate of national issues. Roderic Camp assesses the situation: "A closed, not an open system for public discussion of important issues exists in Mexico. . . . Reporters were beaten, kidnapped, threatened, pressured, and deported for articles critical of the president, his family, and his policies."[26] Further, public sentiment in the 1980s was against the institutional entry of the church into politics.[27]

Middle-level and grassroots activity by Catholic activists was another story. Here the church (as groups of believers) provided structures within which progressive Catholic priests and especially laypersons emerged into the human rights movement.[28] Catholic progressives were not the sole recruits into the human rights movement but played a leading role in cooperation with more strictly secular persons and groups.

A modest group of Catholic progressives had been emerging in Mexico. This trend intensified after the hugely successful 1979 visit of John Paul II and the concurrent celebration of the Latin American Bishops Third Conference at Puebla. The Jesuit Center for Theological Reflection and the Jesuit monthly *Christus*, the Dominican Centro Antonio Montecinos, and especially a growing movement of thousands of basic Christian communities reflected this tendency.[29] These groups and communities furnished the structures in which members formulated political discontents. These circles widely discussed liberation theology, in its mildest forms.[30] For a time at least, most of the bishops kept liberation theology out of seminaries and other institutions under their control.[31]

In this context human rights organizing began. In 1984 human rights was not part of public debate in Mexico. The words were barely known and, if used, were applied to Central or South America where military dictatorships ruled.[32] Also, for the most part, Catholic and secular intellectuals lived apart, largely in separate worlds.[33]

EMERGENCE OF HUMAN RIGHTS ORGANIZATIONS

A brief overview of emerging organizations shows a strong church presence[34] in largely secular human rights activity.[35] In terms of icons, the national human rights award is named for the former bishop of Cuernavaca, Don Sergio Méndez Arceo. An alliance of mostly secular organizations presented the first two awards to a bishop and a priest. The bishop-recipient, Samuel Ruiz García, became a principal link for contemporary human rights activities in Chiapas, Mexico City, and throughout the republic. The Dominican priest-recipient, Miguel Concha, is a principal figure in this account.

Jorge G. Casteñeda, in his description of the Latin American left after the Cold War, *Utopia Unarmed*, notes the disproportionately large Catholic background of NGO activists in many human rights organizations, whether specifically tied to the church or not.[36] In Mexico five of the strongest organizations are related directly to the church: Centro Vitoria and Centro Las Casas (Dominicans), Centro PRO and Comisión de Solidaridad y Defensa de los Derechos Humanos del Estado de Chihuahua (Jesuit and Jesuit/archdiocesan), and Departamento de Derechos Humanos de la Archdiocese de México (archdiocesan). Other important groups include Centro Potosino de Derechos Humanos, Pro Derechos Humanos de Nayarit, and groups in Hidalgo, Tehuantepec, and elsewhere, most of them tied to the church. Teresa Jardí sees in the group members: "A large group of lay persons who wish to have a voice as committed participants in the church and they also wish to challenge the government."[37]

Another sector, students and relatives of the disappeared or exiled, formed the nuclei of two precursor groups to the human rights movement. Both groups' members were concerned with disappearances. After killing hundreds of students in a Mexico City plaza in late 1968, security forces continued to pursue presumptive student leaders. Some were caught and disappeared; others fled Mexico. Among students seeking exile, some sought assistance from Amnesty International (AI), a fledgling institution in the days before it received the Nobel Peace Prize. Amnesty International opened a Mexican section in response to these petitions, backed by foreigners reacting to the prominence and scale of Mexico's 1968 repression. It was thus the first human rights group working on Mexico, but Mexican authorities regarded it as foreign.

The first national group devoted to human rights began in 1978. In the north of Mexico (as in other Latin American countries) small, quixotic guerrilla groups of mostly young urban adults began opposing the government. Security forces rough-handled and tortured dozens of those captured, who disappeared. Rosario Ibarra de Piedra led an organizing effort of mostly mothers of the disappeared. From this effort grew EUREKA; the group was small and limited in objective. The human rights movement needed a further impetus to be born.

One could date the human rights movement from 1984. At that point Mexicans had established three human rights organizations. As mentioned, Rosario Ibarra de Piedra founded EUREKA to search for her son and other disappeared persons and to probe into the inhumane situation of political prisoners.[38] Universidad Nacional Autonoma de Mexico (UNAM), Mexico's largest university, housed Academia Mexicana de Derechos Humanos. They were joined by Centro Vitoria (Centro de Defensa y Promoción de los Derechos Humanos "Fray Francisco de Vitoria"). None of the groups challenged the government to change the Mexican system.[39]

To furnish a narrative thread to the evolution of the human rights movement, attention will focus on Centro Vitoria, a group whose evolution this author has followed since 1979.[40] As an older center, Centro Vitoria is an ''early riser,'' a group that helped trigger cycles of protest and brought other groups into the struggle. Its history allows one to see changes over time in resources and strategies. Centro Vitoria played a pivotal role. It aided in the organization of other centers; it served as a bridge between religious and secular centers; it carried out a major role in framing the arguments of the movement. Miguel Concha, one of its founders, would be a major figure in national movement activities.

Transnational forces and state control of Mexican political activity influenced the first steps of Centro Vitoria. The members began by addressing issues of Central American human rights violations, not *Mexican ones*. Centro Victoria and the Mexican Academy of Human Rights[41] responded to pressures from Central American colleagues who looked to Mexico for advocacy. Pressures also came from many Central American refugees in southern Mexico who were caught in inhumane conditions in southern Mexico and harassed by Mexican security forces.

Concha, other Dominicans, and many lay associates created Centro Vitoria. It was for many of them an expression of liberation theology, as it would be for other centers that followed later. Concha and colleagues described the moral basis of their activism in *La participacion de los cristianos en el proceso popular de liberacion de México*. Siglo XXI, a major secular publishing house, published the work.[42] Activists at this middle level were sensitive to changes in the church outside Mexico, pushed for a stronger public role, and promoted small Christian communities, which, as Camp mentions, often act as grassroots pressure groups.[43]

In terms of progressive trends (and human rights concerns) in the church, Central America and especially Mexico have been late bloomers. Transnational pressures for change influenced changes in the Mexican church. Mexican informants believed impetus for change came from John Paul II who put pressure on the conservative Mexican church to become more involved socially.[44] World leaders of the Dominicans and Jesuits established social justice and collaboration with laity as major priorities. Mexican Dominicans, Jesuits, and active laity searched for ways to carry out the new directions. They formed justice and peace groups which increasingly would focus on human rights.[45]

In the first stage, lacking experience, Centro Vitoria simply diffused information, often clandestinely, from Central American human rights groups for a small Mexican audience. Given the controversies about events in Central America and challenges to interpretations, Centro Vitoria adopted a basic principle to guarantee the veracity of its reports. This it did selectively, relying on Central American agencies that built up credibility over the years. The Mexicans also noted the lives lost in Central America in speaking out about human rights violations.

Again, transnational organizations strongly influenced this activity. Archbishop Oscar Romero, working with lay persons, established a human rights center, El Socorro Jurídico, in San Salvador. In the early 1980s, Roberto Cuéllar, its director, was forced to flee to Mexico City. There the Dominicans provided Cuéllar with an office in their Centro Universitario Cultural, side by side with Centro Vitoria. In turn, Cuéllar played a major role in shaping the work of the center.[46] Amnesty International, housed in the Dominican building, also entered into the process.

INSTITUTIONAL TRAJECTORY/CYCLES OF PROTEST

While members of the Centro Vitoria felt that they had detailed and verified information from Central America, the same was lacking in Mexico. This changed with a sudden shift in physical and sociopolitical environment. The 1985 Mexico City earthquake opened cracks in buildings and the earth. It also exposed, for many who had not seen or cared, the darker sides of the Mexican governmental system. In a word, Mexicans saw the ineptitude and moral bankruptcy of a one-party, paternalistic government slow to respond to urgent needs of those devastated by the earthquake. Mexico had an urban grassroots movement in the 1970s but state patronage and co-optation weakened its independence. Jorge Castañeda, in *Utopia Unarmed*, says: ''The earthquake unleashed a combination of anger, organizational drive, and desire to act independently of the overpowering Mexican state that shook Mexico City almost as much as the earthquake.''[47]

Hundreds of thousands of ordinary persons took the initial stage of rescue and rebuilding Mexico City into their own hands. They gained confidence in the ability of ordinary citizens to do a great deal, in contrast to their customary waiting for action from an authoritarian government.[48] From then on, social movements in Mexico, both grassroots and national, greatly increased their activities.[49] The small human rights movement moved to the forefront.

Further, the political environment would continue to open. A major challenge to the one-party hegemony of the Partido Revolucionario Institutional (PRI) was being mounted in the 1988 elections. For the early risers, Centro Vitoria and Academia Mexicana, an opportunity also opened in the political environment. Foremost, the centers began the collection, verifying, and legal processing of human rights violations in Mexico.

Second, organizations intensified their networking, and division of labor intensified. Two centers that have been pillars of the human rights movements in Mexico, Centro Vitoria and Academia Mexicana, show the changing climate within intellectual and activist networks. These informal networks have evolved into a secular alliance of interest groups promoting democratic change in Mexico, especially through human rights activity. Centro Vitoria has offices in the Centro Universitario Cultural (Catholic chaplaincy), adjacent to the colossal (300,000 student) UNAM. UNAM was the epitome of secular universities in

Latin America, anti-clerical and fiercely maintaining independence from the church. Through the years the walls between individuals working in the university and counterparts working in Catholic schools or organizations began to be lowered. Interaction between journalists and intellectuals led to Concha's appointment in the Facultad de Ciencias Políticas at UNAM.

This, in turn, brought many informal contacts with major figures at the university and resulted in a major collaborative effort. Within the university, a key intellectual center, Centro de Investigaciones Interdisciplinarias en Humanidades, commissioned Centro Vitoria to do research into individual human rights violations in Mexico, "a novelty among research projects in the country."[50] The Mexican Dominicans and colleagues, inexperienced but gifted, learned quickly from Cuéllar[51] and others from Central America. The work was tedious and dangerous. They had to certify details of alleged violations. Months of intensive work by Concha and lay associates went into the effort.

Shaping Public Discourse

Their research formed the centerpiece in a landmark document in Mexican human rights. Pablo González Casanova, prominent intellectual and former rector of UNAM, acted as the publication's coordinator. Social scientists, activists, and theologians published *Primer informe sobre la democracia* (*First Report on Democracy*) in 1988.[52] Miguel Concha's report of fifteen years of human rights violations in Mexico formed the document's empirical core.[53] The *First Report on Democracy* received national and international attention.

Stinging denunciations of the Mexican government by the *First Report* group opened the eyes of Mexicans. Many confessed that they had not known their own society until they began systematically looking into this issue. The inclusion of prominent persons in the volume also gave the work a quality of being untouchable. Further, the PRI administration wanted to emphasize its tolerance, hoping to take its place in the world of free speech and democratic governments.

In social movement theory, shaping public discourse, or, "collective action frames" has been a key consideration. Tarrow summarizes advances made in understanding this aspect of social movements: "Movements frame their collective actions around cultural symbols that are selectively chosen from a cultural tool chest and creatively converted into collective action frames by political entrepreneurs."[54] Full discussion of how symbolic discourse gave power to the Mexican human rights movement is beyond the space allowed here. However, it is important to note that, from the start, leaders in the Mexican human rights movement chose to cast their protest in terms of democratic nation-building. Their first publication with national impact was not *First Report on Human Rights*, but *First Report on Democracy*.

Contemporary understanding of social movements has also emphasized the outsize, often independent, and frequently antagonistic influence of mass media. The media, as Tarrow observes, have as much or more to do with controlling the construction of meaning than states or social actors. Fortunate for the human rights movement, Concha and other authors of *First Report on Democracy* associated professionally with key publishers, editors, commentators, and reporters. Concha gained prominence as a working journalist/intellectual for years. He was a columnist for *Uno más uno* and is a founding shareholder and columnist for *La Jornada* (circulation: 130,000). Many Mexican intellectuals are involved in daily and periodical journalism, attempting to influence societal views. Thus intellectual and journalist colleagues of the authors of *First Report* were quick to conflate two discourses: democracy (the state's new thrust) and human rights (the movement goal) in daily journalism. Human rights entered the Mexicans' vocabulary as applying to their country and was no longer limited to Central and South American countries where military governments had taken their toll.

The slight opening of the political environment allowed the few human rights groups to strengthen their positions. Centro Vitoria and other groups increased professionalizing their work. They did this with special emphases: First, they followed up on individual cases or class actions. They had to observe all the bureaucratic details, since they were dealing with a deeply entrenched Mexican governmental bureaucracy intertwined with the ruling party. Teresa Jardí, now director of the archdiocese of Mexico City human rights office, worked as a federal prosecutor in Chihuahua. She describes the environment of her previous work as corruption permeating the bureaucracy and internal wars being waged. She spent her months there "putting up with the hostilities of administrative personnel, their inefficiency, their arrogance, and their vexations."[55] Nonetheless, she won impressive episodic victories. Centro Vitoria obtained the release of dozens of Indians illegally jailed.[56]

Second, Centro Vitoria put together a larger picture of human rights within the country, a view unknown to most Mexicans. This it did by painstaking efforts to tally cases reported in newspapers and magazines or by national and international groups reporting on human rights in Mexico. The center celebrated its report as an annual event: The year-end report on the human rights situation in Mexico presented at a press conference and published yearly in *Justicia y Paz*.[57]

Publication of the quarterly *Justicia y Paz* became a major work of Centro Vitoria. In a deliberate way the journal continually tested the limits of how much discussion of human rights the state would allow. In part because of the mentorship of Central Americans, editors of *Justicia y Paz* did not limit the journal to traditional concerns of torture and disappearance. They attempted to shape public debate by addressing a full range of issues, from basic economic rights to environmental concerns.

Also, from the earthquake (1985) to the next presidential elections (1988) the division of labor among human rights groups became sharper and better articulated. The Academy of Human Rights, within the academic setting of UNAM, defined itself as devoted to *causas*, not *casos* (causes, not cases). Since the

Mexican press did not use the term human rights, the Academy members set out to define for a wide audience what human rights meant.[58]

Another window of opportunity for human rights organizing opened as the drug enforcement war intensified. Naming Javier Coello Trejo as assistant national prosecutor for the anti-drug fight, and the brutality of the Federal Judicial Police acted as sparks for killings, corruption, and a higher rate of torture in the late 1980s. Teresa Jardí says that generalized violence unknown in contemporary Mexico followed.[59] For some who became active in human rights at this time, the PRI government had gone beyond tolerable limits.

The small human rights movement moved then to mediate between people and government in the turbulence of the drug wars. Also occurring in the 1980s was the lost decade in which millions of Mexicans became poorer and more excluded from the benefits of the economic system. Similarly, human rights organizations increased membership and other resources trying to lessen the secondary harmful effects of the economic process.[60]

However, PRI largely controlled the political process. The PRI government liberalized election laws in 1978. By 1988 Cuauhtémoc Cárdenas and opposition parties mounted an electoral campaign which almost brought Cárdenas to Los Pinos. Cárdenas gained (officially) 31.5 percent of the vote and, some believe, the presidential election in 1988. Denise Dresser points to the 1988 elections as a major factor in the growth of human rights organizations.[61] Turbulence caused by electoral fraud brought many more Mexican human rights groups into existence. The 1988 elections notably increased attention for Mexico from international groups, such as Amnesty International, Human Rights Watch/Americas, and Minnesota Advocates.[62]

International pressures for change to an open capitalist economy increased with the fall of the Berlin wall in 1989. Mexican technocrats listened carefully to foreign comments. Mexico moved from emphasizing national ownership, production, and markets to an open trading zone with Canada and the United States. The Mexican state became more sensitive to criticism of the human rights situation from the United States. In Andrew Reding's view, President "Salinas's domestic vulnerabilities have led him to look to the United States for support," and the U.S. was "in a unique position to support democracy and human rights in Mexico."[63]

The PRI government, with great flourish, created its own human rights group, parallel in many aspects to the nongovernmental human rights movement. President Carlos Salinas de Gotari established the National Commission for Human Rights in 1990 (CNDH). The government published a constitutional law establishing the commission in June 1992.[64] Roderic Camp and others believe Salinas was primarily anticipating public discussion and congressional hearings in the United States on the North American Free Trade Agreement (NAFTA) treaty.[65]

To some respected Mexicans this seemed like a valuable enterprise to be encouraged, since CNDH as an ombudsman agency seemed to have a measure of independence. Jorge Carpizo and Rodolfo Stavenhagen, associated with the

Academy of Human Rights, presided over or joined CNDH; other university-based intellectuals and researchers also participated in its activities. CNDH sponsored many studies and symposia, commissioned a *pastorela* (popular drama), described the notorious prison situation with impressive graphics, and published a range of documents.

The CNDH, conceived as an ombudsman agency, had the power to investigate human rights complaints.[66] By 1993, it would become a monster. Few human rights organizations in the world could match its size: 600 staff members housed in their own building, with prominent signs on the expressway to mark appropriate exits to its location. The PRI government thus attempted to preempt increasingly widespread efforts by the nongovernmental human rights groups. These organizations expressed their concerns about human rights violations, virtually undiminished from year to year.[67]

The interplay of state and nongovernmental groups intensified. Nongovernmental groups seized upon the creation of CNDH to discuss in the public forum government views of human rights. Concha's paper, *La Jornada*, and others of Mexico City's twenty daily newspapers joined the conflict. Independent human rights groups criticized CNDH for excluding political rights from the list of human rights. Although key NGOs had limited liberty, they chose to highlight *la cuestión delicada* (sensitive issue), political rights and fair elections in Mexico. They looked forward to cleaner national and state elections in 1994. As part of this effort, in April 1994, Miguel Concha, Centro Vitoria,[68] *La Jornada*, and Centro de Investigaciones Interdisciplinarias at UNAM published *Los derechos políticos como derechos humanos*.[69]

Jardí believes that CNDH, instead of supporting the work of national and international human rights NGOs, blocked their work.[70] In response, key nongovernmental groups found it useful to band together more formally. Thirty-three of the more active groups, including Centro Vitoria, formed "Todos los Derechos para Todos."

Chiapas, Elections, Repression

The year 1994 brought grave crises and additional controlling responses from the government to human rights activism. For years anthropologists, religious leaders, and juridical activists had been registering the abuse of Indians and various conflicts in Chiapas. Nonetheless, the militant uprising on January 1 caught most observers by surprise. The subsequent events, made clear by Cable News Network and other sources, brought direct attention to human rights violations in the region.

With Chiapas, Centro Vitoria has strong ties to another center with Dominicans, Centro de Derechos Humanos "Bartolomé de Las Casas." This center and its bishop-founder, Don Samuel Ruiz, found themselves attacked ferociously by rightist press, government, and landed-class interests. National and international human rights groups swiftly mobilized mechanisms for the defense of the Las

Casas organization. Concha and others moved quickly from Mexico City to Chiapas. The Minnesota Advocates and other foreign groups also sped to the scene. Further armed conflict was delayed and human rights violations monitored and held in check, for the time being.

Second, Centro Vitoria and other centers chose to make Chiapas a national issue, not one to be hidden in the Lacondón jungle. This, then, was another structure of opportunity to exploit, another phase in the cycle of protest. Human rights centers by now had grown to 300. Many of them sponsored the massive demonstration on January 12, 1994. Their call for participation brought 70,000 persons marching into the Zóolo, the city's largest square. The broad base of support—across class, gender, religious (notable mainline Protestants took part), and political lines—offered a challenge to the state, a deterrent to violent reprisal in Chiapas.

The many groups participating in the demonstration chose Concha as the principal speaker. His twenty-minute, carefully crafted speech[71] drew praise from many interested observers. Ernesto Zedillo Ponce de León, then secretary of education and now president of Mexico, wrote Concha in appreciation for the tone of rebuilding, not defiance, which Concha had taken. Nongovernmental groups added their own response. In April a civic alliance of nongovernmental organizations named Concha as second recipient of the National Human Rights "Don Sergio Méndez Arceo" Award.

To prepare for the crucial 1994 national and state elections, human rights groups mounted months of efforts to train monitors for the election process largely controlled by the government. Salinas and the PRI administration pushed back against the human rights movement. The Chiapas situation and the intense scrutiny of the summer elections triggered the first *systematic* campaign against human rights organizations. In its November 21, 1994 report, Centro Vitoria noted 93 acts against human rights organizations or their members during the year. They believed these were only the certifiable violations, among hundreds of other violations committed. Ten death threats were reported; seventeen offices broken into and documents stolen; and many calumnies and defamations committed. Centro Vitoria characterized this as an attempt at systematic hostage-taking. The 1995 massacre of seventeen peasants in Guerrero also brought publicized death threats to the Miguel Pro Center director.[72]

CONCLUSION: WHAT IMPACT?

Why now a human rights movement in Mexico? The world economic and political environment shifted and the political environment within Mexico opened new opportunities, as transnational pressures toward open trade and democratization influenced Mexico. Human rights organizations moved into new political space, carving niches for themselves. Supported by various social sectors, low to upper middle, they act as vanguards of a civil society unknown in Mexico in contemporary history.

What have more than 300 human rights organizations accomplished?[73] Centro Victoria, in its annual statement of November 22, 1994, noted that 23,623 persons had suffered human rights violations in Mexico.[74] This was a notable increase over the last year. Peasants and Indians were principal victims of the violations. What impact could one point to for all these organizations? One might believe that PRI allowed many groups to organize and to speak publicly, while changing very little behavior by the government or party.

When interviewed in late 1994, Rodolfo Stavenhagen, a world-renowned Mexican anthropologist with decades of work among the indigenous, replied simply that there is no methodology for measuring impact.[75] Nonetheless, in my view, first, human rights groups have helped resolve many individual cases. EUREKA, the first contemporary human rights center in Mexico, obtained the release of political prisoners.[76] Centro Vitoria obtained release of dozens of Indians from prison.[77] The independent Comisión Mexicana resolved favorably many cases of rights violations.[78] Observers report that police are increasingly reluctant to use torture.[79] National elections were, with the exception of Chiapas, more cleanly carried out due to many human rights groups.

Second, human rights groups in Mexico have brought human rights into everyday language. Human rights as a term was virtually unknown in Mexico ten years ago. Teresa Jardí recalls: "No one spoke of human rights because they were considered *burgués*."[80] Jesús Maldonado García of the Miguel Pro Center says: "In 1987 the term human rights was little known in civil society. When it was talked about, it was applied to Central or South America."[81] In this climate it was easy for the government to insist that human rights were an exotic and foreign idea. Some said human rights was a *Yankí* interventionist idea.[82]

Further, human rights organizations have opened public discourse to a much wider range of rights than the government and vested interests wished to address. The rights of the poor and excluded became a prominent issue in the liberalization of the Mexican economy. Political rights became a widely discussed theme. Collective rights, still debatable in world circles, at least entered public consciousness and centered on the landless Indians and their right to land as part of their culture. Human rights groups attempted to protect children and adolescents from a criminal system that granted them very few rights and brought many more issues to public attention.

Third, human rights organizations have opened political space. As organizations, Centro Vitoria and others seized an opportunity to gain a niche in society where none existed previously. These centers arise from various sectors of society and speak in their name to defend their rights, to make present their demands, and to denounce arbitrary action, demanding accountability. These organizations are in the vanguard of social demands.[83]

Fourth, Mexicans sense great symbolic worth to human rights activity. Sara Sefchovich points to hope given (often for the first time) to citizens that human rights violations will decrease. Further, those who commit violations have begun to feel their impunity threatened. The human rights groups have helped generate legitimacy for moral considerations in public debate. Thus, as Celso Lafer says of human rights activity in Mexico: ''The very fact of showing respect for human rights establishes a stabilizing benchmark in society.''[84]

NOTES

An earlier version of this chapter appeared in *Journal of Church and State* 37 (Autumn 1995), pp. 793–812, and is used by permission.

1. Colombia and Venezuela are other prominent examples.

2. Edward L. Cleary, ''Struggling for Human Rights in Latin America,'' *America* 171, 14 (November 5, 1994), pp. 20–24.

3. Interviews with Jesús Maldonado García of the Miguel Pro Center, in Joy Peebles Lane, ''Las organizaciones no gubernamentales de Derechos Humanos en México: Su formación y esfuerzos para realizar cambios socio-políticos,'' Master's thesis, Estudios Latinoamericanos, Facultad de Ciencias Políticos y Sociales, Universidad Nacional Autónoma de México (January 1993), pp. 80–84; and with Teresa Jardí, ''Entrevista,'' *Eslabones* 8 (July–December 1994), p. 66.

4. See discussion of social movements as defined by political practices in Joe Foweraker, ''Popular Movements and Political Change in Mexico,'' in Foweraker and Ann L. Craig, eds., *Popular Movements and Political Change in Mexico* (Boulder, Colo.: Lynne Rienner, 1990), esp. pp. 5–7; and Sidney Tarrow, ''Social Movements in Contentious Politics: A Review Article,'' *American Political Science Review* 90, 4 (December 1996), pp. 874–883.

5. Esp. Charles Tilly's *Contentious French* (Cambridge: Harvard University Press, 1986), and *European Revolutions, 1492–1992* (Oxford: Blackwell, 1993).

6. Doug McAdam, *The Political Process and the Development of Black Insurgency* (Chicago: University of Chicago Press, 1982), and *Freedom Summer* (New York: Oxford University Press, 1988). For an extension of McAdam's model to liberation theology movement, see Christian Smith, *The Emergence of Liberation Theology; Radical Religion and Social Movement Theory* (Chicago: University of Chicago Press, 1991).

7. The work of Herbert Haines on black collective power has been especially useful. He assesses the impact of the civil rights movement in his *Black Radicals and the Civil Rights Mainstream, 1954–1970* (Knoxville: University of Tennessee Press, 1988). Social movement scholars have been making theoretical and historical advances in numerous international conferences. See esp. Doug McAdam, John D. McCarthy, and Mayer N. Zeld, eds., *Comparative Perspectives on Social Movements: Political Opportunities, Mobilizing Structures, and Cultural Framings* (New York: Cambridge University Press, 1996). See also: Enrique Laraña, Hank Johnston, and Joseph R. Gusfield, eds., *New Social Movements: From Ideology to Identity* (Philadelphia: Temple University Press, 1994); and Aldon D. Morris and Carol McClurg Mueller, eds., *Frontiers in Social Movement Theory* (New Haven: Yale University Press, 1992).

8. Sidney Tarrow, *Power in Movement* (New York: Cambridge University Press, 1994). See also his ''States and Opportunities: The Political Structuring of Social Movements,'' in McAdam et al., *Comparative Perspectives*, pp. 41–61.

9. Tarrow acknowledges: ''The social movment has been transnational since the Atlantic Revolution of the eighteenth century'' (p. 61), in his ''States and Opportunities.''

In 1993, Ron Pagnucco argued: ''I would like to add that we also need systematic studies of the *transnational* dimensions of social movements,'' in the *Newsletter of the American Sociological Association's Section on Political Sociology* 10, 2 (Winter 1993), pp. 1–2. Since then Pagnucco, Jackie Smith, and others have added valuable insights into this dimension. See, for example, Pagnucco and David Atwood, ''The Transnational Tactical Repertoire of Social Movements,'' *Peace Review* 6, 4 (1994), pp. 411–418; Smith, Pagnucco, and Winnie Romeril, ''Transnational Social Movement Organisations in the Global Political Arena,'' *Voluntas* 5, 2, pp. 121–154; and Smith, ''Transnational Political Processes and the Human Rights Movement,'' *Research in Social Movements, Conflict, and Change* 18, pp. 185–219.

10. For this analysis I made an ethnographic investigation of the ''early riser'' human rights center, Centro Vitoria, through interviews, observation, and examination of documents in 1979, 1981 (especially of Centro Montecinos, predecessor of Centro Vitoria), 1992, and 1994.

11. A heavy volume of political analyses of Mexico has recently been published. Among often cited works are: Roderic Ai Camp, *Politics in Mexico* (New York: Oxford University Press, 1993); and Héctor Aguilar Camín and Lorenzo Meyer, *In the Shadow of the Mexican Revolution: Contemporary Mexican History, 1910–1989* (Austin: University of Texas Press, 1993).

12. In 1981 the Council on Hemispheric Affairs' *Washington Report on the Americas* reported: ''With some justice, Mexico can be called the 'Iran Next Door' '' (July 14, 1981), pp. 4–5. See also Charles Humana, comp., *World Human Rights Guide*, 3d. ed. (New York: Oxford University Press, 1992), pp. 205–208. See earlier eds. of Humana's *Guide* and Human Rights Watch/Americas Watch, *Human Rights In Mexico: A Policy of Impunity* (New York: Human Rights Watch, 1990); Ellen L. Lutz, ''Human Rights in Mexico: Cause for Continuing Concern,'' *Current History* 92, 571 (February 1993), pp. 78–82; Lawyers Committee for Human Rights, *Critique Review of the Department of State's Country Reports for Human Rights Practices for 1990* (New York: Lawyers Committee for Human Rights, 1991), pp. 155–162; Amnesty International, annual reports, and Minnesota Advocates, various publications.

13. Martin Needler, ''The Consent of the Governed? Coercion, Co-optation, and Compromise in Mexican Politics,'' *Mexican Studies* 102 (Summer 1994), p. 383.

14. Ibid.

15. Tarrow, *Power*, esp. pp. 81–99.

16. For Mexico, see esp. Foweraker and Craig, *Popular Movements* and sources in following endnote.

17. Foweraker and Craig, ''Popular Movements,'' esp. p. 4. See also Alberto Melucci, ''Liberation or Meaning? Social Movements, Culture, and Democracy,'' *Development and Change* 23, 3 (1992), pp. 43–77; Joel Wolfe, ''Social Movements and the State in Brazil,'' *Latin American Research Review* 28, 1 (Winter 1993), pp. 248–258; and Barry D. Adam, ''Post-Marxism and the New Social Movements,'' *Canadian Review of Sociology and Anthropology* 30, 3 (1993), pp. 316–336. A more pessimistic view than many authors is expressed by Diane E. Davis, ''Failed Democratic Reform in Contemporary Mexico: From Social Movements to the State and Back Again,'' *Journal of Latin American Studies* 26, 2 (May 1994), pp. 375–408. For Latin America, see Arturo Escobar and Sonia E. Alvarez, eds., *The Making of Social Movements in Latin America* (Boulder, Colo.: Westview, 1993).

18. Foweraker and Craig, ''Popular Movements,'' p. 5.

19. Nora Lustig provides an account of the impact of adjustment and subsequent economic reform in *Mexico: The Remaking of an Economy* (Washington, D.C.: Brookings Institution, 1992).

20. Alexis de Tocqueville, *The Old Regime and the French Revolution* (Garden City, N.Y.: Doubleday Anchor, 1955), pp. 176–177.

21. An older comparative view is provided by J. Lloyd Mecham's *Church and State in Latin America: History of Politico-Ecclesiastical Relations*, rev. ed. (Chapel Hill: University of North Carolina Press, 1966). More recent descriptions of church and state relations are: Roberto Blancarte, *El poder salinismo e Iglesia católica, una nueva convivencia* (Mexico City: Grijalbo, 1991); Karl Schmitt, ''Church and State in Mexico: A Corporatist Relationship?'', *Américas* 40 (January 1984), pp. 349–376; and Claude Pomerlau, ''The Changing Church in Mexico and Its Challenge to the State,'' *Review of Politics* 43 (October 1981), pp. 540–549.

22. Significant changes were made in January 1992. The changes also affected Protestant churches. See Allan Metz, ''Protestantism in Mexico: Contemporary Contextual Developments,'' *Journal of Church and State* 36, 1 (Winter 1994), esp. pp. 77–78. Even under the old restrictions many priests did vote. See also Matt Moffett, ''In Catholic Mexico, A Priest's Power Is Limited to Prayer,'' *Wall Street Journal* (December 6, 1989).

23. A respected work, *Mexico: Paradoxes of Stability and Change*, 2d. ed. (Boulder, Colo.: Westview, 1987, p. 89), by a North American and a Mexican author, Daniel Levy and Gabriel Székeley, characterized the situation: ''Churches are organizations and they bring individuals together. The regime would not tolerate the church *as a powerful political organization* (emphasis theirs), capable of influencing national policy and even challenging the regime.''

24. Mecham, *Church*, p. 415.

25. See, for example, Aguilar Camín and Meyer, *In the Shadow*, pp. 239 ff.

26. Camp, *Politics*, p. 174.

27. Ibid., p. 86. His later work, ''The Cross in the Polling Bootth: Religion, Politics, and the Laity in Mexico,'' *Latin American Research Review* 29, 3 (1994), pp. 69–100 notes: ''Mexicans believe that the church should openly discuss Third World problems'' (p. 93).

28. Tarrow characterizes in *Power* the role of religion at this level in England and the United States as ''a cradle for associational development'' (p. 56).

29. Tom Barry et al. estimate 150,000–250,000 members of base Christian communities have been active in weekly meetings, in *Mexico: A Country Guide* (Albuquerque: Inter-Hemispheric Education Resource Center, 1992), p. 256.

30. See, for example, Miguel Concha Malo et al., *La participación de los cristianos en el proceso popular de liberación de México* (Mexico City: Siglo XXI, 1986); *Christus*; and various publications of Centro de Reflexión Teológica.

31. Interviews with archdiocesan and seminary officials, Mexico City, February 1981 and November 1994.

32. See Peebles Lane's recounting (''Las organizaciones'') of the difficulties of the citation of human rights violations in newspapers since the press did not use the term ''humans rights,'' p. 72 ff; see also Peebles Lane's interview with Jesús Maldonado García in 1987, pp. 80–84, and discussion of language in final section of this chapter.

33. Interviews with Rodolfo Stavenhagen and Miguel Concha, Mexico City, November 1994.

34. Several organizational leaders prefer ''Christian'' as a designation of the centers.

35. Two studies and sets of interviews are especially useful in tracing human rights

organizations in Mexico: Peebles Lane, ''Las organizaciones,'' and the December 1994 (No. 8) issue of *Eslabones* (Revista semestral de estudios regionales).

36. Jorge G. Casteñeda, *Utopia Unarmed: The Latin American Left after the Cold War* (New York: Knopf, 1993), p. 234.

37. Jardí, ''Entrevista,'' *Eslabones*, p. 71.

38. Abel Guardarrama Juárez, ''La falta de democracia, mayor obstáculo para los derechos humanos: Miguel Concha,'' *Justicia y Paz* 9, 34 (April–June 1994), p. 113.

39. In 1984 the Mexican section of Amnesty International also was established but the section did not concern itself at that time with human rights of Mexicans.

40. See end note no. 6. By interviews and correspondence the author followed the evolution of this group from Centro Montesinos to Centro Vitoria, from 1979 to the present.

41. Sergio Aguayo notes the complementary character, lay and religious, of the two centers in an interview in *Eslabones* 8 (July–December 1994), p. 58.

42. Concha et al., *La participación*.

43. Camp, ''The Cross,'' p. 72. See also Martín de la Rosa, ''Iglesia y sociedad en México hoy,'' in de la Rosa and Charles A. Reilly, eds., *Religión y sociedad en México* (Mexico City: Siglo Veitíuno, 1985), pp. 268–292.

44. Aguilar Camín and Meyer, two of Mexico's leading intellectuals, take up papal influence in their *In the Shadow*, pp. 262–263.

45. See, for example, the history of the Jesuit center, Centro de Derechos Humanos ''Miguel Augusto Pro Júarez,'' in Peebles Lane, ''Las organizaciones,'' pp. 80–84.

46. Interview, San José, Costa Rica, June 12, 1996.

47. Castañeda, *Utopia Unarmed*, p. 224.

48. See, for example, Special Issue on response to the 1985 earthquake: ''Sismo: Disastre y sociedad en la Ciudad de México,'' *Revista Mexicana de Sociología* (April 1986).

49. See, for example, Carlos Monsiváis, *Entrada libre: Crónicas de una sociedad que se organiza* (Mexico City: Ediciones Era, 1988).

50. *Justicia y Paz* (Centro Vitoria) 20, p. 9.

51. See Cuéllar's own account of systematic work in ''Diez años de trabajo del Socorro Jurídico Cristiano,'' *Justicia y Paz* 1, 1 (November 1985).

52. Pablo González Casanova and Jorge Cadena Roa, coordinators, *Primer informe sobre la democracia: México 1988* (Mexico City: Siglo Veintiuno Editores, 1988).

53. Concha, ''La violaciones a los derechos humanos individuales en México (período: 1971–1986),'' in González Casanova and Cadena Roa, *Primer informe*, pp. 115–187.

54. Tarrow, *Power*, p. 119.

55. Interview in *Eslabones* 8 (July–December 1994), p. 66.

56. Sera Sefchovich, ''Los derechos humanos: Teoría, práctica, filosofía, utopía,'' *Eslabones* 8 (July–December 1994), p. 29.

57. See, for example, the reporting in *La Jornada* (November 23, 1994), p. 5.

58. Peebles Lane, ''Las organizaciones,'' p. 72 ff.

59. Jardí, Interview, *Eslabones* 8, p. 68.

60. See Norbert Lechner, ''Los derechos humanos y el nuevo orden internacional,'' in Carlos Portales, ''La América Latina en el nuevo orden internacional,'' *El Trimestre Económico* 19, p. 284.

61. Denise Dresser, ''Folio: La promocción de la democracia en México,'' *Este País* 40 (July 1994), p. 10.

62. See, for example, Human Rights Watch/Americas Watch, *Human Rights . . . Impunity*.

63. Andrew Reding, "Mexico under Salinas: A Facade of Reform," *World Policy Journal* 6, 4 (Fall 1989), p. 725.

64. See Emilio Rebasa Gamboa, *Vigencia y efectividad de los Derechos Humanos en México: Análisis jurídico de la Ley de la CNDH* (Mexico City: Comisión Nacional de Derechos Humanos, 1992.)

65. Camp, *Politics*, p. 174. In 1990 hearings in the United States, the House Committee on Foreign Affairs heard strong denunciations of human rights violations in Mexico. See *Hearing before the Subcommittee on Human Rights and International Organizations, and on Western Hemisphere Affairs, September 12, 1990* (Washington, D.C.: Government Printing Office, 1990).

66. For a brief evaluation of the National Human Rights Commission, see *Human Rights Watch World Report 1994*, pp. 115–117.

67. See *Human Rights World Report 1994*, pp. 115–119, and Amnesty International, *Mexico: The Persistence of Torture and Impunity* (New York: Amnesty International, 1993).

68. Concha was elected in 1993 by Mexican Dominicans as major superior for the country. He has become honorary president of the Vitoria Center and Raymundo Tamayo, another Dominican, its president.

69. *Los derechos políticos como derechos humanos* (Mexico City: La Jornada Ediciones and Centro de Investigaciones Interdisciplinarias en Humanidades UNAM, 1994).

70. Jardí, "Entrevista," *Eslabones*, p. 72.

71. Text published in *La Jornada* (January 13, 1994), p. 9.

72. *National Catholic Reporter* (September 1, 1995).

73. Guadarrama Juárez, "La falta," p. 113. "More than 300" was the assessment also generally accepted at Seminario Regional, "La Construcción de los Derechos Humanos desde los/las Pobres y Excluidos/as," Centro de Derechos Humanos "Fray Francisco de Vitoria," Mexico City, November 23–25, 1994. See also listings of human rights organizations in "Masterlist," *Human Rights Internet Reporter*, Supplement to vol. 15, 1994.

74. Report from Center given media representatives. Report to appear in *Justicia y Paz*. See also *La Jornada*, November 23, 1994, p. 5.

75. Interview, Mexico City, November 24, 1994.

76. Peebles Lane, "Las organizaciones," p. 38.

77. Sefchovich, "Los derechos," p. 29.

78. Interviews with Miguel Concha about Comisión Mexicana, Mexico City, November 21–25, 1994.

79. Sefchovich, "Los derechos," p. 29; Jardí, "Entrevista," p. 69.

80. Jardí, "Entrevista," p. 66.

81. Maldonado, interview in Peebles Lane, "Las organizaciones," pp. 80–84.

82. See Sergio Aguayo, "Naufragan los derechos humanos?", *La Jornada*, February 2, 1994, p. 14.

83. Newspapers, such as *La Jornada*, November 24, 1994, p. 18, seek out the opinion of human rights NGOs ("las principales organizaciones defensores de derechos humanos") as major actors within society.

84. Celso Lafer, *La reconstrucción de los derechos humanos: Un diálogo con el pensamiento de Hannah Arendt* (Mexico City: Fondo de Cultura Económica, 1994), p. 28.

3

Human Rights after the Military: Settling Accounts and Facing Issues

José Aldunate did not agree that Santiago's Vicariate of Solidarity should close its door. Nor did he concur with human rights movement advocates in Chile who moved on to other activities. Aldunate is a Jesuit priest from a privileged class background. His varied career includes acting as Jesuit superior for Chile, theology professor, worker priest, and a founding member of the National Movement against Torture.

Aldunate believed that too many human rights issues remained unresolved for the Vicariate to close up shop. He also held that ordinary citizens were ingenuous to turn over vigilance for human rights to the Chilean government, as apparently many thought would be effective.[1] Public opinion polls showed that most Chileans did not think that human rights problems had been solved.[2] Manuel Antonio Garretón, one of Chile's leading political scientists, put his finger on the fundamental problem for human rights issues in Chile: These issues do not have adequate actors or channels to represent them.[3]

What of the belief that political parties and the government would carry on the human rights movement objectives? The parties and the government did not maintain more than a minimal effort. Garretón says: ''The government's attempts to address these [human rights issues] have been halfhearted and inconsequential, drawing little social or political support.''[4]

Where did persons who had been committed to the human rights movement under military government go? Many prominent members of human rights groups found employment in the Aylwin and Frei governments. In interviews, they were quick to point out that they carry their human rights convictions with them to new governmental or teaching positions.[5] Some believed they assured high-level governmental concern for justice lacking in the military government. Other former participants found positions in universities, high schools, and research centers. Many expended their energies in start-up activities of more than 160 new Chilean universities.

Former members of the Vicariate of Solidarity frequently moved on to closely allied careers. For some time, Gloria Torres directed programs in nonformal education and in local leadership for grassroots groups. Gerald Whelan returned to St. George's, performing a succession of tasks: spiritual director, parent-educator coordinator, and curriculum reformer, all with a strong social emphasis. Christian Precht headed the new Vicaría de Pastoral (Pastoral Vicariate). Later he moved from Santiago to assume a major post at the Latin American Bishops Conference headquarters in Bogotá.[6] Enrique Palet also moved from the Vicariate of Solidarity to become executive secretary at the Pastoral Vicariate.

The dilemmas Chileans face upon return to democracy were repeated in many Latin American countries. All but two nations in South America and all but one in Central America had experienced military repression. The countries have since taken a turn to some form of democracy. What are the human rights issues Aldunate and other Latin Americans believe have not been resolved?

ENCLAVES OF AUTHORITARIANISM

First, enclaves of authoritarian regime remain. To continue with the example of Chile, on the streets, the legacy of repressive military rule continues in police work. Carabineros (national police) typically receive respect from citizens in ways unfamiliar to police in, say, Mexico or Peru.[7] No Chilean interviewed would consider offering a Carabinero a bribe. If a person offered a bribe, Chileans would expect to be jailed for suborning a police officer.[8] But police revert occasionally to repressive habits learned during the Pinochet years. Torture and physical abuse may not be as systematic. However, from October 1993 to September 1994, the Committee for the Defense of the Rights of the People filed nineteen lawsuits against the police for torture and abuse. Police also held some detainees incommunicado for twenty days and denied them due process.[9]

A second authoritarian legacy, a structural one, continues in the broad jurisdiction of military courts over crimes committed by members of the uniformed forces, including police, against civilians. A third holdover compounds this deficiency in a democracy. Civilian authorities in the government lack control over appointments of the military and police. A fourth legacy, Pinochet's heavy hand in Congress, continues. He wrote into the law provisions for military appointments of senators and for disproportionate strength of rightist opposition in Congress.

In Chile, many persons view these legacies as temporary aberrations with which Chileans can live until military influence further diminishes. In sum, the aberrations explain in part why Chile, a society with one of the strongest Latin American civic cultures, gained only an 80 rating in 1992 from the Humana human rights group.[10]

VICTIMS: LIVING ON

Other issues call for attention, as well. From the perspective of mothers, wives, and other relatives of the disappeared, the wounds of many persons have not healed. The psychological condition of many children of the disappeared has grown worse as they grew to adolescence and adulthood. The absence of a parent scarred them. The lack of accountability of why their fathers or mothers merited disappearance left children unusually vulnerable to questions from peers and from themselves. Suicide, school failures, psychic breakdowns occur at a higher than average rate. Psychic and mental health problems have also plagued surviving spouses. Loss of a breadwinner has meant, for many, great decline in economic and social status.

Torture victims had most of the physical wounds healed, although the gait or vision of some will never be the same. Lingering psychological effects differ considerably from person to person. To the discomfort of many victims, sleep and other disorders began occurring years after torture.

In centuries past, torture victims went on with their lives as best they could. Perhaps for the first time in history, in this Age of Human Rights, agencies have provided deep, long-term, and holistic assistance for torture victims. Their comprehensive care has not reached many victims; however, the number of organizations offering care when none existed 30 years ago surprises investigators. Most of the public are unaware of their existence. In Chile a center during the Pinochet regime was called a ''stress-reduction center.''

Only enterprising reporters find them. Such were Stan Grossfeld of the *Boston Globe* and Colman McCarthy of the *Washington Post*.[11] Grossfeld went to Copenhagen where he found Doctor Inge Genefke, founder of the Rehabilitation and Research Center for Torture Victims. The doctors and staff at Copenhagen center treat about 100 patients a year and have helped establish centers in 50 other countries. Doctors and staff offer comprehensive care. Grossfeld believes: ''The restoration of the human spirit is the top priority.''[12] In Minneapolis, Douglas Johnson and many others carry on similar work at a full-treatment Center for Victims of Torture. Since 1985 center personnel have attended some 500 victims.[13]

In other places, small but important groups have grown up to help in the rehabilitation of torture victims. Often no obvious connection to Latin America exists. Rather, these caregivers accepted the argument of the global human rights movement that responsibility for protesting and responding to human rights violations was shared across national borders.

ISSUES THAT CONTINUE

Forgetting or not forgetting, getting even or not getting even with torturers or ''tormentors'' (those who caused victims to disappear, leaving torment): These questions continue not only for victims but for society. The Chilean bishops may have represented the sentiments of many when they urged telling the truth, offering forgiveness, and expecting accountability.[14] Besides the fundamental issue of truth and reconciliation, three other issues continue as unresolved from the military era: socioeconomic misery, gender issues, and reform of the judicial system. The following sections continue using Chile as the focus of issues that many Latin American countries face.

Socioeconomic Misery

Chile does not rank among Latin American nations with the highest percentages of the suffering poor. Nonetheless, poverty has been a major concern for the country. First, the years of military rule in Chile and in much of Latin America were years of acute suffering. Some regimes, such as Chile's, attempted to force economically rational plans that involved basic readjustments. The negative effects of this policy fell disproportionately on the lower classes.[15]

Second, virtually all governments, military or civilian, were subject to global economic changes over which they had no control. The 1980s became the "lost decade" for Latin Americans, military government or not. Real income fell and many families fell into acute poverty.

Third, beginning in the late 1980s many Chileans began to enjoy a relatively high level of prosperity. Structures of inequality continued. The top 20 percent of households in 1987 received 56 percent of income and in 1992, 55.1 percent of Chile's family incomes. No change occurred at the bottom where the lowest 20 percent of families received 4.5 percent of income in 1987 and 1992. The contrast of income levels and access to goods and services between rich and poor thus accentuated those left behind in the economic resurgence.[16]

Initially, many critics attacked the Pinochet regime because of its economic model and its effect on much of the population. Members of the human rights movement and many allies were in the forefront of protest on these grounds.[17] However, as time progressed many Chileans moved to support the economic model. Garretón believes that complacency effectively hinders meaningful debate about pressing social issues.[18]

Ideological conviction, rather than complacency, apparently holds the Catholic Church back from public stands about misery in Chile. The church, through the Vicariate of Solidarity, had taken leadership in various parts of the country to promote a wide range of human rights. From its inception in 1975, the Vicariate provided many services, including health and occupational assistance, to more than 700,000 persons in one four-year period.[19]

But the Chilean bishops now are strongly inclined to create or to support independent or semi-independent organizations to deal with social and economic issues. Gradually, specialized groups, often associated with the church, absorbed many activities previously supported by the Vicariate. However, the bright promise of some groups has diminished. A major autonomous group continuing the church's social orientation is the renowned Center for Investigation in Education (CIDE). Patricio Cariola, its charismatic founder and director, organized the center that a few years ago employed a professional staff of more than 70 persons. Now many of the staff, including Gloria Torres, have been dismissed. The fragility of autonomous nongovernmental organizations dependent on North Atlantic funding became painfully evident.

Enrique Palet, who served the Vicariate of Solidarity as executive director, explains why it closed: "The church trusts in civil society (the government and civic organizations) to carry on functions that the church previously fulfilled. The church occupies a space mostly outside politics. Its public space is reduced. Frankly, the church does not have much resonance in public life. If the church were to take public positions, hardly any one would listen."[20]

However, small, prophetic enclaves persist within the church. One, the Justice and Peace Commission, operates within the National Bishops' Conference. This small group of lay persons and a few bishops continue to raise questions about inequality and poverty within Chile. They built on ideas in the Chilean church's National Plan (1991), which affirmed the church's option for the poor.[21] In 1992, the Justice and Peace Commission addressed misery that continues in Chile: *Desafíos de Chile: Reflexiones y sugerencias de accion para superar la pobreza.* In 1994 the group sponsored a major conference, attended by bishops, priests, and laity, drawing the participation of President Frei. They then published a statement, *Superación de la pobreza en Chile* (Overcoming Poverty in Chile).[22]

While Palet believes the bishops continue to be preoccupied by poverty in the country, other observers raise questions about the reluctance of the national episcopal conference to speak. Katherine Gilfeather O'Brien, who has worked for years as a social scientist at Centro Bellarmino in Santiago, expresses this: "One would think that the bishops could at least help frame the public debate over misery in which many persons live, as bishops in the United States have raised questions about the Republican "Contract with America."[23]

In the Chilean debate, observers point out that Chile has led Latin American countries in improving their economy. Then, too, Chile made notable gains in reducing poverty in terms of measurable income.[24] But many observers fail to recognize that the condition of the poor has not changed much, because income figures do not express more profound aspects of poverty. The editors of *Mensaje* attempt to track the situation of the poor, especially through periodic reports of Jaime Ruiz-Tagle. In his review of 1994, Ruiz-Tagle refined his statistics to show presence or absence of basic necessities in a household. Measured in this manner, he shows: "Some 8.5 million persons (of a total of 14 million) either do not have sufficient income to satisfy basic necessities or they have to face basic deficiencies that do not permit them to carry on a humane existence."[25]

Thus the dilemma continues for a society in which the voice of the voiceless is not well heard. "Many Chileans fall between the cracks, having no one to represent their interests," as one official of the Inter-American Development Bank believes.[26] For some human rights activists such as Gerald Whelan, the human rights movement declined too early to address the needs of the poor.[27]

Gender Issues

Whelan believes the same about gender issues. However, in this area forceful groups continue to work.[28] Women were, as mentioned in the first chapter, a major element in the human rights movement in Chile. Women formed the majority of workers in the movement, at least in Santiago. They also guided some organizations as chief executives.[29] Women in politics have a long history in Chile,[30] but, for the most part, they were not visible, appearing in the background. They formed part of mobilizations and supported male leadership. Major issues about women and politics only became fully evident in the 1970s and 1980s.

Eduardo Frei Montalva's centrist government (1964–1970) created Mothers' Centers, government-supported efforts. During the Allende years, El Poder Femenino organized to protest his socialist government. One member said: "Women felt their fundamental values of family and motherhood threatened at the onset of Marxism."[31] When Pinochet came to power in 1973, he capitalized on those fears. His government reorganized Mothers' Centers (Centro de Madres) and created a National Secretariat for Women. Pinochet's wife, Lucía Hiriart, directed both groups.

Hence, from the beginning of military government, officials attempted to enlist women. This largely meant mobilization from above, the use of women from the upper classes to reach out to lower-class women. These Mothers' Centers numbered as many as 10,000 with 230,000 members.[32] Documentary footage from the era shows elegantly dressed ladies attempting to show less privileged women how to conserve food in a time of economic belt-tightening.[33] Strong paternalism and ignorance of the living conditions of the poor marked these efforts.

Socioeconomic distress brought gender issues special consideration in Chile and throughout Latin America. The double weight of being a poor woman in a discriminatory society became clearer during the Pinochet years.[34] Opposition to government policies brought women a greater sense of who they were in Chilean society and who they might be. One mechanism of change was the reflection group. There women learned a method of seeing, judging, and acting. Women began perceiving themselves as invisible in public life. In a patriarchal society women did not count in politics, except as numbers to be mobilized and counted.

The Pinochet government's strong drive to mobilize women and to reinforce their traditional roles through Mothers' Centers helped to focus oppositional efforts. They protested not only a repressive government but society as heavily patriarchal. This consciousness took time to grow. The members had to shield the process from public view, given the military's tight control.

In poor neighborhoods and shantytowns, *pobladores* showed unusual creativity. Women led the way toward forming communities of persons who would share whatever food they had on a particular day. The ups and downs of the poor resulted largely from erratic circles of work, such as construction work when money was available and weather allowed, short harvest period, and resources for externally funded, short-term projects. Throughout Latin America, *ollas comunes* grew from women's desire to share in the face of uncertainty. Women gathered whatever they could afford to give and put food into common dishes which neighbors could share.

In poor neighborhoods where security forces made periodic sweeps, women took leadership roles in responding to government actions. Security forces often detained for short periods many persons caught up in these sweeps. Some prisoners needed legal defense and medical assistance. Women, especially through CODEPU (already described), did what they could to seek assistance and to publicize the terrorizing. *Solidaridad*, the Vicariate's magazine, routinely carried reports from these neighborhood committees.

For the women of the *poblaciones* the churches sponsored small craft workshops. Marjorie Agosín lovingly tells the story of Chilean women weavers in *Scraps of Life: Chilean Arpilleras*.[35] Among the workshops were several set up for women who had lost family members through disappearance. These women, brought together by loss, told their stories by embroidering small wall hangings, *arpilleras*, from old clothes and fabric remnants. Arpilleras are commonly found in Chile and Latin America. But, as Agosín believes, initially only women from the neighborhoods surrounding Santiago created the political arpilleras.

The Vicariate of Solidarity furnished raw materials, sponsored the workshops, bought their finished goods, sold the products abroad, and distributed the profits equally to group members. Agosín describes the product: "Each arpillera is a small scene from the life of the woman who creates it; just as their lives have been torn to pieces, the arpillera consists of scraps of leftover material, put together slowly and in sorrow."[36] For some women it takes one week to complete an arpillera, another a month, and a few because of deep sadness never completely finish one. These women say that these workshops are "their life, their daily bread, and a way of feeling accompanied in their sadness."[37]

Some 30 workshops turned out arpilleras. The weavers expressed a story of Pinochet's Chile that was not supposed to be told. Therefore, government officials forbade sale of arpilleras in Chile. Missionary priests and sisters returning for leave to their home countries and other empathetic travellers clandestinely served as couriers to sale-points in Massachusetts and elsewhere. Many small messages of repression thus found their way to foreign and influential audiences.

Noteworthy nongovernmental organizations grew out of these efforts. The groups were especially important in the latter years of the Pinochet government and during the democratic transition of the Aylwin years. Social empowerment and economic enrichment resulted. Brian Smith notes: "Despite . . . caveats about the *political* power of non-profit organizations in developing countries, there clearly have been some forms of empowerment in the poor as a result of their activities. . . . Grassroots non-profit organizations have been particularly helpful for women to advance their social power throughout developing countries."[38]

Through the years of dictatorship, then, women took part valiantly in the human rights movement, joined movements of women (as in the *poblaciones*), and created feminist groups. They are no longer invisible in Chilean public and political life.

Women have slowly transgressed into worlds of men's power. This transgression is not an ultra-feminist one but another typical of Latin America, conveying a sense of "being in this together." Catherine Boyle believes the transgressions were made "with solidarity for men's struggles, a solidarity built in the knowledge that equality and respect between men and women was and is the only progressive way forward."[39] As Boyle concludes: "There has been a palpable change in the presence of women in Chile."[40]

President Frei Ruiz-Tagle has appointed two women ministers in his cabinet. Both appointments have significance for gender issues. One woman's position is attorney general and she has special concern for devising laws to benefit women's interests. The president charged the other minister with wide responsibility to look into issues affecting women. The two ministers do not stand alone. A small and vital women's movement supports, criticizes, and encourages them.

Judicial Reform

Before the Pinochet years, Chile's judges were an honored group and trust was high in the system itself. Of Chile, Tina Rosenberg says: "Democracy was not just an empty exercise in voting; people used democratic channels such as the courts and political parties to solve their everyday problems."[41] A longtime observer of the system, Carmen Garretón, now executive director of the Vicariate archives, says: "We were fanatics in believing in the judiciary system. We would spend all kinds of money defending cases in the courts."[42]

Thus many Chileans were shocked to observe the passivity of judges during the Pinochet years. Worse, in José Luis Cea's eyes, were judges and lawyers who tried to relativize human rights under authoritarian government. In his view they twisted ideas of justice. "It is a deplorable work of manipulation and fitting in," he wrote.[43] Constable and Valenzuela assessed the situation: "The military takeover exposed Chile's distinguished juridical tradition as a charade of eloquent phrases and prodigious paperwork."[44] A few heroic judges did begin, in about 1980, to take an increasingly activist stance, by overseeing investigations. However, the generally poor performance of the judiciary during the military regime forced a reevaluation of the system. Many human rights advocates in Chile (in contrast to some Latin American countries) believe the judicial system is key to the solid foundation of justice and of democracy itself.

The system needs wide reform. Carlos Peña González captures this in "Informe sobre Chile."[45] His report and commentary forms part of a larger Ford

Foundation project. Three aspects stand out: the best law teachers and lawyers do not become judges (poorly paid is one reason); the courts are partly paralyzed with caseloads; and, above all, the prevailing positivist system has proven increasingly inadequate.

Under the contemporary system the law as written comes first; jurisprudence a distant second. So judges are reported as saying, in effect: ''I apply the law. I cannot worry about justice.'' The system traps judges. Not only did the Pinochet regime show the system as lacking independence, but technological changes in society demand a greater latitude in jurisprudence than that provided by the nineteenth century model that governs Chile's legal system.

Peña González examines the discussion about reforming the judicial system and finds that politicians and judges inadequately carry on the debate. What Chile lacks, he says is an ''academic class'' within the legal profession, persons trained to diagnose and correct the deficiencies.[46]

THE FUNDAMENTAL ISSUE

The fundamental issue in human rights, one hears not only in Chile but elsewhere in Latin America, is *impunidad*. Society has to hold someone accountable. When interviewed in 1989, most Chileans expressed a strong opinion that what Argentina, Uruguay, and Brazil had done was enough to settle accounts with repressive governments.[47] That was before Chileans tried to set their record straight.

The question of settling accounts with torturers has been an issue from the beginnings of human society. If Chileans had reached further back in history than Argentina to *la madre patria*, Spain, they might have been less demanding. A million died in Spain and human rights abuses abounded in a civil war and succeeding years that left deep cleavages in Spanish society. In the view of *The Economist*, Spaniards formed *un pacto de olvido*, an agreement to forget. In *The Economist*'s view: ''Almost every one tacitly decided that Spain could move ahead only if the past remained undisturbed.''[48] This is only partly true but represents a major impulse in dealing with the past.[49]

Many Latin American countries have not been satisfied with large-scale forgetting. Selective memory has been carried out. In the process, settling accounts has involved divisible tasks. Some countries take initial steps and find that latter tasks become progressively harder. Ultimate accounting seems beyond reach. In Latin America, among countries with repressive histories, one-half have taken major steps toward truth and reconciliation. Eight countries, for a variety of reasons, have not.[50]

In the view of many observers, the most basic step is for some agency, not necessarily governmental, to tell the truth in some fashion. In her review of truth commissions, Priscilla Hayner states: ''A growing consensus [exists] that human rights crimes cannot be ignored during a democratic transition; a perceived need [exists] to institute truth commission-like bodies in various countries around the world.''[51]

Proof for that assertion is lacking. Some Latin American countries have made creative efforts to come to terms with past horrors. One might exclude countries where military governments aimed more at reform than repression (Peru[52] and Panama), or where military rule was limited (Ecuador), or where militaries still exercise strong control (Guatemala and Cuba). Then one could focus on clear cases (in order of retreat from the presidential palace): Brazil, Bolivia, Argentina, Uruguay, Paraguay, Honduras, Chile, and El Salvador. These are countries where human rights violations were common, where repressive rule accounted for many violations, where citizens wish a turn toward democracy, and where governments have taken some first step toward rectifying past wrongs.

Brazilian Drama

These countries made important steps toward recognizing the record and setting it straight. True to stereotype, Brazilians made their first step in the most dramatic way possible. They did it as did no other Latin American country, or perhaps any country in the world. They established the record *out of military files*. In a tale of intrigue worthy of the best thrillers, a small group of Brazilians borrowed files of the military, photographed them, and published the record. All the while they maintained absolute secrecy for five years while the group carried on the project. They guarded secrecy about the report's authors for another year and a half after publication.[53]

A Portuguese and Spanish legacy to the ''Latin American way'' is bureaucratic record-keeping. Any visitor to Latin America twenty years ago or anyone dealing with customs officials has experienced the need to have official stationery purchased, seals affixed, copies signed by many officials, and papers filed. Record-keeping found a life of its own in Latin America. To this tendency add Brazilian ambitions of becoming technologically advanced as a military power. Since most trials took place under military jurisdiction, this meant careful record of charges filed, imprisonment endured, confessions obtained, appeals made, and reasons for judgments noted.

The military transported records made in various parts of the vast country to the national capital. In Brasília, clerks carefully sorted, filed, and stored records. ''Records were better kept than prisoners,'' was a common complaint heard in Latin America during military dictatorships. One can then imagine the storehouse of materials built up from 1964 to 1979 in Brasília.[54] As the generals thenceforth extricated themselves from governing Brazil, the military began in 1979 to selectively allow lawyers use of its archive. Lawyers could take out files on individual cases for 24 hours.

Astute lawyers, sympathetic to human rights causes, approached Jaime Wright, a Brazilian of parents from the United States. Wright was moderator of the Presbyterian Church/U.S.A. in Brazil. He lost a brother to military repression. Lawyers proposed to him the idea of photocopying large batches of records from the military archives. This would provide a view previously hidden to the public of what had been going on for many years. Wright explained: "We sat in the car mulling over the existence of that archive, and the chances of our having access to it. One of the passengers of the car was a staff member from the World Council of Churches, visiting Brazil from headquarters in Geneva. He became enthusiastic about the idea.

"We hatched the whole plan right there in the car. . . . We realized, of course, that everything had to be handled with the utmost secrecy. The next day I went into the Cardinal's [Arns] office and presented the plan to him. He immediately endorsed it, and volunteered his personal sponsorship."[55]

The World Council of Churches (WCC) granted over $350,000 over time. The Catholic archdiocese of São Paulo, 1,000 kilometers from Brasília, furnished safe storage. After three years of borrowing files, photocopying them, transporting them to São Paulo, the small band had put together a million-page record.

Next came the more difficult stage: putting these pages in order and printing a report. This was accomplished, with no leak, except as the publication date grew near, to inform reporters about what was to happen. The report appeared first in Portuguese as *Brasil: Nunca Mais* (Brazil, Never Again).[56] The publication of the most unusual of all Latin American records caused a strong impression in the public. As Lawrence Weschler comments: "These accounts of torture were thus doubly astonishing: first in the indisputable authoritativeness—the undeniability—of the testimony; and secondly, in the very fact, the virtual scandal, that such testimony existed at all."[57]

A few years before the Brazilian bombshell was set off, Bolivians were wrestling with setting their record straight. Still under military rule in the early 1980s, human rights advocates managed to have Jack Anderson in his syndicated newspaper column, and CBS's *60 Minutes* reveal a bit of what Bolivians call "distortions of justice."[58] After Bolivia restored a civilian presidency, the country's attempt to tell the truth differed from Brazil's. Other Latin American countries have followed Bolivia's form of truth-telling.[59]

Bolivia became the first Latin American country to establish a truth commission.[60] The number of disappearances (about 155) was small, compared with what was taking place farther south in Latin America. The commission never had enough resources nor political support to complete its work and disbanded after a few years. Its partial results in locating bodies and in having governmental acceptance of responsibility produced what Americas Watch characterizes thus: "The search for truth and justice has been recognized, not only as a legitimate endeavor of human rights organizations, but as an obligation of the state."[61]

Bolivia's example inspired Argentinean efforts.[62] Argentina's presidents after military rule, Raúl Alfonsín and Carlos Saúl Menem, both were members of a prominent human rights commission before being elected president. Their behavior about human rights while in office would differ greatly.

Alfonsín acted quickly to establish the National Commission on the Disappeared (the Sábato Commission). Similar groups also set to work in some provinces. The Argentine military had called the period *El Proceso*; others called it "The Dirty War."[63] Estimates range from 10,000 to 30,000 citizens disappeared and 30,000 imprisoned, at least for short terms.[64] If Argentina had the worst period of repression in Latin America, its first civilian government attempted to go further than most other countries in setting the record straight.

Members of the National Commission on the Disappeared reviewed extensive files from human rights organizations. Sábato Commission staff members investigated detention centers, cemeteries, and police stations. Some half million Argentines had gone into exile during the repression. Some returned to give testimony or those still abroad gave testimony at embassies or consulates. The Sábato Commission members felt that they had to agree with the figure of 9,000 disappeared.[65] (The number has since been increased by another 1,000.) A two-hour national television program summarized testimony presented. Argentineans snatched up the Sábato Commission's report *Nunca Más*, issued in 1984, and made it a best-seller.[66]

Argentina, under Alfonsín's leadership, pushed further. Argentine judges indicted and convicted top military officers for their roles in repression. (No other Latin American country attempted systematic trials.) As David Pion-Berlin observes: "The trials of the former members of the military juntas that ruled Argentina between 1976 and 1982 engendered intense curiosity and scrutiny in the international community. Not since the Nuremberg trials of the Nazi criminals of World War II had a trial of this nature anywhere in the world captured so much attention."[67] At the end of the 1980s the director of the Human Rights Watch said: Argentina's was "the most successful effort of the decade anywhere in Latin America, and perhaps worldwide, to hold accountable those who committed gross abuses of human rights."[68]

However, the political consequences were severe. Military pressure soon after the trial brought closure, through the Punto Final (End Point) Bill in late 1986. Even these terms were not enough to satisfy younger officers. Military insubordination followed. The first of four military uprisings occurred in early 1987. Junior officers organized rebellions against their superiors. Alfonsín had to negotiate with junior officers and had to agree to end human rights trials. Alfonsín was wounded politically in the exchange, lost legitimacy, and resigned the presidency about a half year early. By 1990, Menem (who had spent six years in prison because of human rights activities) completed a chapter in the story. He granted pardons to all military officers accused or convicted of human rights violations.

In Uruguay the military had terrorized a greater reach of its people than other military governments. It did so in its own special way: torture and prolonged imprisonment. (One estimate of disappearances placed the number for Uruguay at 164.)[69] In a population of then less than three million, 300,000 to 400,000 Uruguayans went into exile. Weschler reports: ''Of the remaining, according to Amnesty International, one in every fifty was detained at one time or another for interrogation; and one in every five hundred received a long prison sentence for political offenses.''[70]

The treatment received from Uruguayan security forces was especially cruel. They tortured prisoners with a clear purpose: to inspire fear in others and to extract information about others.[71] Prisoners were brought to the point of death, revived through medical attention, and brought to the point of death again.[72] Some 4,000 Uruguayans were given long-term imprisonment. In most cases, they were tortured.[73]

Uruguay's[74] official investigations were so limited and inadequate that, in Hayner's view: ''Many writers reviewing the Uruguayan case have stated that no official investigation took place, which indicates the small impact the [government] commission had.''[75] A nongovernmental group, Service for Peace and Justice, managed to put out a report called *Uruguay: Nunca Más*, resembling Argentina's report of similar title. Hence, Uruguay took a basic step in settling accounts.

This was true in Paraguay and Honduras,[76] as well. The Paraguayan Committee of Churches sponsored a series of publications, *Nunca Más*. The Honduran National Commission for the Protection of Human Rights issued a lengthy report of human rights violations between 1980 and 1993.[77]

Chile's Truth (or Rettig) Commission issued the Rettig Report with strengths and weaknesses, as noted. Chile took another step not noted in other countries. Aylwin's government created the National Corporation for Reparation and Reconciliation. This meant a follow-up on the work of the Truth Commission. The organization held the door open for continuing work on certifying victims, for compensating families, and for accomplishing the Truth Commission's other recommendations. As Hayney notes, Chile furnishes an excellent model for systematic reparation for other countries.

A more recent truth commission in Latin America, El Salvador's, was highly unusual.[78] All members of the commission were foreigners, maintained by the United Nations, and were part of the U.N. intermediary effort in the country. The commission strongly worded its report. Further, it named more than 40 individuals as responsible for human rights violations. Five days after publication of the report, its effect was greatly dampened. The legislature passed a general amnesty for crimes noted in the report. However, the report would become part of a larger transformative process of speaking in public about secret crimes.

Philosophical versus Political

The debate, represented by José Aldunate and ex-president Patrico Alywin, is not finished. Alywin met head-on Aldunate's dissatisfaction with excluding torture or criminal responsibility from the Rettig Report. (In Chile, politicians often craft political options before taking office. These are not primarily hurried compromises engineered in cloakrooms or the Oval Office.) Before assuming the presidency, Aylwin published his positions in *Un desafío colectivo*.[79] Aylwin was, as Pion-Berlin says, a harsh critic of those who are prepared to defend nonnegotiable truths at all costs.[80] Alywin originally aimed criticisms at Salvador Allende for being unyielding as president. In time Alywin's arguments found targets in those who wished full ethical satisfaction for crimes committed in Chile. Aylwin as president was the principled pragmatist.

Menem claimed the same mantle. After Alfonsín pushed the military toward insubordination, Menem mollified the military to the extent that the military chief of staff told *The Economist* that the armed forces were mellower now and had a limited place in Argentine society.[81]

However, when Alejandro Scilingo came forward in 1995 with stories that he helped to throw drugged prisoners out of helicopters, the military's agreement to *un pacto de olvido* began to shatter. First the army chief of staff made public confessions of the military's ''unnecessary suppression of life,'' chief among other crimes. Then commanders of other forces came forward. Uruguay's ghosts, unnamed guilty perpetrators of rights violations, also stirred.[82]

Human rights work, even about the relatively distant past, was far from accomplished. The issue of *impunidad*, a question of conscience in countries wrestling with basic questions of democracy, continues.

NOTES

1. Transcript of filmed interview by Robert S. Pelton, Santiago, January 6, 1995; see also ''Carpintero Segundo'' (interview), in Aníbal Pastor et al., *De Lonquén*, esp. pp. 126–127.

2. Manuel Antonio Garretón, ''Redemocratization in Chile,'' *Journal of Democracy* 6, 1 (January 1995), p. 153.

3. Ibid., p. 156.

4. Ibid., p. 150.

5. Interviews, Santiago, March 1992 and March 1995.

6. Precht moved on to become secretary general of the Latin American Bishops Conference (CELAM), headquartered in Bogotá.

7. Chile stands alone among Latin American countries near the top of the least corrupt countries on the worldwide index constructed by Transparency International. See the *New York Times*, August 13 and 20, 1995.

8. Nina Rosenberg's description of Chileans as citizens is esp. useful. See her ''Beyond Elections,'' *Foreign Policy* 84 (Fall 1991) and ch. 6 of her *Children of Cain* (see note 41).

9. Human Rights Watch, *Human Rights Watch World Report 1995* (New York: HRW, 1994), p. 78.

10. Charles Humana, comp., *World Human Rights Guide*, 3d ed. (New York: Oxford University Press, 1992), p. 69.

11. *Boston Globe*, July 3, 1994; *Washington Post*, July 19, 1994.

12. Grossfeld, *Boston Globe*, p. 22.

13. As McCarthy notes (*Washington Post*, July 19, 1994, p. D10): ''The comparative neglect of the treatment side of the human rights movement shows up in the international lack of financial support.''

14. See esp. *Nueva evangelización para Chile: Orientaciones Pastorales 1991–1994* (Santiago: Conferencia Episcopal de Chile, 1990), pp. 75–81.

15. See Pilar Vergara, ''Market Economy, Social Welfare, and Democratic Consolidation in Chile,'' in William C. Smith et al., eds., *Democracy, Markets, and Structural Reform in Latin America* (New Brunswick, N.J.: Transaction, 1994), p. 244.

16. Jaime Ruiz-Tagle, ''Dimensions de la Pobreza en Chile,'' in Comisión Nacional Justícia y Paz, *Superación de la Pobreza en Chile* (Santiago: Comisión Nacional Justícia y Paz, 1992), p. 25.

17. Manuel Antonio Garretón, ''The Political Dimension of Processes of Transformation in Chile,'' in Smith et al., *Democracy*, p. 231.

18. Garretón, ''The Political,'' p. 232.

19. Brian Smith, *The Church and Politics in Chile: Challenges to Modern Catholicism* (Princeton, N.J.: Princeton University Press, 1982), pp. 318–319.

20. Interview, Santiago, March 15, 1995.

21. Conferencia Episcopal de Chile, *Nueva*, nos. 156–165 (30,000 copies of the document were published.)

22. *Superacíon de la pobreza on Chile* (Santiago: Comisión Nacional Justicia y Paz, 1992).

23. Interview, Santiago, March 16, 1995.

24. See, for example, Alejandro Foxley, ''Mis vaticinios,'' *Hoy* 806 (December 28, 1992), p. 24.

25. Ruiz-Tagle, ''Dimensiones críticas de la pobreza en Chile,'' *Mensaje* 435 (December 1994), p. 630.

26. Interview with official from Santiago office, Washington, D.C., Latin American Studies International Congress.

27. The dissatisfactions with partial results of social movements is well described by Sidney Tarrow, *Power in Movement: Social Movements, Collective Action and Politics* (New York: Cambridge University Press, 1994), pp. 168–186.

28. Latin America women and their political activism have received increased attention. See esp. Nancy Saperta Sternbach, Marysa Navarro-Arangurén, Patricia Chuchryk, and Sonia E. Alvarez, ''Feminisms in Latin America: From Bogotá to San Bernardo,'' *Signs* 17, 2 (Winter 1992), pp. 393–434; Marysa Navarro-Arangurén, ''The Construction of a Latin American Feminist Identity,'' and Helen l. Safa and Cornelia Butler Flora, ''Production, Reproduction, and the Polity: Women's Strategic and Practical Gender Issues,'' both in Alfred Stepan, ed., *Americas: Interpretive Essays* (New York: Oxford University Press, 1992), pp. 137–151 and pp. 109–136, respectively.

29. Orellana's estimates of women's participation in the movement are given in Orellana and Hutchinson, *El movimiento*, pp. 46–47. Note that tables presented in Anexo 11 do not fully agree with Orellana's earlier text.

30. For history and commentary, see esp. Teresa Valdes and Mariza Weinstein, *Mujeres que sueñan: Las organizaciones de pobladores 1973–1989* (Santiago: Facultad Latinoamericana de Ciencias Sociales, 1993); and Patricia M. Chuchryk, ''From Dictatorship to Democracy: The Women's Movement in Chile,'' in Jane Jaquette, ed., *The*

Women's Movement in Latin America: Participation and Democracy, 2d ed. (Boulder, Colo.: Westview, 1994), pp. 65–107.

31. María de los Angeles Crummett, ''El Poder Feminio: The Mobilization of Women against Socialism in Chile,'' *Latin American Perspectives* 4, 4 (1977), p. 110.

32. Norbert Lechner and Susana Levy, *Notas sobre la vida cotidiana lll: El disciplinamiento de la mujer* (Santiago: FLACSO, Materia de Discusión No. 57, July 1984).

33. Americas Project, The Annenberg/CPB Collection (P.O. Box 2345; South Burlington, VT 05407–2345).

34. For Latin America and the Third World, see Lourdes Benería and Shelley Feldman, eds., *Unequal Burden: Economic Crisis, Persistent Poverty, and Women's Work* (Boulder, Colo.: Westview, 1992).

35. Majorie Agosín, *Scraps*, subtitled: *Children, Women, and the Pinochet Dictatorship* (Trenton, N.J.: Red Sea Press, 1987).

36. Ibid.

37. Ibid.

38. Brian Smith, ''Nonprofit Organizations in International Development: Agents of Empowerment or Preservers of Stability?'', in Walter W. Powell and Elisabeth Clemens, eds., *Private Action and the Public Good* (New Haven: Yale University Press, forthcoming).

39. Catherine Boyle, ''Touching the Air: The Cultural Force of Women in Chile,'' in Sarah A. Radcliffe and Sallie Westwood, eds., *Viva: Women and Popular Protest in Latin America* (New York: Routledge, 1993), p. 156.

40. Ibid.

41. Nina Rosenberg, *The Children of Cain: Violence and the Violent in Latin America* (New York: Penguin, 1992), p. 339.

42. Interview, Santiago, March 15, 1995.

43. José Luis Cea, ''Derecho, justicia y derechos humanos,'' in Augustín Squella, ed., *La cultura jurídica chilena* (Santiago: Corporación de Promoción Universitaria, 1992, reprinting 1988 ed. with additions), p. 74.

44. Constable and Valenzuela, *A Nation*, p. 122.

45. Carlos Peña González, ''Informe sobre Chile,'' in Jorge Correa Sutil, ed., *Situación y políticas judiciales en América Latina* (Santiago: Escuela de Derecho, Universidad Diego Portales, 1993), pp. 285–423.

46. Peña González, ''Informe,'' pp. 422–423.

47. Author interviews, Santiago, July–August 1989.

48. *The Economist* (April 8, 1995), p. 48.

49. See ''Letter to Editor,'' *The Economist* (May 13, 1995), p. 8.

50. Guatemala, Nicaragua, Panama, Ecuador, Peru, Cuba, Haiti, and Mexico. Mexico is included because of its one-party domination and repression; in other countries, repression is associated with military regimes. Disappearances in Mexico have been numerous. A German agency estimated 536 disappearances before 1987. See Paul W. Zagorski, *Democracy versus National Security: Civil-Military Relations in Latin America* (Boulder, Colo.: Lynne Rienner, 1992), p. 66, n.9.

51. Priscilla Hayner, ''Fifteen Truth Commissions—1974–1994: A Comparative Study,'' *Human Rights Quarterly* 16, 4 (November 1994), p. 605.

52. Peru here refers to the period when military men were president; violations by military forces under civilian presidents became much greater in the 1980s and 1990s.

53. See esp. Lawrence Weschler, *A Miracle, A Universe: Settling Accounts with Torturers* (New York: Penguin, 1991).

54. In comparison to other Latin American countries, Brazil's record of military violence was lower. Disappearances were estimated at 250 persons and other victims at some 20,000. See Zagorski, *Democracy*, p. 99.

55. Weschler, *A Miracle*, p. 17.

56. English translation: Joan Dassin, ed., *Torture in Brazil: A Report* (New York: Vintage Books, 1986).

57. Weschler, *A Miracle*, p. 10.

58. Interviews with Arthur Sist, Bolivian Commission on Human Rights, and members of the Washington Office on Latin America, Washington, D.C., 1980–1982.

59. For truth commissions, see Hayner, ''Truth Commissions''; Justice and Society Program of the Aspen Institute, *State Crimes: Punishment or Pardon* (1989); David Weissbrodt and Paul W. Fraser, ''Report of the Chilean National Commission on Truth and Reconciliation,'' *Human Rights Quarterly* 14, 4 (November 1992), pp. 601–622; a book review which includes reports on other commissions; Juan Méndez, review of Weschler's *A Miracle* in *New York Law School Journal of Human Rights* 577 (1991); Aryeh Neier, ''What Should Be Done about the Guilty,'' *New York Review of Books* (February 1, 1990), p. 32 ff.; Jamal Benomar, ''Confronting the Past: Justice after Transitions,'' *Journal of Democrarcy* (January 1993), and *Coming to Terms with the Past: How Emerging Democracies Can Cope with a History of Human Rights Violations* (Atlanta: Carter Center, 1992).

60. Bolivia's group was called The National Commission of Inquiry into Disappearances. See Hayner, ''Truth Commissions,'' pp. 613–614; and Americas Watch, *Bolivia: Almost Nine Years and Still No Verdict in the ''Trial of Disappearances''* (December 1992).

61. Americas Watch, *Bolivia*, p. 1.

62. Hayner, ''Truth Commissions,'' p. 615.

63. For background, see David Pion-Berlin, *The Ideology of State Terror: Economic Doctrine and Political Repression in Argentina and Peru* (Boulder, Colo.: Lynne Rienner, 1989); Martin Edwin Andersen, *Dossier Secreto: Argentina's Disappeared and the Myth of the ''Dirty War''* (Boulder, Colo.: Westview, 1993); and Alison Brysk, *The Politics of Human Rights in Argentina* (Stanford, Calif.: Stanford University Press, 1994).

64. One estimate given is from John P. King, ''Comparative Analysis of Human Rights Violations under Military Rule in Argentina, Brazil, Chile, and Uruguay,'' *Statistical Abstracts on Latin America* 27 (1989). His estimates are lower than those typically given.

65. See Alison Brysk's important discussion: ''The Politics of Measurement: The Contested Count of the Disappeared in Argentina,'' *Human Rights Quarterly* 16, 4 (November 1994), pp. 676–692.

66. *Nunca Más* (Buenos Aires: Editorial Universitaria de Buenos Aires, 1984). English version: *Nunca Mas: Report of the Argentine National Commission on the Disappeared* (New York: Index on Censorship/Farrar, Strauss, and Giroux, 1986).

67. Pion-Berlin, ''To Prosecute or To Pardon: Human Rights Decisions in the Latin American Southern Cone,'' *Human Rights Quarterly* 16, 1 (February 1994), p. 105. Persons in human rights movements in other countries frequently expressed, in interviews with the author, a belief that Argentina was able to bring officers to jail for the extraneous

reasons that the Argentine military ''disgraced itself'' in the Malvinas war against Britain and therefore could more easily be humiliated.

68. Aryeh Neier, ''An Overview of the Issue and Human Rights Watch Policy,'' *Human Rights Watch* (December 1989), p. 2.

69. Pion-Berlin, ''To Prosecute,'' p. 109. See his note 8.

70. Weschler, *A Miracle*, p. 88.

71. Servicio Paz y Justicia Uruguay, *Uruguay: Nunca Más: Human Rights Violations, 1972–1985* (Philadelphia: Temple University Press, 1992), p. 84.

72. Ibid., p. 179.

73. Pion-Berlin, ''To Prosecute,'' p. 108.

74. For transition from military to civilian rule in Uruguay, see Martin Weinstein, *Uruguay: Democracy at the Crossroads* (Boulder, Colo.: Westview, 1988); and Charles G. Gillespie, ''Uruguay's Transition from Collegial Military-Technocratic Rule,'' in Guillermo O'Donnell et al., eds., *Transitions from Authoritarian Rule* (Baltimore: Johns Hopkins University Press, 1986), pp. 173–195. See also Luis E. González, *Political Structures and Democracy in Uruguay* (Notre Dame, Ind.: University of Notre Dame Press, 1991).

75. Hayner, ''Truth Commissions,'' p. 616.

76. See esp. José Luis Simón, *La dictadura Stroessner versus los derchos humanos*; and Guido Rodríguez Alcalá, *Testimonios de la represión pólitica en Paraguay 1975–1989* (1990).

77. Comisionado Nacional de Protección de los Derechos Humanos, *Informe Preliminar sobre los Disaparecidos en Honduras: Los hechos hablan por sí mismo* (1994).

78. Mark Ensalaco provides excellent insights into both Chile and El Salvador in ''Truth Commissions for Chile and El Salvador: A Report and Assessment,'' *Human Rights Quarterly* 16, 4 (November 1994), pp. 656–675.

79. Patricio Alywin, *Un desafio colective* (Buenos Aires: Planeta, 1988).

80. Pion-Berlin, ''To Prosecute,'' passim.

81. *The Economist* (September 24, 1994), p. 46.

82. *Latinamerica Press* 27, 14 (April 20, 1995).

4

Contemporary Democracy and Efflorescence of Human Rights Organizing

On an average night 200 children and adolescents come by the square in front of São Paulo's cathedral. They linger for a while and move on. The few who stay overnight are periodically vigilant for sudden and threatening movement. They, and most of Brazil, remember the slaughter of sleeping children and adolescents. The "Candelaria incident"[1] remains forever fixed as the centerpiece killing in what Gilbert Dimenstein describes in his *War against Children*.[2]

HUMAN RIGHTS IN NEW DEMOCRACIES

This chapter traces the highs and lows of movements centering on human rights in contemporary democracies, imperfect, turbulent, but somehow offering a glimmer of hope. It searches for reasons why human rights advocacy became a movement, after centuries of violations. Then attention centers on a movement that illustrates contemporary struggles. The streetchildren's human rights movement became notable for seizing opportunities, framing action, and cycles of protest within the contemporary context. Discussion of the interplay of government response and movement objectives concludes the chapter.

In Brazil, Sister Michael Mary Nolan has buried young people she once taught. She remembers them all, especially the six buried on the same day. It was also her birthday. The lives of these children, trapped in poverty, had taken a foreseeably bad turn for the poorest streetchildren. The change in Sister Michael's life was less predictable. Nonetheless, what she has turned to follows the general direction of an influential sector in Brazil.

Sister Michael left the classroom and became a lawyer. She arrived at a critical point in her life (39 years old). She felt she had to turn from working directly with children to making the legal system more responsive to the needs of the young. Some Brazilians do not like her legal advocacy. A few have threatened her life. However, she has staked everything on the rule of law.[3] This, according to many human rights participants, is the dividing point between the era of military dictatorship and the present era when a turn toward democracy has occurred in Latin America.

After military men withdrew from presidential palaces, many observers expected human rights to diminish as an issue. Many groups in the United States tied to Central America, Chile, and Brazil closed their doors or turned to other issues. By contrast, hundreds of groups in Latin America have come forward to confront human rights issues.

Human rights violations continue in peril. Human Rights Watch summarized the Latin American situation as: "the persistence of egregious, systematic human rights violations in countries with institutional democracies."[4] In Human Rights Watch's view, these countries achieved neither respect for human rights, nor political tolerance, nor the rule of law. "Torture, police abuse, assassinations of political activists and 'disposable people', electoral irregularities, and threats against the press co-existed with nominally democratic governments and were tolerated by them. . . . Torture was commonplace throughout the region."[5]

The expansion of nongovernmental human rights organizations shows both the good and the ugly aspects of Latin American democracies. In the view of Joseph Eldridge, executive director of the Lawyers Committee on Human Rights: "Violations of human rights in many countries are just as bad under democracies as under military rule."[6] Governments, showing a facade of democracy to the world, cannot admit human rights breakdowns, for fear of ostracism. The main victims now are not the sons and daughters of the white middle class but the poor and the marginalized. These are not glamorous victims and have few mass-media reporters to defend them.[7] So, human rights groups and the poor are learning together.

The work of the Washington Office on Latin America (WOLA) never abated. Started as an ecumenical effort of Catholics and mainline Protestant laypersons and financially supported by many church groups, WOLA has had many admirers and critics.[8] Many local groups in the United States interested in Nicaragua and other Central American causes in the 1980s collapsed for many reasons. They suffered fatigue, depression (over multiple Sandinista failures), or misread victory (elections in Haiti and elsewhere).[9] WOLA continues. Peru and Colombia became as ardent causes as Brazil and Chile had been. New democratic openings for helping to assure human rights in El Salvador and Guatemala motivated intense efforts there.

Contemporary Response: Expansion of Human Rights

Some 3,000 organizations (a conservative estimate), some with large memberships, some with small, have sprung up in Latin America to address human rights issues. Core groups are often national or provincial in scope but many

Table 4.1
Growth or Decline of Core Human Rights Organizations in Latin America and the Caribbean

	1994	1989
Brazil	84	50
Peru	77	14
Mexico	68	20
Chile	45	52
Ecuador	44	12
Costa Rica	40	9
Colombia	39	11
Argentina	29	24
Bolivia	29	4
Venezuela	23	11
El Salvador	22	4
Panama	21	0
Guatemala	18	1
Uruguay	18	5
Haiti	17	2
Dominican Republic	15	4
Nicaragua	15	7
Honduras	15	3
Paraguay	14	6
Cuba	7	0
Totals	640	241

Sources: For 1989, Patricio Orellana and Elizabeth Quay Hutchinson, *El movimiento de derechos humanos en Chile, 1973–1990* (Santiago: Centro de Estudios Políticos Latinamericanos Simón Bolívar, 1991), p. 202; for 1994, *Human Rights Internet Reporter Masterlist* (Ottawa: Human Rights Internet, 1994), passim.

more are working at the grassroots level. Many groups work at special issues, such as children in danger. Most groups have come into existence in the last ten or fifteen years. Some are struggling to become organized. Within clusters of human rights organizations are key groups. They function as anchors within computer and other networks. Their growth or decline is shown in Table 4.1.

Many of these groups work at different issues but they are forging ties for greater strength. They have to, for they often conflict with controlling groups who have the arms of the state at their disposal.

However, entrenched power holders have shown themselves vulnerable. The opening to democracy in Latin America, "ceremonial" or incipient representative democracy, has given Latin Americans permission to scrutinize public behavior of the ruling elites. The new groups, allied with investigative journalists, have technical means to trace the flow of money in ways not possible before the proliferation of computers. Members of the new groups have been persistent in their investigations.

WHY HUMAN RIGHTS NOW?

Why human rights? Why now? After all, human rights violations have been part of the Latin American condition for centuries.[10] Human rights as an issue in world politics dates only from the middle third of this century. Jack Donnelly points to the Holocaust as the catalyst for raising human rights for the first time as an issue in world politics. In his recounting, the Nuremberg Trials were followed by the unanimous approval of the keystone document, the *Universal Declaration of Human Rights* (1948). Latin American governments signed the document but years passed before *derechos humanos/direitos humanos* became commonly used by Latin Americans. Joseph Eldridge, executive director of the Lawyers Committee on Human Rights, believes he first heard the expression "human rights" while working in Latin America in 1973.[11]

A comprehensive view of the reasons behind the human rights explosion is difficult to gain, because the activity is new and growing. But one can point to four factors. First, Latin America has suffered major social breakdowns. These breakdowns greatly increase the incidence of human rights violations.[12] Human rights advocates criticize governments for indiscriminate repression, torture, and denial of *habeas corpus*. They also oppose governments for not promoting wide participation of ordinary citizens in the countries' political life. The socioeconomic woes of the classes at the bottom have meant, as Latin Americans were saying, that many poor went from being marginalized to being excluded.

In their assessment of the Brazilian situation, researchers at the Universidade de São Paulo point to the wearing effect of the continual deterioration of life for most Brazilians. They summed up: "One of the most striking effects of the socioeconomic situation is the lack of hope. . . . Brazilians do not see the possibilities of a better future. This attitude has great repercussions on the mobilization, construction of solidarity, and participation."[13]

Second, views of many Latin Americans about human rights and tolerance of rights violations have changed. Jorge Castañeda, in *Utopia Unarmed*, says that many members of human rights groups acquired this orientation from being Catholic.[14] For them human rights activity is an expression of their faith, as surely as Mother Teresa expresses her belief through caring for the sick. In 1994, Sister Nohemey Palencia from Colombia, in religious habit, and Father Matías Camuñas Marchante from Venezuela, in clerical black, went to the podium in New York to receive Human Rights Watch awards.

For Sister Nohemey and Father Matías, Vatican II and Medellín cast their Catholicism as a this-worldly religion.[15] The test of fidelity (orthopraxis) became the response to the needs of others as the needs presented themselves. If one said human rights activity is the expression of theology of liberation for the contemporary age, many liberation theologians might agree while the practitioners might not know what that meant. Gustavo Gutiérrez, the father of liberation theology, said: "Not recognizing a person's full human rights was one way to kill a person, to cause a cultural death."[16] Social Christianity permeates religious life for many in Latin America.

The same motives that led Catholics a decade ago to support democracy instead of military governments find expression today in human rights activities. Catholics have wanted to make an imperfect democratic process better, more responsive to ordinary citizens, not just elite members of a country. The Brazilian Paulo Freire, in his *Pedogogy of the Oppressed*, hoped to evoke the same impulse in the fatalistic peasant.[17]

For many participants, human rights involvement builds on years spent in base Christian communities or similar groups. Neil MacDonald, in his extensive travels for Oxfam, found: "The vast majority of today's citizen activists had their first experience taking control of their lives through the church's grassroots Christian communities in the 1960s and 1970s."[18] In the early days of human rights efforts in Latin America, the Latin American bishops held their pivotal Medellín Conference (1968). In the much-read Medellín document on peace,[19] the bishops urged the church to "favor the efforts of the people to create and develop their own grassroots organizations for the redress and consolidation of their rights."[20] The bishops also recommended that universities conduct studies on human rights in the light of the U.N. "solemn declaration of human rights."[21]

The result of the church's efforts was impressive. In 1987, Murray Kempton, writing in *The New York Review of Books*, said: "In the thirteenth century, Catholicism was unknown outside of Europe, but it is now a universal force. . . . In Poland and Nicaragua, Chile and El Salvador, churchmen stand reproaching and resisting the excesses of the state. Even unbelievers like myself have to conclude that the Catholic Church has become the steadiest, and in many places, the only defender of human rights the wide world can show."[22]

Third, most governments in Latin America lag in investigating and defending human rights. The strong bureaucratic tradition in Latin America and the contemporary corruption within governments accounts in large part for governmental hesitancy. As noted, in Chile observers criticized the turning over of human rights protection to the government as a mistake. Governmental agencies lack the independence needed for public accountability.

Fourth, North Atlantic countries are now influencing human rights groups in Latin America. The Human Rights Declaration of 1948 initially affected First World countries. Human rights were a First World luxury. For many years Brazilians adamantly opposed policies that would limit pollution of the environment, water, and air, such as the immense burnings in the Amazon. Socio-

Table 4.2
Relation between Initiation of Dictatorship/Repression and Functioning of First Important Human Rights Groups

Paraguay	1954	1976
Guatemala	1957	1984
Brazil	1964	1972
El Salvador	1967	1977
Uruguay	1972	1981
Chile	1973	1973
Argentina	1976	1980
Bolivia	1971	1976

Source: Patricio Orellana and Elizabeth Quay Hutchinson, *El movimiento de derechos humanos en Chile, 1973–1990* (Santiago: Centro de Estudios Políticos Latinoamericanos Simón Bolívar, 1991), p. 152.

economic development had to take precedence over environmental concerns and over the rights of Indians and others affected by contamination. Now many Brazilians no longer are willing to tolerate unbridled environmental destruction.

Widening the Field

Human rights activities by nongovernmental organizations were virtually unknown before military dictatorships appeared in the 1960s. When Patricio Orellana surveyed the history of human rights organizing, he found that human rights organizations existed in a few countries before the 1960s. Their role was mainly symbolic or the organizations existed merely on paper. The Argentine League for Human Rights, tied to the Communist Party, existed as early as 1937 but became ''very inoperative'' when military dictatorship took over. In Chile, in 1972, the year before the coup, the labor patriarch Clotario Blest presided over the tiny Committee for the Defense of Human Rights. The organization ceased activity from 1973–1976.

Rather than single groups, movements to defend human rights began to appear in Latin America in the 1970s. However, a lag generally occurred between military takeover and the first effective activities of an important human rights group. Chile was the notable exception (see Table 4.2).

The turn from military government toward democratic elections unfolded gradually (see Table 4.3).

In contrast to generally slow rising of human rights organizations under military repression, societies with democratically elected governments offered an immediate and fertile context for human rights organizing. The new groups built

Table 4.3
Turn to Democratically Elected Governments

South America	
Ecuador	1979
Peru	1980
Bolivia	1982
Argentina	1983
Brazil	1985
Uruguay	1985
Paraguay	1989
Chile	1990
Central America and Panama	
Honduras	1982
El Salvador	1984
Nicaragua	1985
Guatemala	1986
Panama	1989
Caribbean	
Haiti	1994

Source: *Veja*, No. 1326 (February 9, 1994), p. 70.

on the strong backbone of mature organizations from the military era. Other human rights groups sprang into existence and joined the florescence of non-governmental groups in Latin America. These groups have reached major proportions. Brazilian newsmagazines similar to *Time* and *Newsweek* have given great play to 5,000 NGOs dedicated to "defense of social causes."[23]

Ernesto Bernardes and Kaíke Nanne, writing in *Veja*, found that, by the end of 1993, social-cause NGOs had doubled in two years.[24] The variety of groups they reported on seemed limitless and were highly inventive. Bernardes and Nanne pointed out the sophistication of an organization working in the forests of the Mato Grosso. With the aid of satellites, the group showed Indians how to identify the limits of their reservations. In Baixada Fluminense the reporters found not only groups working with streetchildren, but also learning to protect witnesses.

Democracy in Brazil and other countries has meant a widening of human rights issues, far beyond torture and disappearance. (As wide as the Latin American imagination, one might add.) *Veja*'s report shows a wide spread of issues (see Table 4.4).

Table 4.4
Causes to Which More than 5,000 Nongovernmental Organizations Were Dedicated in Brazil, 1993 (Percent)

Cause	Percent
Ecology	40
Popular movements	17
Women's rights	15
Racial justice	11
Children in need	6
AIDS	3
Indians	1
Other causes	7

Source: *Veja*, No. 1326 (February 9, 1994), p. 70.

Bernandes and Nanne estimate that these organizations administered about $U.S. 700 million a year.[25] This total is greater than the internal product of four of Brazil's poorer states. More than half, probably $U.S. 400 million, comes from outside Brazil. Brazil was clearly in crisis, especially economically, and these movements arose from both need and opportunity. The Brazilian state did not provide for many urgent needs. Or, alternatively, the state provided services, but did so poorly or at extravagant cost. In one site the state spent ten times what private agencies did to care for streetchildren.[26]

Advances Made

Notable advances in human rights protection have been made. In 1994, Amnesty International reported "Most countries of the region have active and mature human rights organizations. Stronger civil societies mean that human rights victims are not at the mercy of the state as easily as in the past. . . . In many countries the new freedom of the press has seen the growth of an independent media prepared to challenge the authorities."[27] The inter-American system of human rights protection has also been strengthened.

Beyond the surface story, social movement theory leads to probing further. Questions arise about the way movements frame issues. Outside forces, such as the media, are crucial in shaping issues in contemporary society. Further, governments typically do not welcome the challenges of nongovernmental groups. Governments will often attempt to co-opt or to control human rights activity. "Many governments . . . persistently labor to limit formal access and participation of nongovernmental human rights organizations and to challenge the legitimacy of their findings," remarks Felice D. Gaer.[28]

STREETCHILDREN AS HUMAN RIGHTS ISSUE

Among human rights causes in Latin America none seems more urgent than lack of care and torture and killing of homeless children and adolescents.[29] To furnish insight into the current workings of human rights organizations, I pursue this issue as revealing the ups and downs, the cycles of protest and decline. The issue also shows the political moves governments make to ward off the sharing of power.

An evident difference between North Atlantic countries and most Latin American countries is the large number of children on the street at any time of the day. In Brazil 4.3 million 7- to 14-year-olds have no school to attend. Many others drop out after a time or attend irregularly. Children not enrolled in schools have been hanging around Latin American streets and plazas for centuries. However, the category and the magnitude of "streetchildren" have a more recent history. Most children before, say, 1970 had a place where they belonged at night. For centuries extended family or strangers typically cared for children after premature death of parents, even abandonment by parents. Within networks of villages or small urban communities, many Latin American families took in children who were not their own. Women who acted as mothers argued to complaining males that another mouth to feed added little burden.

Orphanages, often run by religious groups, cared for limited numbers of children not living with families. Even convicted young criminals often found a substitute for jail in low-security alternatives run by groups, such as the Sisters of the Good Shepherd.[30] For decades courts had remanded girls and young women to these *hogares* found in most larger cities of Latin America.[31]

Father William Wasson's Cuernavaca orphanage encouraged remarkable mutual care among orphans. National magazines in the United States took notice.[32] Reporters chronicled Wasson's efforts to seek release of juvenile prisoners. Wasson and associates provided for hundreds of Mexican homeless ex-prisoners through open acceptance and gradual assumption of responsibilities. Such efforts were possible because the scale of the problem was small.

Another kind of orphan began appearing in Latin America's streets. In Europe postwar shoeshine orphans have mostly disappeared. However, in Latin America shoeshine boys, known as *gamines*, increasingly gained attention. Their numbers grew, to the anxiety of religious groups, caring adults, and police. They were a new breed of orphan, independent and older, difficult to deal with. New approaches were tried. Kindly religious order members, such as Vicente Blake from Des Moines, Iowa, opened houses "without locked doors." Blake operated his house in Santa Cruz, Bolivia. Street boys could initially maintain their fierce independence and gradually learn "to fit in."[33]

The new phenomenon drew social scientists. G. Tellez published *Gamines* in 1976, followed by V. G. Pineda's *El Gamín* in 1978, and Jackson K. Felsman wrote his dissertation, "Street Urchins of Cali."[34] The door was opening for understanding *menores de la calle* in ways other than delinquency and social control.

Building on this research, Louis Aptekar undertook systematic psychological research for his *Street Children of Cali.*[35] Presuming similarities between situations throughout Latin America, Aptekar provides a penetrating look at the wide phenomenon of streetchildren. Children and adolescents are in the streets for differing reasons. Most of them maintain contact with at least their extended families. Some are runaways from abusive parents. A smaller number have been abandoned. At a minimum, government policies to meet the problem would have to take differing reasons for being in the streets into account.

Equally, the age of the young persons matters. Many persons called streetchildren are not children but adolescents. [36] Children and adolescents often mix in *galladas* (gangs). Younger ones provide income and older ones provide protection in a mutual support system. Rather than being just ragtag outfits, the groups have a complex organization for meeting the physical and emotional needs of members. As Mark Lusk, who has studied streetchildren in San José, Costa Rica, says: The closeness within the group ''provides much of the friendship and intimacy that they miss by having to live outside their families.''[37]

Evolution of Issue

When most of a nation's population lived near farms, extended-family living arrangements made sense. When Juan Usipanqui's family moved to Lima in 1975, food became harder to obtain. Juan watched how uprooting from familiar social circles made more difficult the long-standing custom of sharing food. When one household had a windfall of abundance, they shared their food with extended families under nearby roofs. In 1984, Juan lost steady employment and joined millions of unemployed. His family could no longer shelter and feed children of his extended family. Thus, for many, the 1980s brought the final blow to the open family structure. Poor families closed in on themselves for survival. Children appeared increasingly on the streets at night.

Military governments tried to control the problem with force. Military and police enforced nightly curfews and put homeless children and adolescents in detention centers. When the military left governing directly, children and adolescents poured out in the streets. The problem was no longer *gamines* or street urchins but streetchildren. Even here the practiced eye could distinguish between *menores en la calle* (minors hanging out) and *menores de la calle* (minors with no other place to go).

Not all the impetus drawing minors toward life in the streets came from being abandoned by impoverished or abusive adults. Children and adolescents went to the streets to make money for their families, earning perhaps 20–30 percent of family income.[38] They found temporary work or joined the steadier routines of street hawkers. The informal sector of the economy became a bailing-pump for family survival and an enhanced opportunity for exploitation of children.[39]

The last two decades also brought attractive and dangerous wealth to the streets through trade in native-grown coca and marijuana. This commerce demanded structure and networking. So, too, did thievery. Thus, mafia-like families of organized street gangs demanded regular payments from shopkeepers. The groups also marked off their territories for mugging and theft. They patrolled tunnel exits between Rio's beaches and shopping centers. They made the elevators between upper and lower Salvador, Bahía, a risky transit. The most notorious areas are in Brazil and Colombia. However, nights are unsafe in Central American capitals, such as Guatemala City and San Salvador, as well.

Reactions to young people's crimes, real or suspected, has been swift and lethal. Children and adolescents have been killed by the hundreds each year. An investigation by the Brazilian congress reported 4,611 young persons (most of them black) killed between 1990 and 1993.[40] Thousands of others were beaten and tortured.

When Gilberto Dimenstein was putting together his widely read *The War on Children*, he and a photographer visited six of Brazil's largest cities.[41] "It was," he said, "impossible not to be affected by the stories we heard of the torture, ill-treatment, and murder of children. . . . We often spent the day in the sun and many places we visited in the shantytowns stank, but I needed a bath not so much to get rid of the sweat or the smell. It was more a need to wash away all that I had heard; a vague, useless attempt to expunge from my memory words I did not want to hear, like trying to shake the dust from my clothes."[42]

SEIZING OPPORTUNITIES: BRAZILIAN MOVEMENT FOR STREETCHILDREN

To view characteristics of contemporary human rights movements in Latin America, one can examine more closely groups working with streetchildren in Brazil. This specialized movement, as older human rights movements, arose under military government (1964–1985).[43] Human rights groups protested against state inaction, against covert state killings or approval of killings, and against the larger socioeconomic system that produced these by-products.

In Brazil military control tightened gradually. From a benign *dictablanda* (soft dictatorship) military governors became increasingly closed to civilian opposition. By 1970 only slight traces of representative politics remained. With authoritarian decrees (especially Institutional Act 5 and succeeding decrees), the military limited oppositional activity of political parties and brought a halt to many civil rights guarantees. Arbitrary detentions, extralegal killings, and torture became systematic.

In this context the Catholic Church was virtually the only institution in society left with public rights. As Ronald M. Schneider says: "The Catholic church became the chief critic of human rights violations, and to an increasing degree, of social injustice as well."[44]

With the protection of the church, human rights groups engaged in protecting persons and groups at risk. Despite efforts of the military to dress its repression in legality by decrees, the regime was vulnerable to charges of illegitimacy, of arbitrary rule. Human rights groups justified for themselves opposition to the regime on these grounds. A precedent for future action within democracy was being set.

Human rights was virtually an unknown idea in Brazil until military repression tightened in the late 1960s. The rights of many children had been violated for as long as anyone could remember; nor had Brazilians mounted systematic protests.

When the military took over in 1964, it inherited a repressive system for dealing with the abandoned and the streetchildren. The notorious Assistance Service to Minors (SAM) conducted correctional facilities. These facilities were intended to be frightening "branches of hell." The press occasionally reported scandals in the decade before the military took over but little reform occurred.

General Humberto Castello Branco and early military leaders favored a technocratic approach. This led the government to a short-lived emphasis on assistance-oriented policy.[45] In practice, however, the military was stuck with the same buildings and staff from the SAM system. Increasingly, too, the military felt the need to control society more tightly. Thus the military enacted important new laws that gave the government power to intervene in the lives of minors in "irregular circumstances." As Anthony Dewees and Steven Klees remark: "This policy criminalized the activities of millions of young people, whether they had committed a crime or were simply in the streets seeking to survive."[46]

Military men and other nationalists did not want children on the streets. Order was disturbed by unruly children and adolescents. Further, Brazil's burning desire to become a respected world power fueled a need for a suitable image. Brazil's winning the World Cup in soccer in 1970 fit that image; urchins in large numbers did not. Children and adolescents were swept into jails and prisons to get them off the streets. Almost 700,000 children and adolescents would be locked up in FEBEMs (State Foundations for the Welfare of Minors) or related reform schools.[47] These actions helped mobilize groups in defense of minors. Human rights advocates watched the often callous routines of the child welfare institutions called FEBEMs. Incarceration in Latin America has historically been a grim experience, meant to punish and to terrify.

Movement Commences

Adults working with young street people typically organize themselves into neighborhood groups, take turns being on the street, and offer acceptance and friendship as the first steps toward more extended care in diverse settings. Many adults mobilized as a force through base Christian communities and similar neighborhood groups, some that had enough structures to be called NGOs. Their dissatisfactions with the growing problem, the violence of security forces, and callousness of governmental agencies served as the basis for organizing on a wider scale beyond their neighborhoods and cities. Group members who often thought of themselves as nonpolitical found themselves drawn into an increasingly large political arena. They began mounting their discontents as challenges to the system. Their efforts led them into national prominence in ways they would not have dreamed of.

Of all Latin Americans, Brazilians mounted the most prominent human rights movement for children. The environment was not favorable for organizing. Military governors wanted to atomize society, to keep voluntary nongovernmental groups from joining together, and to dictate national policy without opposition. Like their best soccer players, adept Brazilian grassroots groups found subtle ways to express and to channel their deeply felt frustrations over human rights violations. Out of an impulse for charity came a movement for structural change and justice.

Deodato Rivera, with members of the Catholic Justice and Peace Commission, saw for themselves how these conditions affected young prisoners. They found cells contaminated;[48] the rooms had no mattresses, chairs, sheets, or soap; inmates were often forced to sleep on damp cement floors.

Night was the worst; weeping and groaning often filled the air. Young persons who had never been in trouble and were not used to being detained gave in to heartbroken feelings in the dark. Other adolescents who had been in jail for months groaned involuntarily, overwhelmed by degrading conditions. Sexual abuse and violence recurred in dreams.

Human rights activists, in increasing numbers, aided children in prison, police centers, and on the streets. They worked at alleviating the worst hardships suffered by the children and adolescents. They provided medical attention, comfort, and aftercare for torture and other abuses.

In working for homeless children's welfare, human rights workers observed even laws used as instruments of oppression for Brazilian children. UNICEF noted: "Thousands [of children] were sent off to harsh correctional institutions simply because they were poor and abandoned. Such children had no legal rights, and abuse by police and other authorities had become the norm."[49]

Public Space Opens

Two hundred human rights and activist groups working on behalf of street-children had been formed by the time military governments would give way to popularly elected leaders in 1985.[50] Public space opened for the specialized movement for children and adolescent rights. This occurred during the long run-up to civilian rule, known in Brazil as *distensão* (decompression).

Within the military government, first under General Ernesto Geisel and then General João Baptista Figueiredo, some policy makers were searching for alternatives to correctional approaches. Other groups, too, especially the Social Secretariat of the Catholic Church and UNICEF, shared similar convictions about new choices. In the early 1980s, these disparate groups pulled together in a common project, the Alternative Project.

Given the size of Brazil and the atomizing effect of military control on society, organizations working for human rights had been isolated from one another. As the military allowed more political space, groups working with the Alternative Project opened for public debate the correctional model and alternative programs. Working for long months on the Alternative Project brought these groups a common sense of purpose, crucial for social movements.

By November 1984, with the military government winding down, the groups brought the Alternative Project to the final reporting stage. The military's national pride aided the project. Brazil's commanders thought of themselves as the leaders for Latin America and of Brazil as the first nation of the region. Thus, the military government sponsored a meeting on streetchildren for all of Latin America.[51] The media, attuned to reporting what the government fostered, applauded Brazil's leadership and widely publicized the meeting.

The media's interest was key in framing the issue for the movement. Brazilians had referred to streetchildren as *moleques*, as ragamuffins or worse.[52] Now the media portrayed these children in a more favorable light. For the human rights organizers the timing and the media attention were decisive. The movement for streetchildren was able through the media to gain a collective identity. Through published and televised interviews members of the sprawling movement talked with one another.

Second, movement members projected to the Brazilian public an image of an issue taken seriously by national (including military men in uniforms) and international "authorities." The media attention, then and through the next few years, allowed movement participants to project a strong collective image to opponents. They were trustworthy adults openly critical of government programs. Activists also emphasized children and adolescents as able to speak clearly about the conditions of their lives, the reasons (often survival) they went to the streets, and the nightmarish violence they faced.

Allowing children and adolescents to speak for themselves before national audiences was a master stroke of the movement. Antonio Carlos Gomes da Costa, UNICEF's representative to the Alternative Project, said: "Brazilian society was accustomed to looking at these children exclusively as needy, seeing what they did not have, what they did not know, what they were incapable of, a totally negative profile compared to the middle-class norm. The movement presented streetchildren in a positive light, emphasizing what they could do."[53]

The period of political *abertura* that followed decompression led to full transition to civilian government. A window of opportunity for the movement opened more widely due to a temporary power vacuum. The military was receding from overt wielding of power. However, political parties did not yet have control over political patronage.

Shaping the Issue

Democracy posed a major challenge to nongovernmental organizations. Nongovernmental organizations, human rights groups among them, had to adapt to new political arrangements. Internally, many groups sought greater organizational strength. They increased professionalization of staff.[54] New external challenges forced human rights groups to redefine their agenda. In terms of psychological adjustment, the shift was enormous: from fighting a common enemy in small splintered groups to creating a positive program, a national vision. The process resembled efforts of Republicans in the United States to change from reactive to front running leadership.

In public, activist groups participated in government-controlled meetings in which they expressed their opposition to the correctional approach. Within the organizations, members debated how to recast the issue. They decided to shift from emphasizing assistance to rights. In many senses, the movement would succeed or fail based on this objective.

In the process, human rights groups participating in the Alternative Project became a national political movement. They created the National Movement of Street Boys and Street Girls (MNMMR) in 1985. The movement gained premier status around the world, and became first among equals in the Brazilian human rights movement.

With the turn to democracy, the larger rights movement[55] began to diminish.[56] The coalition of groups began to fall apart.[57] However, some groups continued to mobilize members by specialization.[58] The streetchildren's movement served as a leader for other specialized groups.

With the country's political structure in flux, the streetchildren's movement forged ahead. Movement leaders aimed at shaping a new constitution for the country. They envisaged a legal foundation for Brazil's democracy distinctive from the one that had governed the past. Children and adolescents had few rights and many handicaps. The movement would build intellectually on the International Declaration of the Rights of Children promulgated by the United Nations. First World countries pushed this declaration. Fitting in with the First World drew in Brazil's political leaders.

Brazil has a long human rights agenda to work on before approaching comparison with North Atlantic countries. Brazil ranks, in my view and that of Humana associates, among the more troubled Latin American countries, though not the worst.[59] In terms of human rights violations Charles Humana and colleagues ranked Brazil twelfth lowest of nineteenth Latin American countries evaluated.[60]

Brazilians in large numbers are working on the agenda, issue by issue. In addressing the streetchildren's issue, MNMMR served as the point of the lance in the mobilization to follow. MNMMR joined the National Conference of Brazilian Bishops, the National Front for the Defense of Child and Adolescent

Rights, the National Order of Attorneys, and other groups to form a loose and effective coalition. They aimed at mobilizing public opinion and at electing appropriate candidates to the assembly to write a new constitution. They pushed for a still wider coalition, this time seeking closer partnership with the government. Six government ministries joined with nongovernmental groups to form the National Commission on the Child and the Constitution.

Coalition leaders gained national attention for the initiative. In May 1986, they held the First National Meeting of Street Boys and Street Girls. Five hundred children and adolescents came as delegates from various corners of Brazil. The media featured the children and adolescents as speaking for themselves. ''These silly faces now talking sense about fundamental issues,'' is the way one streetperson advocate remembers the impact.[61] The country was saturated with media coverage of the meeting.[62] In the last six months of 1986 the media ran almost 3,000 print articles and 72 television programs on children's rights.[63]

Massive mobilization followed. Two hundred thousand adults and 1.3 million children signed petitions favoring constitutional changes in favor of children's rights. The process duly impressed members of the constitutional assembly, convened in 1988. The assembly approved the article covering children's rights the following year. Article 227 resembled the U.N.'s International Convention.

However, observers believed general statements of rights had little worth. Brazil needed a delineation of rights expressed at length in a subsequent statute. Movement leaders set up as objectives educating a broad range of constituents and anticipating oppositional moves; they needed a still wider coalition of groups. Many nongovernmental organizations, within or outside MNMMR, pulled together into the Child and Adolescent Forum.

Framing Action

Next, movement leaders had to devise a national strategy. They lacked experience in democratic settings. However, they had at hand transnational mentors, as United Nations advisers, to tutor them. Leaders looked over the modern repertoire of collective action; they chose public meetings and seminars as their instruments. They conducted thousands of meetings and seminars throughout a country larger than continental United States. The meetings ostensibly sought public support for new and detailed legislation; however, the meetings also aimed at showing Brazilians the central place of rights and of the rule of law in democracy. They borrowed dominant themes (representation, sharing, and other democratic themes) used by Brazilian political parties. This repertoire rendered less effective the opposition of conservative political actors.

The media again played a vital role. Television, press, and radio gained attention for movement objectives. They also provided, in Tarrow's term, a diffuse vehicle for consensus formation. From a ''correctional remedy'' frame, they shifted the issue to ''human rights.'' The movement brought about passage of

Table 4.5
Street Children and Adolescents Killed in Rio

1990	442
1991	306
1992	424
1993, through May	320

Source: *Isto É* 1243 (June 28, 1993), p. 16.

key legislation. President Fernando Collor de Mello signed the Child and Adolescent Statute (with 267 articles) in July 1990.

Change of perspective between the old Minor's Code and the new Statute was radical.[64] Emphasis was placed on ''child'' and ''adolescent'' as categories referring to all Brazilians in certain age categories. In Brazil rich persons' offspring had been called children and adolescents. Poor offspring were called *meninos* (minors). Paul Jeffrey recalls a headline in Belém: ''Minor Attacks Child'' (a poor, thieving kid attacked a rich kid).[65] Doing away with *menino* in the Statute allowed emphasis on basic rights of children and youth as human beings. Given their vulnerabilities, young persons were accorded highest priority in policy considerations. Judges now could halt pork barrel projects until the state provided for children's basic needs (such as elementary education).[66]

Institutional Inertia and Presidential Countermoves

The accomplishment of the movement—change in constitution and establishment of statute—is exemplary (human rights groups in other countries hope to do the same) but, opponents say, empty. They charge that the same machinery, people, and infrastructures are responsible locally for taking care of the children.

Systematic violence by police and parapolice forces has not ceased. Even the glare of international publicity has not been strong enough to diminish its occurrence. (Murders of children and adolescents in Río de Janeiro, as documented in the mass-circulation Brazilian newsmagazine *Isto É*, are shown in Table 4.5.)

By the end of 1993 the *New York Times* reported both greater outcry *and* increase in murders of the young.[67] Child labor, often under inhumane conditions, also continues. Some estimates show children as 18 percent of the work force.[68]

One might judge that the movement has been suitably tamed and rendered ineffectual by traditional political repertoires of the government. What was granted by the government under extreme pressure and public scrutiny were words and laws. These were nothing of grave consideration, especially for President Collor and associates. Patronage and cronyism quickly took hold in the ''new'' national politics of Brazil. In effect, Presidents Collor and Itamar Franco (1990–1995) played an excellent hand: They cooperated in a traditional decentralization-without-resources strategy. Proponents of change in the care of streetchildren and adolescents argued for and were granted localized control. Few monies followed.

Further, power holders within the political-bureaucratic apparatus carried on the authoritarian past. Eli Diniz and Renato Boschi point to features that persist: closed style, low transparency, little accountability, strong clientalistic ties, and low capacity for achievement and enforcement.[69]

Human rights activists faced not only strongly entrenched enclaves but also profound corruption of presidential power in Collor de Mello's administration. Inflated anticipation of the turn to democracy heightened the disappointments that followed. Grassroots activists, as from the base Christian communities, began saying: ''A democracia e um engano [Democracy is a deception].''

The Brazilian situation was repeated elsewhere in Latin America. Democracies seemed to unravel. Venezuelans, celebrating 30 years of democracy, found themselves faced with a magnitude of corruption they had not experienced, even under General Marcos Pérez Jímenez. Venezuelans were saying that democracy is a license for a party to steal, not just a group around PJ (Pérez Jímenez). Even Latin American bishops at their major Santo Domingo meeting (1992) tempered their enthusiasm for democracy, saying: ''Its exercise is more form than reality.''[70]

Gains Made by Movement

Public pressure, fueled by human rights organizations, helped to bring down President Fernando Collor de Mello. *No president in Latin American history had ever been impeached or stepped down because of corruption before 1992.* Carlos Andres Pérez and Jorge Serrano Elías followed Collor out of presidential palaces in Venezuela and Guatemala. Observers felt something new in the air. Hence bureaucratic entrenchment and presidential power are no longer unshakable in contemporary Latin American democracies. Human rights groups, investigative reporters, and a host of other actors showed corrupt governors could be rooted out. This small victory (the system remained in place) gave courage to human rights workers that presidential power did not confer absolute privilege.

In Brazil many small steps at the municipal governmental level have taken effect. Here the interplay between nongovernmental and governmental actors continues as a political battleground. NGOs have wrested a measure of power in newly created municipal councils in a some cities. In many others NGOs are ignored, held at arm's length, or their initiatives incorporated in local government programs for children where benign aspects of the program die.

Nonetheless, human rights activists point to a fundamental achievement: change in the law, by which they are willing to live and die. Willingness to trust the rule of law continues to drive human rights activists and marks a sea change in Brazil and many Latin American societies.

Moreover, if a law is on the books, a good chance exists that public prosecutors will enforce the laws. As Dewees and Klees remark, they do so "in part simply because the new law exists and their responsibility and personal orientation is to enforce laws."[71] Human rights activist lawyers, such as Sister Michael Mary Nolan, march on, presenting case after case, seeking justice for the killers of children. They helped to bring down celebrated *justiceiro* (vigilante) Cabo Bruno, a former policeman who had bragged to the media about getting away with more than 50 killings.[72]

Advisers and educational consultants interviewed at United Nations Fund for Children (UNICEF) and the Interamerican Development Bank in Brasília believe that the Child and Adolescent laws are having a notable effect in Brazil.[73] They see an improvement on the streets in the treatment of children and adolescents by government agencies. More, they point to the use of existing laws by parents to force school officials to respond to the needs of previously neglected children.

The laws provide political justification for creative programs to entice children to schools. The governor of the Federal District, a member of PT (Workers Party, supported by many churchmen), has devised a program to keep children off the streets and in school. Parents in dysfunctional families often use children as sources of income, keeping them out of schools. Further, Brazilian lower-class schools typically have rates of repeating grades as high as 70 percent. This waste greatly increases the cost of education. To remedy the situation, the governor's program provides parents with a month's minimum salary if students attend school daily. This has reduced nonattendance drastically.

Brazilian human rights activists are, in general, a hardy and inventive lot. They set up SOS telephone numbers for children and adolescents in peril. Institutions are beginning to provide training and help with income-earning opportunities. Many educators are training young people where they are, on the streets, in literacy and other basic skills. Persons and groups have responded by the thousands, to the extent that observers, such as Duncan Green, believe that most children and adolescents have a place to go at night.[74]

International Gift Pathologies

One recent criticism of the Brazilian children's rights movement bites deeply: The streetchildren's movement has become an industry. This charge stems from the large amounts of foreign assistance available for remedying the situation. Even friendly observers have been dismayed by hundreds of millions of dollars sent to Brazil and by their effect on organizations.

Some observers view a distorting effects on NGOs. One said: "A certain pathology takes over. Foremost, organizations should be turned outward, to the benefit of their clients. Instead some become more interested in their own functioning and welfare. They spend much time justifying their activities before foreign funding agencies. They have to compete for funding with other groups. So attention goes on winning grants. Further, foreign benefactors (mostly European of various nationalities) have their own agendas to which Brazilians have to conform. Sometimes these agendas are out of touch with the Brazilian situation.''[75]

A frequent charge made is that streetchildren as an industry offers full-time employment to persons who would not otherwise have a job. Given the high unemployment rates, in the 25–30 percent range, Brazilians look for employment anywhere they can find it. Questionable assumptions thus are made: Being paid for working with children is only to keep adults busy or that the work with young persons should be a work of charity (not justice) and implies voluntary employment.

José Goldemberg, ex-rector of perhaps the best university in Brazil, Universidade de São Paulo, in a front-section interview in *Isto É*, agreed that NGOs had become an industry in Brazil.[76] This was especially true, he felt, in Rio among organizations devoted to resolving the problems of streetchildren. ''There are almost as many organizations as streetchildren. One judge in town said that if each of these organizations would adopt two or three children, the problem would disappear. In this sense, NGOs today are an industry, since they live by their activity. They ought rather to fight the problem. At least they were created to do so.''

Late 1990s

Funding from Europe and other places for NGOs in Latin America is drying up. Attention of the funding groups has been diverted closer to home in Central Europe or to Africa. Funding agencies have also expressed the belief that Latin American countries, such as Brazil and Chile (virtually a First World country), have enough resources to take care of themselves.

Nationalist criticisms of outside assistance are commonly heard, as well. The criticisms are heightened because of foreign intervention in environmental issues. For 30 years outsiders have been trying to tell Brazilians how to manage their environment. This criticism carries over to other human rights areas, as well. Nationalist Brazilians often make the assumption that Brazil has the ninth largest economy in the world and should take care of itself.

Any night of the week on Brazilian streets members of the Pastoral da Menor (Catholic Church) and groups from other churches and organizations sit under street lights on park benches, waiting for streetchildren and adolescents to come by. For young people who wish a roof for the night, one can typically be found. Hundreds of educators reach out to children during the day, too. Brazilians are closing in on improved care.

Many caregivers understand better than their critics the virtually intractable nature of the issue. Poverty and homelessness, for them, result from basic inequalities of economic organization. In their view a peaceful challenge to the prevailing distribution of wealth and power has to be made.

CONCLUSION

Thus far, what has been accomplished? Above all, the human rights movement achieved a fundamental change in Brazilian law. This allows streetworkers to protect children and adolescents in more adequate fashion, such as by community service as an alternative to incarceration. More fundamentally, the movement put in place a building block for democracy through focusing on law and rights.

Some, such as Dewees and Klees, believe that the movement has fostered improved public attitudes toward street- and working children. They offer no survey data to confirm this assertion. Moreover, public attitudes are notoriously volatile, especially when crime is blamed on whole sectors, such as streetchildren. Brazilian police and death squads seem to have wide support in the Brazilian public for violent treatment of streetchildren.[77]

NGOs have entered into partnership with government agencies in some locations and at various levels, changing public practice for many homeless or runaway young persons. The partnership has opened the way to more open, locally determined, and successful practices to deal with street- and working children.[78]

In sum, human rights advocates believe that legal changes mean essential foundations for progress have been established. The weeping and groaning of young persons at night has been heard. Abuse of children in Brazil and much of Latin America no longer goes unprotested.

NOTES

1. A concise account is in *The Economist* (July 31, 1993), p. 39.

2. Gilberto Dimenstein, *Brazil: War on Children* (London: Latin America Bureau, 1991).

3. See extended interview, ''Getting Away with Murder,'' CBS News, *60 Minutes*, December 1, 1991.

4. Human Rights Watch, *Human Rights . . . 1995*, p. 65.

5. Ibid.

6. Telephone interview, February 3, 1994.

7. By contrast, newspapers and magazines in various parts of the world gave wide coverage to Jacobo Timerman, the Argentine writer and editor.

8. A description of WOLA's evolution follows in Chapter 7.

9. See Edward T. Brett, ''The Attempts of Grassroots Religious Groups to Change U.S. Policy Towards Central America: Their Methods, Successes, and Failures,'' *Journal of Church and State* 36, 4 (Autumn 1994), pp. 773–794.

10. The bishops at the Medellín Conference (1968) described Latin America as an unjust society. See Second General Conference of Latin American Bishops, *The Church*

in the Present-Day Transformation of Latin America in the Light of the Council, vol. 2: *Conclusions* (Washington, D.C.: U.S. Catholic Conference, 1970), passim.

11. Interview, February 10, 1994.

12. See Alexander Wilde and Coletta Youngers, ''Latin America: The Challenge of the 90s,'' *Peace Review* 2, 1 (Winter 1990), p. 25.

13. *Os direitos humanos no Brasil* (São Paulo: Núcleo de Estudos da Violência, Universidade de São Paulo, and Comissão Teotônio Vilela, 1993), p. 44.

14. Jorge G. Casteñeda, *Utopia Unarmed: The Latin American Left after the Cold War* (New York: Knopf, 1993), p. 234.

15. See story and photographs, *The New Yorker* (January 10, 1994), pp. 70–73.

16. Gustavo Gutiérrez, ''Church of the Poor,'' in Edward L. Cleary, ed., *Born of the Poor: The Latin American Church since Medellín* (Notre Dame, Ind.: University of Notre Dame Press, 1990), p. 16.

17. See Paulo Freire's *A Pedagogy of the Oppressed* (New York: Seabury Press, 1970).

18. Neil MacDonald, *Brazil: A Mask Called Progress* (Oxford: Oxfam, 1991), p. 102.

19. Marcos McGrath, ''The Medellín and Puebla Conferences and Their Impact on the Latin American Church,'' in Cleary, *Born*, p. 77; and interview, University of Notre Dame, March 17, 1989.

20. Second General Conference of Latin American Bishops, *The Church in the Present-Day Transformation of Latin America in the Light of the Council*, Volume II (Bogotá: Latin American Bishops Council, 1970), p. 81.

21. Ibid., p. 82, noting the twentieth anniversary of the Declaration of Human Rights.

22. Murray Kempton, quoted by Fleming Rutledge, *Commonweal* (January 14, 1994), p. 10.

23. *Veja*, No. 1326 (February 9, 1994), pp. 70–77; and *IstoÉ*, No. 1315 (December 14, 1994), pp. 3–5.

24. Ibid.

25. Ibid., p. 70.

26. Ibid.

27. Amnesty International, *Americas: The Continent in which We Want To Live* (New York: Amnesty International, 1994), p. 1.

28. Felice D. Gaer, ''Reality Check: Human Rights Nongovernmental Organizations Confront Governments at the United Nations,'' *Third World Quarterly* 16, 3 (1995), p. 389.

29. Among the many useful accounts of streetchildren are Dimenstein, *War on Children* (endnote 2); Anthony Dewees and Steven J. Klees, ''Social Movements and the Transformation of National Policy: Street and Working Children in Brazil,'' *Comparative Education Review* 39, 1 (February 1995), pp. 76–100; Nancy Scheper-Hughes and Daniel Hoffman, ''Kids Out of Place,'' *NACLA Report on the Americas* 27, 6 (May–June 1994), pp. 16–23; UNICEF, *Childhood and Urban Poverty in Brazil: Street and Working Children and Their Families* (New York: UNICEF, 1992); Anthony Swift: *Brazil: The Fight for Childhood in the City* (Florence: UNICEF, 1991); Ben Penglase, *Final Justice: Police and Death Squad Homicides of Adolescents in Brazil* (New York: Human Rights Watch, 1994).

30. For their history and methods, see Robert Gabriel Quinn, ''The Reeducation and Rehabilitation of the Difficult Problem Girls under the Direction of the Sisters of Our Lady of Charity of the Good Shepherd of Angels,'' unpublished manuscript, Providence College Library, 1953.

31. Locations cited in Quinn, ''The Reeducation,'' pp. 309–315.

32. Jean Dorcy, ''From Prisons to Playgrounds,''*Sign* 47 (April 1968), pp. 20–27; Ruth Mulvey Harmer, ''Father Wasson's 'Little Brothers,' '' *Ave Maria* 89 (June 13, 1959), pp. 11–14; I. Sternberger, ''Father Wasson's 'House of Love,' '' *Jubilee* 6 (January 1959), pp. 12–15; and H. Ferguson, ''Mexico's Homeless Ones,'' *Extension* 61 (October 1966), pp. 32–53.

33. Interview with Vicente Blake, Santa Cruz, May 24, 1989.

34. Jackson Kirk Felsman, ''Street Urchins of Cali: On Risk, Resiliency, and Adaptation in Childhood,'' Ed.D. diss., Harvard University, 1982.

35. Louis Aptekar, *Street Children of Cali* (Durham, N.C.: Duke University Press, 1988).

36. Implications of age differences cannot be explored fully here.

37. Mark Lusk, ''Reviews,'' *Grassroots Development* 14, 2 (1990), p. 46.

38. William Myers, ed., *Protecting Working Children* (London: Zed Books/UNICEF, 1991), p. 31.

39. The violent character of both the formal and informal economic sectors for children is noted in Núcleo, *Os direitos humanos*, p. 42.

40. Paul Jeffrey, ''Targeted for Death,'' *Christian Century* (January 20, 1993), p. 155.

41. Besides Dimenstein's *Brazil*, see Elizabeth Hillman, ''Some Hope for Brazil's Abandoned Children,'' *Contemporary Review* 264, 1539 (April 1994), pp. 190–196.

42. Dimenstein, *War*, p. vii.

43. For earlier history of voluntary organizations, see, for example, Alexandrina Sobreira de Moura, ''Non-governmental Organizations in Brazil: From Opposition to Partnership,'' paper for Latin American Studies International Congress, 1994.

44. Ronald M. Schneider, *Order and Progress: A Political History of Brazil* (Boulder, Colo.: Westview, 1991), p. 264.

45. These changes were embodied in two major laws: The National Policy for the Welfare of Minors (PNEBEM) (1964) and the Minors Code (1979).

46. Dewees and Klees, ''Social Movements,'' p. 84.

47. See note 10 of Scheper-Hughes and Hoffman, ''Kids.''

48. Reported in Dimenstein, *War*, p. 41.

49. UNICEF, *The State of the World's Children 1993* (New York: Oxford University Press, 1993), p. 38.

50. UNICEF, *State*, p. 38

51. Called the First Latin American Seminar on Community Alternatives in Attention to Street Boys and Street Girls, and held in November 1994.

52. Scheper-Hughes and Hoffman, ''Kids,'' p. 16.

53. Antonio Carlos Gomes da Costa, quoted in Anthony Swift, *The Fight for Childhood in the City* (Florence: UNICEF, 1991), p. 18.

54. Sobreira de Moura, ''Non-governmental,'' p. 9.

55. For a careful overview of the human rights situation in Brazil, see Núcleo, *Os direitos humanos*. See also Edite Faial, Guilherme Delgado, and Rosita Milesi, *Direitos Humanos no Brasil 1992–1993* (São Paulo: Edicões Loyola, 1993); and yearly and occasional reports of Amnesty International and Human Rights Watch. An evaluation of Brazil's performance on a range of issues is found in Charles Humana, comp., *World Human Rights Guide*, 3d ed. (New York: Oxford University Press, 1992), pp. 48–51.

56. In interviews conducted in Brazil in May 1994, human rights advocates attributed the diminishing, in part, to the loss of a common foe. The *Os direitos humanos* research

group cites loss of hope and structural and behavioral constraints as formidable obstacles, passim, esp. p. 44. The decline of militancy in the women's movement is traced by Natalie Lebon, "The Emergence of Non-Governmental Organizations in the Brazilian Feminist Movement," unpublished paper.

57. Dewees and Klees, "Social Movements," p. 96.

58. Zander Navarro delineates the trajectories of four rural movements in the transition to and first years of civilian government, in "Democracy, Citizenship, and Representation: Rural Social Movements in Southern Brazil, 1978–1990," *Bulletin of Latin American Research* 13, 2 (May 1994), pp. 129–154.

59. Humana, *World Human Rights*, esp. pp. xvii–xix and 48–51.

60. Indicators used allow only rough comparisons. Employing statistics or other evaluative measures in human rights are only approximate guides. For a discussion of statistics and human rights, see Thomas B. Jabine and Richard P. Claude, eds., *Human Rights and Statistics: Getting the Record Straight* (Philadelphia: University of Pennsylvania Press, 1992).

61. Interview, São Paulo, Brazil, May 17, 1996.

62. Dewees and Klees, "Social Movements," p. 85.

63. UNICEF, *State . . . 1993*, p. 38.

64. Dewees and Klees, "Social Movements," p. 87 ff.

65. Jeffrey, "Targeted," p. 158.

66. Innovations of content, methods, and decision making in the Statute are considered by Dewees and Klees, "Social Movements," pp. 88–89.

67. James Brooke's report in the *New York Times* (January 3, 1993).

68. Robin Wright, "Nations Selling Their Futures into Economic Slavery," *Los Angeles Times* (January 16, 1994), p. 1a, cited by Dewees and Klees, "Social Movements," p. 95, n. 51.

69. Eli Diniz and Renato Boschi, "A consolidacão democrática no Brasil: Atores políticos, processos sociais e intermediacão de interesses," in Diniz, Boschi, and Renato Lessa, eds., *Modernizacão e consolidacão democrática no Brasil: Dilemas da Nova República* (São Paulo: Edicaos Vétice, 1989), pp. 58–59.

70. Fourth General Conference of Latin American Bishops, *Conclusions*, nos. 190–191, in Alfred T. Hennelly, ed., *Santo Domingo and Beyond* (Maryknoll, N.Y.: Orbis, 1993), p. 126.

71. Dewees and Klees, "Social Movements," p. 91.

72. "Getting Away with Murder," CBS News, *60 Minutes*, December 1, 1991.

73. Interviews, Brasília, May 30, 1996.

74. Interview, London, December 14, 1995. Green is conducting a survey of child abuses in several countries.

75. Interview, Brasília, May 30, 1996.

76. *Isto É*, No. 1315 (December 14, 1994), pp. 3–5.

77. Hillman, "Some Hope."

78. Dewees and Klees, "Social Movements," p. 97.

5

Contemporary Societies under Siege: Peru, Politics, and Public Secrets

Five plagues arose within Peru, bringing great suffering to millions. Out of war and ethnic conflict has arisen one of the most unified of human rights movements in Latin America. However, Peru shows more than the movement's ability to rise above partisan and ideological divides. The Peruvian situation also displays profound ties of human rights to culture.

Many in the United States concerned about human rights in Latin America turned to other interests after 1990. By contrast, staff workers and managers at Human Rights Watch, Amnesty International, and the Washington Office on Latin America found their work never abated. Concern about Peru, Colombia, Guatemala, and Haiti never diminished and, at times, intensified. Peru stands here as a vivid example of these societies under siege.

The sentencing of a U.S. citizen to life imprisonment brought further attention to human rights issues in Peru. Hooded judges in a military court sentenced Lori Berenson, a native New Yorker, in 1996.[1] The existence of such courts points to unresolved human rights issues, not only for Berenson but for thousands in Peru.

This chapter stresses the embedding of human rights discourse within politics and culture. Thus the first section traces political and other issues buffeting Peru. Then, focus shifts to movement organizing. Since organizing occurs within an intensely partisan and ideological context, politics and human rights are examined. Several sections treat cultural aspects of human rights, such as framing of issues, terror, and uncovering secrets.

PLAGUES DESCEND ON PERU

Peru's recent history is unique only in combining all the worst ills of Latin America and in adding native guerrilla movements. The 1980s were very difficult for many Latin Americans. Repayment of a large external debt and other causes brought almost uncontrolled inflation and great loss of employment in Peru. Lima became a scene of street vendors, panhandlers, car-window washers, and petty thieves. Peru has also suffered violence, cholera, a weakening party system, and corruption.

Embezzlement by President Alan García and some of his APRA (Alianza Popular Revolucionaria Americana) government cronies reached a scale that may be unknown in Peruvian history (and was exploited by political opponents). Peru, as a major grower of coca, became deeply embroiled in narcotrafficking and military control and corruption.

Unhealthy conditions of the poor contributed to the spread of cholera. However, home-grown Marxist guerrilla movements, such as Sendero Luminoso (SL) and Movimiento Revolucionario Tupac Amaru (MRTA) brought even greater devastation to Peru through crude, widespread, and spectacular violence. By 1992, Peru had become the country no one wanted to visit or chose to live in, if there was a choice. Jeffrey Klaiber, a Jesuit teacher, returned that year to Peru where he was assigned and where had spent most of his professional life. When he arrived at Lima, he was one of only two persons who disembarked from the plane.

While armed forces occupied the presidency and controlled the political direction of the country for thirteen years (1968–1980), military men did this with wide civilian participation in government. Peru's military had a much better human rights record than the harsh dictatorships of Argentina or Chile.[2] Peru's military had been formed with a French military vision, *tour de horizon*, depicting a society that needed reform. Dependency analysis led the military to believe that a landholding oligarchy created an incendiary situation. Viewed within a military framework, vast differences between rich and poor threatened national security from within the country.

Peru's military undertook land reform with a wider impact than any other Latin American country, except Chile and Cuba.[3] They also attempted other, more short-lived, reforms. The first military administration, that of General Juan Velasco Alvarado, spent freely on government programs and borrowed generous amounts of foreign capital. False economic assumptions of his government led the second military administration of General Francisco Morales Bermúdez to stop reform experiments.

The Morales Bermúdez government, guided by international advisers for loan repayment, began a series of misadventures that Catherine Conaghan and James Malloy describe as the International Monetary Fund's (IMF) Vietnam.[4] IMF demanded deep budget cuts. Peru was one of the first nations to submit to budgetary surgery in response to the worldwide debt crisis. Its ministers chose an austerity-package approach, repeated five times.

Huge spending by the military remained largely untouched. This unnerved groups upon which the greatest burden fell. These measures were but preludes to more severe steps. Increases of 50–60 percent in food and public transport costs brought on nationwide riots in 1978. The military government turned tougher and repressed resistance, expressed mostly by working-class groups.

Human Rights Groups Appear

Human rights activities began during the second military administration. As government control of the economy continued to falter badly, statist provision for lower classes greatly diminished. The state became vulnerable to protest and political oppositional actors moved in. Human rights became an issue politicians could use against the military administration.

Public discourse about human rights as a persistent issue thus began in Peru in the latter half of the 1970s. Patricia Abozaglo Jara and Martín Vegas Torres believe that before that time: ''Human rights were not an issue either in popular movements or in intellectual circles.''[5] Human rights as part of the Peruvian common speech was virtually unknown in the 1960s, according to Brian K. Goonan.[6] Living in Peru since 1966 and former director of a human rights group, Goonan is editor of *Latinamerica Press*. In Goonan's view human rights in Peru came into more common currency in Peru because Jimmy Carter placed strong emphasis on rights as part of U.S. foreign policy.

Opponents of military governments thus seized upon a now sensitive ''human rights'' as an issue of protest. The U.S. government had been supporting military takeovers throughout Latin America, putatively supplying even the key ideological basis for military governments through the ''doctrine of national security.''[7] Latin Americans perceived Carter's initiative as a major shift in foreign policy, one they could use against their own government.

In the late 1970s one of the first human rights groups, the Centro de Información, Estudios y Documentación (CIED), undertook its Human Rights Project. The project attempted to chronicle increased repression by the military government. The focus became *luchas populares* (working-class protests) and government repressive response. A spur to action came in 1977 when the government detained and fired more than 5,000 union members who had partaken in a disruptive general strike.

Both the protests and the publication were signs of a degree of liberty achieved under a weakened military administration. The CIED noted the many, mostly small, incidents one might interpret as conflicts between government and people. Opponents made demands for changes in political economy and against imposition of new repressive measures. The CIED described the protests as spontaneous and dispersed. However, CIED analysts read the events as preludes of a rising popular movement.

The chronicles and analysis of 1977–1978 did not appear until June 1979, in the waning days of military governance. The CIED report writers acknowledged Carter's strong influence and attempted to disparage his efforts. The CIED described these ''as the million-dollar and extensive campaign 'in defense of human rights' put forth by North American Imperialism by Carter, as a way to expand its neocolonial policy.''[8]

Civilian government returned with Fernando Balaúnde Terry as president in 1980. Human rights activity diminished. The National Commission of Human Rights, with branches in Lima and elsewhere, lost the target of its protest, the military government, and fell quiescent. Opposition parties gained public space and resources they lacked under military regimes: representation in Congress, party office headquarters, publishing sources, and greater opportunity for public protests.

Simultaneously, the Sendero Luminoso (SL) guerrilla movement so vicious as to be compared to the Khmer Rouge was taking shape. Abimael Guzmán, a middle-class philosophy professor from Arequipa, gathered disciples around him at Universidad de San Cristobal de Huamanga. In 1959 this university reopened in remote Ayacucho in Peru's central south. It became a suitable breeding ground for revolutionaries. Through the 1960s, Guzmán took a leading role in university politics. He and his disciples went underground in 1978.

The Sendero Luminoso opened war with selective strikes in 1980. Belaúnde and his government blindly followed a policy of minimization. In August 1981, Belaúnde said that only a minority was involved and that they were heavily financed from outside the country. He sought to depict them as an irritant, not an ominous threat. The national press did little to record or to interpret what was happening. The SL was growing into an ultrasecret movement of some 5,000 men and women.[9] Guerrilla leaders were also forming a smaller Túpac Amaru Revolutionary Movement (MRTA). MRTA caused notable damage but would nearly collapse over its confused goals and tactics.[10]

The SL founders recruited well among urban slum dwellers, peasants in less socially organized regions, and, above all, among high school teachers and students in public schools. John Gitlitz has observed human rights violations and rural organizing in Peru for many years. He believes that SL's greatest attraction was from sons and daughters of lower classes who achieved a relatively high educational level but still found themselves branded as ''country hicks.''[11] Other analysts agree.[12] Michael L. Smith has described this group: ''Rural youth are no longer satisfied being peasants but cannot find adequate employment or opportunity in urban Peru.''[13] Cultural and economic exclusion from desired positions disposed a number of recruits to the Sendero message.

Support for SL forces in rural areas, apart from coca-producing areas, was often superficial. Here, Gitlitz sees regional differences in support due to strength or weakness of social organization. In places where peasants had not organized well, people watched with approval as SL members stopped cattle rustling and punished corrupt judges. Peasants offered support initially and later withdrew their help when SL demanded active participation in the armed struggle.

In areas where peasants organized themselves strongly, once peasants discerned the SL cause, they resisted. In Cajamarca and northern Peru, villagers had organized to enforce local justice and to stop cattle rustling. Eventually, some half million, mostly peasants, organized in *rondas* (rural protective groups). Gitlitz believes that these northern groups were 95 percent effective in keeping SL forces out. This wave of peasant organizing produced a force that struggled alongside the army to reduce the SL presence in key areas.[14]

Billie Jean Isbell, a Cornell anthropologist, has chronicled the evolution and unfolding of the SL farther south, in the heart of the SL territory, the Ayacucho Department, and, even more, the effects of the war on a populace.[15] The village she has studied for years, Chuschi, found itself caught up in early activities of the SL, which attempted to prepare the ground for a revolution, in part because this area lacked the organization of haciendas. In 1980, before national elections, SL masked adherents seized and burned ballot boxes in defiance of the national government.

Isbell subsequently traced the swirl of events surrounding the spread of terror through Chuschi and Peru. Many villagers of Chuschi were displaced. For the first time as a group they experienced ethnic and racial antagonism. By necessity, many group members became bilingual, educated in the workings of the national system, and politicized.

The war in the shadows was being conducted by the SL but national attention was still focused on civilian politics in Lima. There, major opposition figures seized the new freedoms as opportunities to exploit opposition to Belaúnde and the alliance of his Acción Popular and the Partido Popular Cristiano. Parties depicted Belaúnde's administration as a "civil dictatorship."[16] They charged that Belaúnde substituted presidential and cabinet decrees for congressional legislation and used repressive measures.

Crisis of Statism

Budget cuts, price rises, loss of subsidies for basic materials, all led to the worst economic crisis in Peru since the 1930s. Protests against the government intensified. Popular frustrations with economic policies took shape in Belaúnde's middle years. Two nationwide strikes took place in 1983 and another two general strikes in 1984. Many Peruvians remember even the police, municipal workers, and bus drivers in Lima going on strike. The strikes gave the appearance of public disorder.

The public thus perceived the state to be under siege, and for good reason. For a long time Peruvian governments had indulged themselves in statism in economic affairs.[17] Governments, including Belaúnde's, not only established economic policy but attempted to act as leading actors in economic development. The government became a target of protest when economic failure set in as bitter realities for many Peruvians.

This view of the state under siege explains, in part, the degree of adversarial relations between various governments and human rights organizations. Presidents and those around them (cabinet ministers, party officials, and military advisers) perceived human rights groups as being out of order. They were, presidents believed, harmful to the interests of the state (as defined by the administration).

The shock of economic maladjustments and restructuring had profound effects on Peru's grassroots population. Peru's poor (the majority of citizens) began to respond creatively to the crisis. Peruvian writer Hernando Soto described for millions of readers in Latin America and the United States the informal economy. This sector governed the economic lives of many Peruvians and Latin Americans.[18] Out-of-work Peruvians took to the streets in droves, hawking wares, exchanging currencies, and bartering labor for food. Women in *barrios marginales* (slum neighborhoods) and *pueblos jóvenes* (new towns) around 1978 began joining in survival movements, such as *comedores populares* (neighborhood kitchens).

Millions of Peruvians were joining in social movements, most of them peaceable. Ordinary Peruvians were responding to the same economic and social processes as the SL. They too were becoming active agents of their visions of political change. Susan Stokes traces the change in ethos among the urban poor.[19] In her account the period of nationalist military rule in the 1970s contributed to breakdown of conservative ethos among the poor. Urban groups became assertive, making demands for participation in decision making and distribution of resources.

During this early period of response to human rights violations, recruits for human rights organizing tended to come from two camps: progressive Catholics and political leftists, such as those on congressional commissions for human rights.[20] The leftist camp had entered the field of human rights first. They then dominated the public discussion of rights. They *did not clearly condemn* the violence of SL.

FROM GROUPS TO MOVEMENT

Phase 1: Recognition of Guerrilla and Government Violence (1983–1985)

Human rights organizations began pulling together as a movement in 1983.[21] From that time to the present, three phases in the history of the movement can be delineated. The first began in response to Sendero Luminoso. The SL had initiated its violent attacks against selected targets in the early 1980s. Peru's major police force, the Guardia Civil, had been acting as the main agency dealing with the SL until late 1982. In the revolutionary timetable SL leaders had a long view in which the military campaign jumped to a strong start in 1983.

The SL gained sufficient force to be reckoned a national menace. This recognition brought a fateful change in government response. The administration transferred primary responsibility for controlling SL and other guerrilla threats from police to military command. The change was inevitable. Peru's national police force, underfunded, largely stationary, and lacking firepower and political clout of the armed forces, could not meet the growing challenge of the SL. The police receded to a largely localized but important role.

Escalation of violence and human rights violations by Peru's military and police brought human rights protests and systematic organizing against state violence. Within two years, 5,000 persons died in political violence, more than 500 disappeared, and an unknown number died in extrajudicial killing. President Belaúnde blundered early and seriously. He did not perceive the Peruvian character of SL and blamed foreign subversives.

Worse, Belaúnde's government put in place an anti-terrorist law. From March 1981 this ill-conceived law acted as a sixth plague for the country. The law allowed the detention of suspected terrorists for fifteen days without charges. Another provision made "speaking out publicly in favor of a terrorist" a crime punishable by up to 25 years.

Anti-terrorist measures could thus mute legitimate opposition, especially on the left. James Rudolph reports: "Thousands of opposition figures, particularly Izquierda Unida militants and peasants and labor leaders, were in fact detained under the law's provisions during subsequent years."[22] In reviewing the evidence in the mid-1980s, Susan C. Bourque and Kay B. Warren found: "Sixteen thousand of the nation's prisoners had not been found guilty of anything."[23]

Human rights activists saw in the anti-terrorist measures occasion to mount protests against the government. Transnational human rights groups attempted to add their weight. Belaúnde ridiculed Amnesty International. From the beginning of human rights organizing, military and police saw human rights activity as unjust and aggravating.

In January 1983, an event shook many Peruvians. Peasants from Uchuraccay killed visiting journalists, apparently believing them to have been members of SL. After that, the violent conflicts gained greater attention in Peru's sensationalist television and newspapers. Human rights became part of Peruvians' ordinary language.

Human rights were again made a form of political opposition. In the Chamber of Deputies the Comisión de Derechos Humanos pursued human rights violations that had not been carried out in public in Peru. However, these parliamentary investigative commissions were ill-suited instruments for human rights protests, either for framing issues or mounting protests. As ad hoc committees they did not have professional staffs nor unassailable testimony. Further, these commissions operated within the whirlwind of multiparty parliamentary conflicts. As Alfred Stepan notes, this "tends to increase the paranoia latent in most military organizations of the world with respect to political 'interference' in their activities."[24]

The cavalier tactics offended Peru's military. The confrontational attacks obstructed satisfactory civil-military relations needed in the transition from military to civilian rule. Further, the largely unaccountable power of the military continued as an unresolved issue in Peru. By contrast, Stepan argues, the routinization of legislative-military transactions would have reduced "mutual fears and ignorance of military and party leaders alike."[25]

Nonetheless, Amnesty International reports that since 1983: "Special commissions of inquiry appointed by the Senate have played a major role in the clarification of past human rights violations."[26] The Bernales and Accomarca Commissions brought light to hidden military abuses, if not prosecution.[27]

A pioneer human rights group, APRODEH (Association for Human Rights), published a report[28] based on work from the parliamentary commission and written by Javier Diez Canseco, vice president of APRODEH. Diez Canseco also acted as leader of a leftist party within the coalition, Izquierda Unida. Javier Valle-Riestra, president of APRODEH, wrote the Prologue to the report. Valle-Riestra inadvertently reveals the intensely ideological and partisan basis of human rights work at the time. Valle-Riestra refers to Diez Canseco's Marxism and his Aprismo (doctrines of Raúl Haya de la Torre) as impelling these politicians to work for human rights defense. He ends his interpretative prologue, brazenly conflating all organizations working for human rights, including the churches, as "Aprismos."[29] The fuller measure of objectivity needed for human rights advocacy eluded the early organizers.

As the number of persons affected grew, new players entered the human rights struggle. Four sets of organizations joined in the mobilization for action. Catholic progressives began entering the human rights field in small numbers. Catholic lay organizations acquired several decades of experience in university and national political conflicts.[30] Members of these groups migrated to human rights defense using existing structures, such as the national Episcopal Commission for Social Action (CEAS). In 1979 CEAS held the first national conference on pastoral work in human dignity, a precursor to human rights work.

The entrance of these church-related groups, with their less conflicted "defense of life platform," widened the human rights movement's focus. The issue of human rights became less politicized. Further, the defense of *rights* drew in other sectors of civil society, especially the poor and workers, to become participants. The political playing field thus became wider and the movement's focus widened to promotion and defense of life and rights.

Another set of groups, made up of lawyers and other legal professionals, focused primarily on legal defense and on making formal complaints against abuse of governmental authority. These groups, say Abozaglo and Vegas, at the time lacked a social recruitment base and had slight effect.[31]

Mostly women who were relatives of the disappeared formed a third set of organizations. They formed two especially prominent groups: ANFASEP in the Ayachuco area where the violence was then greatest, and COFADER in Lima in 1983–1984. Fortuitous modeling took place the previous year when a salient transnational movement brought representatives to Lima. The Latin American Federation of Relatives of the Detained-Disappeared (FEDEFAM) held its congress in Lima. The Catholic bishop-chairman of CEAS inaugurated the event.

In contrast to the narrow recruitment base of these groups, a fourth set of organizations sought membership from a wide social base. Regional and local human rights commissions sprouted up in regions where armed violence was growing. Peruvians of various backgrounds including experienced grassroots activists, professionals, union members, and church members formed the leadership and ranks of the groups.

Paralysis and Struggle for Vision and Consensus. Widening the social and political base of membership brought on internal debate about goals and vision. Lack of a common vision led to organizational paralysis, as groups were unable to agree on the manner of framing their protests. Arguments over disbursement of monies from overseas sources flared up. Further, attempts of cliques within the groups to put a partisan cast on organizational activities led to further disagreements and deeper paralysis.[32]

Through the months that followed, many participants stuck with the groups until they painfully forged a minimal consensus about methods and goals. In a sense, Peru's human rights movement thrashed out, first within groups, the working consensus that became the hallmark of the movement. Then the next step of national coordination was possible.

Probably nowhere in Latin America was the debate among movement members more acute than in Peru. What rights would the movement emphasize? Social, political, or economic rights? Activists could not defend them all effectively. What grounds would they use as the basis of rights? Peru's activists were swept into a cauldron of conflicting discourses that had been brewing in Latin America. Several emphases emerged in the conflict of ideas. Peru's deeply entrenched political left saw rights as instrumental: a way of shielding activists until a better society was achieved. These secular leftists emphasized civil and political rights. Conservative and progressive tendencies initially divided Catholics. Jeffrey Klaiber says: "Coexistence without dialogue seems to characterize relations between many in the two camps."[33]

To the surprise of outsiders, progressive Catholics were also divided among themselves. Some wished to join in the transnational human rights movement. Others, such as those trained in liberation theology, rejected First World versions of human rights as inadequate and wrong-headed and wanted to emphasize the "rights of the poor."

Many enthusiastic followers of liberation theology in the United States had equated liberation with human rights. The vast CICOP (Catholic Inter-American Cooperation Program) meeting for years drew North and South American participants. When the meeting took place in 1970, organizers chose the theme of rights and liberation.[34] When two leading mission scholars, Gerald Anderson (Protestant) and Thomas Stansky (Catholic) devoted their annual review, *Mission Trends*, to liberation theologies, human rights were presumed to have a key place in liberation theology.[35]

The conflict pitched these North American elitist, First World views of rights against contrasting Third World theologies of the poor. In a word, some noted liberation theologians strongly opposed human rights language used by Jimmy Carter, the United Nations, and modern Catholic popes.[36] The conflict also drew in conservative and progressive Protestants.

The debate raged for a time through North and South American circles.[37] The Jesuit Woodstock Center at Georgetown University had taken a lead in developing theological and historical studies of human rights in the Western tradition.[38] Third World Jesuits, such as Juan Luis Segundo, Aloisio Pieris, and Ignacio Ellacuría found Woodstock views inadequate. The Ecumenical Studies Center in San José, Costa Rica, took to publishing volumes against neoliberal human rights conceptions.[39] In their view, human rights advocates wanted to free mostly middle-class prisoners and did not see the larger picture of the unjustly suffering poor.

Several historical and contextual factors help to place the debate in Peru at this time. Human rights organizing was late in Peru, compared with Brazil and other southern neighbors. Human rights issues took shape in Peru during the "lost decade" of the 1980s when socioeconomic conditions had grown desperate. Physical survival was more important for many persons than political rights.

Through four decades, Catholic lay movements had grown strong in Peru, especially among the poor. "Option for the poor" was evident in vast slum-cities, such as Villa El Salvador and other subregions of Gran Lima. Maryknoll priests, Jesuits, sisters of many congregations, and lay leaders had highly organized networks of religious and humanitarian activities. Thus some priests and lay leaders of the Peruvian church had embraced the this-worldly orientation of the church in the modern world. By the 1980s many progressive Catholics embraced the Peruvian expression of this orientation: grassroots movements, options for the poor, and liberation theology. (These ties are especially salient in the discussion that follows.)

Peru was home to liberation theologian Gustavo Gutiérrez. Many progressive Catholics were strongly under his influence. Through Catholic schools and lay associations Peru had built a critical mass of educated Catholic intellectuals.[40] Many of them had absorbed liberation theology at one of its principal centers in Latin America, the summer theology course at Lima's Catholic University. Yearly enrollment ranged as high as 3,000 to hear Gustavo Gutiérrez and biblical scholars. Historian Jeffrey Klaiber says: "The course, offered now both in summer and winter, has over the years imparted a critical biblical-social-consciousness to thousands."[41]

"Questions of justice are central to the pastoral and theological work of liberation theologians," says Ismael García, a North American Protestant professor, in his full-length study of the question.[42] However, major liberation theologians strongly resisted "human rights" as a term. Gutiérrez has not one reference to human rights in his classic statement, *A Theology of Liberation*. He uses "human rights" only twice in more than 600 pages of his magnum opus, *Las Casas*. (Las Casas is regarded as a great defender of human rights.) Juan Luis Segundo was vitriolic in the debate. He spoke about Western countries manipulating ideologically human rights discourse to justify global maintenance of unjust economic systems.[43]

Language and cultural differences between First and Third World are paramount considerations here.[44] Liberation theologians recognize the human rights movement as the West's specific contribution to the understanding of human liberation. However, in the view of these Third World theologians, "human rights" reflects a culture that is too individualistic, too "liberal," and neglectful of economic rights. Nor does human rights language reflect directly or fully biblical language. By contrast, Gutiérrez and Segundo both choose biblical language and speak of the rights of those favored by God, the poor.

Both sides of the debate have learned from one another. The Catholic Church, with liberation theologians among its ranks, threw itself into resisting the most flagrant of human rights abuses. Also throughout Latin America, now that military regimes have receded from direct rule, the movement pursues a much wider agenda of human rights protection.

The most prominent liberation theologian of Brazil, Leonardo Boff, has shown by example the pulling together of the two perspectives. Boff has been a tireless worker for human rights in Brazil. In 1994 he won the National Award for Human Rights. Simultaneously, he was showing how to reconcile conflicting perspectives into a biblical basis for human rights work.[45]

Many Latin American Protestants agree with the literal statement in St. Paul's Letter to Romans, Chapter 13: One should obey lawful authority. In Peru the major political thrust of Protestants for years had been the gaining of freedom of worship and a measure of equality. Younger Protestants, trained at state universities, brought pressure for a greater Protestant presence in society.

From 1980 to 1984, Protestants, as other Peruvians, were becoming aware of the human rights violations which guerrilla and state forces were causing. Intense debates brought a vision of human rights protection as an integral part of the mission of the churches. The National Peruvian Protestant Council (CONEP) gave birth to the Comisión Paz y Esperanza in 1984. With Pedro Arana as president and Samuel Escobar as vice president, the group began its dynamic work, especially in the most conflictive areas of the country.

Some observers see Peru as a closed society. New ideas, they say, do not permeate easily. Thus, Peru's left, both secular and Catholic, shared a measure of disdain for human rights, as "Mr. Carter's" campaign.

Another Peruvian characteristic, the drive for widespread education in human rights, intensified the debate. Progressive Catholics were strongly tied to grassroots organizations. Members of these groups felt the blows of the guerrillas and the security forces that fell hardest on the poor. Grassroots organizations thus took the lead in demanding human rights education.

But what rights should activists teach? Five groups were notable for their common efforts to provide human rights education: Episcopal Commission for Social Action, Andean Commission of Jurists, Center for Studies and Action for Peace, Institute for Legal Defense, and the Peruvian Institute for Education in Human Rights. As basic propositions for their work they agreed: (1) economic and social rights are an essential dimension of human rights, and (2) civil and political rights are the other face of human rights.[46]

From the mid-1980s, strong belief in human rights education marked the human rights movement in Peru. Activists emphasized education [47] not only as the basis for human rights work but also as the foundation of democracy. By 1985, they put together teams specialized in human rights education. They spread through Lima, Ayacucho, and many other regions of the country. Among various groups, teams from the Andean Commission of Jurists tailored their courses to grassroots leaders, jurists, law students, and the police.

What was most distinctive about Peru was merging membership in popular organizations, human rights education, and legal defense. Priests, sisters, and lay workers spent years helping the poor to organize themselves in the vast slum-cities, such as Villa El Salvador in southern Lima. These groups served as ready networks for new educational emphases.

Internalization and Talking Politics

Both the grand debate over rights and the massive educational efforts had two major effects for the human rights movement: internalization of norms and framing issues. First, those joining in the dangerous work of human rights protection had a special need of a conversion-like process. They required convictions strong enough to sustain them through public apathy and personal fear.

On the surface the strong Peruvian emphasis on education represents a common and naive Third World response: problems will be resolved by education. A more personal motive emerged in interviews: group members felt that dealing with case after case of human rights violations was not enough.[48] They needed what Latin Americans call ''reflexión,'' or ''toma de conciencia.'' Why were they doing what they were doing? Why were they engaged in dangerous and disruptive activities?

Historical factors contributed to this deeply felt need. Many Peruvians gained experience in Catholic Action or base Christian community techniques. In those groups the see-judge-act method had formed a rhythm in their lives. They habitually took the second step: the process of examining reasons—biblical, theological, legal—for convincing themselves to continue in difficult work and for framing their message to attract thousands of others to their work.

This inductive methodology was present as early as the 1950s and shows up in the landmark 1953 Chimbote meeting.[49] Later formulations of Gustavo Gutiérrez and other liberation theologians refined the methodology. The Latin American bishops in their Medellín and Puebla conferences routinely used description-reflection-action in their deliberations and thousands of other church groups followed their example.[50]

Another factor in the need for internalizing convictions was the newness of ''human rights.'' Although human rights was becoming a life-and-death issue, it but had been virtually unknown. Peruvians felt the urgent need to educate both in schools and more commonly in adult circles. Here was a key element in Peru, the vast social movement for informal education, intersected with the human rights movement. Since the late 1960s, many groups had already become the natural outlets for adult learning. Many human rights activists were members of credit unions, cooperatives, microenterprises, church schools, and women's groups; they began to educate them with sophisticated ideas about rights.

Third, the heated debate over the basis for rights became for Peruvians what William Gamson calls "talking politics." They searched for acceptable "frames for action," to motivate members who would take chances in a hostile environment.[51] The time spent in debating which rights to emphasize and on what intellectual foundation was more than a conflict over words or educational methodology; the groups were forging a political consciousness.

"Reflexión" produced a message of injustice. Members' goals became the stopping or ameliorating of extensive suffering that security forces and guerrillas were inflicting. Injustice, then, in the suffering of human rights violations by innocent people became the target. "Injustice," as Gamson says, "focuses on righteous anger that puts fire in the belly and iron in the soul."[52] Peruvian human rights activists emerged from the reflective process with the "hot" motivation they needed for the long fight.

However, another issue impeded the acceptance of human rights. The idea of law and of law being the basis of society had not been a central part of Peruvian political discourse, either on the right or on the left. However, as John Gitlitz remarks, without a discourse on law, a realistic discourse on human rights is impossible.[53] In the 1980s, justice served as a stepping-stone idea and perhaps emerged more strongly because of the absence of a discourse on law. But it was inadequate to serve as the basic support for human rights protection.

The human rights groups chose the government as the principal target of protest. This brought heavy criticism on the movement. Why did not the human rights groups attack the vicious SL? Human rights activists did make many protests against SL and had them rejected.[54] Human rights advocates believed SL to be fanatics, impervious to arguments from people who supported the system, lacking in a sense of reality, and unavailable for direct communication.

Human rights groups in Peru and in Latin America aimed at vulnerability in the government. Their argument: Forces of the state have as their role and mission the protection of citizens. When the state injures its citizens, especially the innocent through indiscriminate violence, this directly counters its role and is a doubly grave injustice. Also, when the state used the same tactics as SL—torture and massacre—this added force to SL anti-government rhetoric. The government did not try to win over the minds and hearts of the civil population and to isolate the enemy psychologically and politically. Further, democracy requires accountability by state forces. Hence, military and police were held to minimum standard of behavior. Human rights groups were only asking for the rule of law.

For military and police these arguments, while correct, did not hold for them. Peruvian police and military personnel viewed themselves also as victims, for several good reasons. President Belaúnde and his government ignored the main body of police, the Guardia Civil. Peruvian police were among the most poorly paid in Latin America.[55] Besides better pay, they were badly in need of reform and rearming. But Belaúnde chose to ignore the problem. The SL were cutting down police. In the first five years (1981–1985) of confrontation the SL killed 175 police.

Ineffectiveness of the police force was a factor pulling the army and marines into anti-terrorist work. The military also felt abandoned by the civilian administration. In 1984, Americas Watch characterized the Belaúnde administration as ''abdicating authority.''[56]

In sum, during this period human rights groups began recruiting from a much wider clientele. Recruits from the left-center to liberal right in 1984 organized the Commission for the Rights of Persons and the Construction of Peace. Members included bishops, priests, retired generals, and a number of lay Peruvians. Public debate shifted from emphasis on strongly anti-government politics and began centering on Catholic versions of respect for the human person as the basis of rights.

Key groups emerged from their period of internal debate with a conviction that the movement needed a massive social response. They would mount demonstrations at critical moments to attract new members and to call national attention to the cause.

Phase 2: New Political Opportunities and One Voice (1985–1989)

In the second period, new political opportunities presented themselves, critics intensified their attacks on human rights organizations, and the movement consolidated under a national coordinator. Belaúnde was nearing the end of his term in 1985. Presidential weakness and the turbulence of the preelectoral period opened new opportunities for movement organizing. Activists staged the first national congress of human rights advocates. Primer Encuento Nacional de Derechos Humanos issued a major statement in February 1985. By now many organizations were associated with the Catholic Church. Together the groups condemned SL and the spiral of violence that had taken place in Peru.

Participants in the congress took the next step of creating a central coordinating body for the movement. Coordinadora Nacional de Derechos Humanos (CNDH) thus took life in 1985. Christian activists, lay and religious, have led this central group.[57] It has continued since 1985 to pull groups together and to attempt to speak with one voice.[58]

CNDH organized its first massive demonstration, the March for Peace. It was typical of the new unity: University rectors, some Catholic bishops, leftist parliamentarians, Christian Democrat leaders, and other prominent Peruvians marched at the head of the column. Rank after rank followed. These included thousands of relatives of the disappeared, leaders and members of grassroots organizations, lower-class Catholic parish members, and members of human rights, professional, and labor organizations. In the Latin American traditional repertoire, demonstrations end in a declaration, announcing the political demands of the marchers. In the first March for Peace, a bishop-member of the Commission for Peace read the agreed-upon proposal. Thousands thus came from all over the country to demand observance of human rights by the state. In this and subsequent demonstrations, progressive Christians helped to organize and lead the marches.[59]

During his 1985 inaugural address, Alan García made human rights protection an issue, perhaps for the first time in Peruvian presidential history. He promised to control human rights violations by police and military. The new minister of war, General Jorge Torres Flores, took a similar stand. García's efforts increased public attention to human rights observance. Americas Watch noted, however, that "the quality of discussion has not necessarily improved."[60]

García believed that corruption, poor discipline, and widespread criminal activity marked Peru's police. García made strong efforts to reform the police. His government unified the three police agencies, provided new weapons, increased their pay, and purged more than 1,800 policemen from the ranks, charging many of them with infractions. These reform moves were obscured by efforts to shield police and military from criminal charges and especially by police continuing in their largely ineffectual and sometimes corrupt ways.

Human rights violations by security forces diminished for a time. Human rights organizations made gains through some governmental officials' allowing monitoring of the human rights situation.[61] This was a period of consolidating public space for human rights within Peru. Core groups[62] were pulling away from identification of human rights with partisan politics. They were becoming more professionalized and recognized within Peru. Courts, ministries, and other government agencies called upon them to provide information. Human rights groups typically offered humanitarian and legal assistance to victims and survivors, as well.

By 1986 two central groups, the Andean Commission of Jurists and the Catholic Bishops Commission for Social Action (CEAS), were especially able to display human rights work as salient for important sectors of Peruvian society: professionals and Catholic activists. The Andean Commission of Jurists held out the promise of constitutional reform and observance of law. CEAS and similar groups turned the attention of Catholic Action or base Christian community members toward human rights as expressing their social Christianity.

Within CEAS twenty full-time lawyers, social workers, and activists took on the dirty work of becoming a main channel for verifying disappearances and violations of human rights. They also acted as advisers for Bishops Luis Bambarén and Miguel Irizar, successive presidents of CEAS. Bambarén and Irizar became the most forceful spokespersons for human rights among the bishops.[63]

Alan García shackled the armed forces with some restraints. However, García too left the military without clear leadership. As Carlos Iván De Gregori states: "The armed forces felt they were bearing the brunt of a conflict which was becoming bloodier without the support of the politicians."[64]

The armed forces had contributed to the problem by an image of luxury with the repetitive demands for large budgets which included Mirage fighter aircraft and other glamorous hardware. García began reducing military prerogatives.[65] Unsupported and bloodied, the armed forces were reported to be grossly *underpaid.* Salaries had slipped to the lowest in South America in 1991, with a general commanding a division receiving $U.S. 210 a month. Junior and middle-grade officers found they could not sustain their families on their salaries alone.[66]

By 1991, lack of support for the armed forces had resulted in the army's growing difficulty in feeding, clothing, and providing medical care for its soldiers.[67] De Gregori reported: "Requests for retirement multiplied at an alarming rate. Mediocrity and the temptations of narcotics trafficking threatened the institution of the armed forces."[68]

The army contributed to its poor performance through ignorance of the enemy, disinterest in domestic conditions while focusing on border conflicts with other countries, failed strategies of "strategic hamlets," making combat assignment a career detriment, and belated and inadequate intelligence.[69]

The decision to turn the conflict with the SL over to the military was fateful for many ordinary Peruvians. Peru's military made neither a good anti-subversive unit nor police force. It responded to guerrilla forces by surprise detentions, military sweeps through areas, quick and indiscriminate response to suspicions, secrecy, and cover-up. Its intelligence reports were unrefined, based on rumor and vengeful denunciations, and often ignorant of specific geographical situations. Many of Peru's recruits came from coastal areas. They were unfit for understanding the ways of living and responding to crises in the Central Sierra. Ethnic intolerance compounded the subordinate and vulnerable position of Indian peasants.

Parliamentary commissions investigated mass killings of peasants, such as by the garrison of Huanta and at Accomarca in 1984 and 1985. The Ames Commission of the Senate looked into the mass killings in three prisons in 1986. The Bernales Commission, also from the Senate, looked into the larger causes of extended political violence. Given the small number of nongovernmental groups at the time, these governmental bodies performed a small but vital function of showing government as a major human rights violator. Other parliamentary commissions remained under control of García's party and adroitly obfuscated evidence, such as at Cayara.[70]

This formula for disaster was compounded by the nature of guerrilla warfare and the exceptional stealth of the SL. Military strategists had long discredited the traditional formula of ten uniformed men for every guerrilla to achieve military victory; many more uniformed men would be needed. Peru's police and military understood poorly the history, modus operandi, and ideological appeal of the SL. Years passed before military intelligence achieved clarity about the leaders' identities or SL's chain of command.

Ayacucho, the seat of the SL, was remote, unimportant to Lima where a third of Peruvians lived and which drew most of the government's attention. Moreover, governmental and other development specialists bypassed the Sierra. They favored enhancing coastal agriculture for export (similar to Chile's central valley) or developing the tropical interior (with petroleum and other extractive riches).

The SL leaders built on decades of neglect. The SL trained its recruits in relative isolation and sent them out to destroy key figures in Peruvian local society. It perceived social movement leaders as enemies, slaughtering hundreds of them. Special targets of the SL were mayors, public school teachers, neighborhood leaders, Protestant ministers, nuns, and priests. They executed María Elena Moyano, a noted grassroots leader in Lima, and Sister Irene Teresa MacCormack, an inconspicuous Australian nun, among many others. They also attacked major pillars of modern Peruvian society through spectacular car bombings in urban districts, attacks on police stations, and explosions of electrical pylons. After the attacks the guerrillas vanished, indistinguishable from peaceable neighbors.

The Peruvian security forces caused almost as many human rights violations as the SL. More was involved than indiscriminate killing in the field. Peru had the world's worst record from 1988 to 1991 for the number of persons detained who then disappeared. After reaching a high in 1988 of 549 persons disappeared, the number fell to less than 100 in the first six months of 1993.[71] Thousands detained by security forces were being kept in prison without due process.

Phase 3: Expansion of Movement (1989–Present)

The third phase witnessed many human rights groups flooding throughout the country. The number of core groups quadrupled from seventeen in 1989 to seventy-seven in 1994, the second largest number in Latin America.[72] They ranged from local, regional, and national. Many groups were recruited from Catholic Church affinities, other groups from political networks, and some groups from networks of peasant communities.

Recruitment from the middle and lower levels of Catholic and other activists expanded strongly beyond Lima. In 1987 in Piura, Bishop Oscar Cantuarias Pastor opened an office for human rights, in part to forestall the incursion of SL.[73] Other dioceses opened "vicarías de solidaridad," resembling those of Chile.

The Piura office, with a staff of seven, reached beyond traditional concerns to the administration of grassroots justice. In Peru justices of the peace now form more than 80 percent of juridical corps. Paco Muguiro, the Jesuit priest in charge of the Piura office, and associates have sought to enlighten and strengthen the justices of the peace. They made similar efforts to train rural community members in nonviolent conflict resolution methods.

Progressive Christians were key in seizing opportunities to stage demonstrations. When SL threatened to disrupt local elections in 1989, some 200,000 took to the streets in Lima. Human rights activists organized similar marches in Huancayo, Piura, and elsewhere.

The human rights movement expanded during acute conflict imposed by the growing numbers of SL and the immense havoc they inflicted. Despite divisions over counterinsurgency policy in the military,[74] advocates of the "Argentine solution" prevailed. The military engaged in an annihilation strategy. French military practices in Vietnam and Algeria heavily influenced Peruvian strategy. The military and paramilitary produced almost as many casualties in the general populace as did SL. Some 30,000 Peruvians would perish in the fifteen years of political violence.[75]

Human rights groups addressed their protests to both sides. Again they found themselves attacked by SL, the military, and the ruling APRA party. Attacks on persons defending human rights were especially acute from December 1988 to December 1989. Americas Watch noted nineteen cases of persecution of members of rights organizations, witnesses, or legal representatives. Attacks diminished but the following year Fujimori's justice minister complained that human rights groups "only contribute to a climate of demoralization."[76]

To conduct war against the SL, the military created emergency military zones to control more than half of Peru's population.[77] These zones included the eight million inhabitants of Greater Lima. For more than ten years Peruvians lived in the emergency zones without customary rights, such as habeas corpus. By 1992 the Humana group classified Peru, along with El Salvador and Cuba, as the worst human rights offenders in Latin America.[78]

Besides long-standing forms of violations—torture, prolonged detention without trial, and disappearance—human rights groups protested new legislation and continuation of military tribunals. New laws from the Fujimori government threatened the press with life imprisonment for "apology of terrorism." The government then jailed four reporters on such charges in 1992.

Especially worrisome have been the continuation of military tribunals where terrorism or treason are alleged. Lori Berenson found herself trapped in this structure. The process is secret and swift. Judges are hooded to protect themselves from retaliation. Only one judge is an attorney. Active-duty military officers, with little or no training in the law, serve as the other judges.[79] Compounding the gravity of possible injustices, national referendum instituted the death penalty in 1992.

WIDENING OF PERSPECTIVE: CULTURE, POLITICS, AND HUMAN RIGHTS

The effort of pulling together for human rights challenges to the government brought on substantial change for the secular left. In Peru this sector had focused on the political economy. They did not express a consistent interest in law. In the last ten years many of the secular left, along with other Peruvians at the elite and grassroots levels, have been shifting to stronger reliance on law. The Andean Commission of Jurists is leading the way not only for Peru but for the region as well. At the grassroots level, researchers, such as Isbell, have observed much more recourse to law.

This represents a major change within Peruvian culture, if Tina Rosenberg's analysis is to be followed. Rosenberg, a MacArthur grant recipient, contrasted Peruvian with Chilean society. Chileans have a measure of trust in the judicial system and spend large amounts of money in judicial processes. Peruvians, she asserted, lack faith enough in their judicial system to want to use or to depend upon it.[80]

The shift toward greater reliance on law accompanies a widening of geographical perspective of human rights protection, as well. Ordinary Peruvians now have recourse to *denuncias* (legal complaints) beyond local boundaries. They carry their *denuncias* to human rights organizations for legal assistance in provincial capitals and beyond. In 1991 four elected officials disappeared after a lieutenant and troops took them away from Chuschi.[81] Relatives and friends attempted to determine their whereabouts through provincial authorities. Unable to find them, relatives and friends made the arduous trip to Lima. They made two visits, one at APRODEH, a national human rights organization. The second visit was made at the U.S. embassy to have a formal conversation with the political attache. There the villagers made their protest: Aid to Peru was not to be given if human rights are abused. Did not the U.S. Congress *by law* have to stop such aid?

The influence of the U.S. government on human rights protection in Peru cannot be evaluated adequately here. Embassy advisers did not agree on many emphases, especially military solutions or human rights protection. But Peruvians, such as newspaper editor Manuel d'Ornellas and think-tank researcher Fernando Rospigliosi, believe that U.S. pressure to investigate human rights violations has been a strong counterweight to Peruvian military resistance to do so.[82]

Further, says Rospigliosi: "The influence which foreign governments and institutions can exercise over Peru is enormous. This influence has been apparent often in recent years, particularly concerning human rights violations by the security forces, which have diminished almost exclusively because of international pressure."[83] Other observers believe a combination of national and transnational pressures have been essential.

Anthropological Probings for Meaning

Deeper probing of changes in cultural perspectives, such as of Chuschi villagers, is needed. Here I relate findings wider than those from Peru. This is not to conflate culture into a Pan American unity but to note striking similarities. Accounting for changes occurs at a fortuitous conjuncture. North American and national field researchers from a third generation of anthropologists have been returning to Andean and Mayan communities. Some anthropologists have been observing the same villages, as often as possible, since the late 1960s. Their careful records mark the changes. Further, first-generation Peruvian, Guatemalan, and Mexican *indigenous* social scientists are making their own interpretations.

First, human rights activists, especially from North Atlantic cultures, may not easily grasp the profound internal shift for Peruvian peasants involved in reacting to human rights violations. The manifestation of injustice that ''must'' be made involves the *denuncia.* In doing so Peruvian peasants gain a different sense of time than culturally given. Time is no longer circular, just the past repeated. Time becomes linear: It leads to the future and allows for a global sense.[84]

Second, probing cultural perceptions also enlarges the narrow focus of reporting by rights activists. Since the beginning of this human rights era, say, in 1961, AI and similar transnational groups have had to emphasize factual accounts of repression. National and local groups followed AI's lead. They had to document facts, impeccably. They were, after all, mounting protests against hostile targets.

However, as governments have allowed anthropologists to return to contested areas in Peru, Guatemala, Chiapas, and elsewhere, something more became evident. Warren says: ''The [human rights] movement's understandings conveyed in realist narratives . . . are not the only way to represent the impact of human rights violations on local communities.''[85]

Robin Kirk of Human Rights Watch agrees: ''Much eludes human rights reports. Not facts, but the fabric, not the accuracy of numbers but the high accuracy of sense, experience, passion. . . . True 'balance' lies in . . . a story, a witnessing, a point of view.''[86]

Deeper probing of cultural expressions of terror is needed. Peasants were displaced from Chuschi, as were 600,000 others from the military zones. Some sought exile in Chile. Through the Chilean Vicariate of Solidarity, women began to learn *arpilleras*, folk art forms that could be used for protest. Returning exiles carried the *arpillera* back to highland Peru. These woven wall hangings encapsulate life stories. They typically recount loss and recovered hope. They now grace the halls of office buildings in New Haven, Conn., and Ithaca, N.Y., as they do adobe homes in Peru.

The *arpilleras* are cultural constructions of terror. They are both personal and social statements of experience and protest. Weavers may also experience a therapeutic effect. Violations of human rights are also manifested by victims with a degree of artistic permanence.

Silence and Public Secrets

Reticence by indigenous speakers has been a long-standing theme of anthropologists dealing with both Andean and Mayan cultures. Given the racism of

Peru and Guatemala since the conquest, Indians have had to shield their rituals and their thoughts. Repression that fell on contemporary generations greatly increased this guarded quality. As Warren notes: Their "language is often veiled or oblique, often condensed into cryptic observations with unspecified agents."[87]

Another medium for constructing terror, besides *arpilleras*, is the cultural narrative. These narratives convey even deeper meanings than wall hangings. In Guatemala, Warren attempted to discern how Mayans shape their understandings of the militarization of civilian life with frequent torture and death. To enter into this world, Warren emphasizes analysis of traditional narratives to convey their horrors, as reshaped by Mayan families and community storytellers. These stories assume central importance, because, as Warren notes: "These narratives are Mayan histories, portraying events that are said to have happened in the town."[88]

In Peru, too, long-standing beliefs and experiences with repression are expressed through traditional stories applied to terror experiences. Shining Path members become *ñaqa*, supernatural beings who rob body fat to harm villagers. Peruvian military and police are perceived as foreigners who know no fear and who are savage.

The narratives illuminate central issues arising from experience of militarization and repression. One issue, silence, emerges with special importance for the human rights movement. Rural dwellers witnessed repression and death. Sometimes death was seen firsthand. More typically, bodies of strangers increasingly were found on roads, or as in Quiché, floating in nearby rivers.

Further cultural meaning is involved, beyond horror over brutality. These bodies were "out of place." Persons (who had inhabited these bodies) were gone from their homes (where they belonged). In addition, empathy was felt for the others "at home" who would be missing this disappeared person.

Warren notes: "*La violencia* still comes up in every conversation, in every meeting or event."[89] Silence operates, though, to deny involvement of any one in particular. Villagers were caught between two armies. No agent from army, guerrilla, or civil patrol or any neighbor who brought death through being an informant may be named. Isbell, too, notes the strong tendency to denial in Peru.[90]

David Stoll returned to his research in the Ixil triangle in Guatemala where army and guerrillas had been especially belligerent. Stoll found what Michael Taussig, Warren, and Isbell call the public secret: "What every one knows but cannot talk about in public because of the prevailing distribution of power. Hence, the public secret is a way of remasking the truth in order to avoid confrontation and reprisal."[91]

This public silence protects the impunity of killers, torturers, and those who aided the targeting of victims. Does this mean the telling of truth will never occur? Not until a dramatic change in the way power is exercised by the Guatemalan army, Stoll believes. Stoll is also convinced that: "Memory of army abuses is nurtured by the entire population." Nor do their judgments "point exclusively to the army.''[92] What is lacking for expressing the truth is political opportunity, a vulnerability to be exploited.

Warren, who is a major figure in modern anthropology, adds her own conclusion: ''For many Latin Americanists, social research needs to address social inequalities, local culture, and human rights. Our contribution is to give a voice to those who are muted by cultural difference and the politics of marginalization.''[93]

Giving voice in Isbell's case has meant performance art. She believed that telling the truth would have to be in a form other than realist narratives. In Peru human rights violations continue at a pace that will not allow truth commissions. Even more, sources have to be protected. Isbell has chosen to tell the truth through drama. She has written a performance piece for actors in several acts. Dialogue is drawn directly from interviews, quoting from Peruvians and U.S. embassy personnel. Her play, ''Public Secrets from Peru,'' has strongly affected audiences.[94]

Uncovering Secrets

The subtleties of culture and human rights have become clearer in the recent and highly valuable contributions of physical anthropologists. Clyde Snow at the University of Oklahoma and Karen R. Burns at the University of Georgia have taken the lead in human rights–oriented forensic work.

Snow trained forensic anthropologists such as Mercedes Doretti and Luis Fonderbrider, who founded the Argentinean Forensic Anthropology Team. This team, now composed of a dozen members, originally began work in their own country to determine the fate of thousands for the National Commission of the Disappeared. A similar group, led by Guatemalans Federico Reyes and Mariana Valdiz, looked into the much wider field of hundreds of thousands killed in Guatemala.

In the fall of 1995, both Argentines and Guatemalans made up part of the team attempting to establish what occurred in a three-year period of terror in Haiti. Burns acted as scientific leader for the Haitian mission. Earlier she had accepted an invitation from the Minnesota Lawyers International Human Rights Committee to prepare guidelines for forensic work. Her work proved to be outstanding and became the basis for adoption by the United Nations in 1991.

Detective work with knowledge of ethnology and linguistic structures helps culturally sensitive interviews that yield reliable evidence from survivors and witnesses of repression. In Latin America patron-client relations often control meaning. Interviewers have to be extraordinarily aware that initial responses to direct questions are often false, ones calculated to please the patron-questioner. Even descriptions of evidence, such as right-or-left side of anatomy or color, demand linguistic sophistication.

Establishing a record of what occurred in Argentina, Guatemala, and Haiti has two striking effects: Not knowing with certitude about the death of loved ones and not being able to bury relatives have left profound scars on survivors. Uncovering the truth has brought a measure of closure to their loss.

From now on, as the *Anthropology Newsletter* says, they "no longer live in an emotional limbo bereft of social power."[95] They bury their dead with dignity. Identification and confirmation of injustices furnishes survivors with evidence that can be used against oppressors. In this way forensic anthropology empowers others with information for effective human rights protests.

A final issue dogs human rights defenders. Conflicts occur when questions are raised about which rights are to be emphasized. Do rights to food, housing, and health come before fair trial and imprisonment without torture?

Ordinary Peruvians have sometimes chosen to emphasize rights which transnational human rights groups do not. As Kirk says of Human Rights Watch: "The majority of Peruvians probably do not believe that the human rights we champion are the most important ones." In fact, "there has been wide popular support for Fujimori's antiterrorist laws" (and subsequent human rights violations).[96]

CONCLUSION: CLEAVAGES AND COOPERATION

Recruitment for human rights organizations took place especially among persons from Peru's left-center.[97] Despite surface unanimity, deep ideological cleavages separated them. The two most prominent affiliations among human rights activists were religious and secular.[98] Historically, these differed greatly in outlook and goals.

Many of the secular left were driven by Marxist visions. They saw a Peru with intermediate state domination and an evolution to a rational world without religion. The religious left was more interested in a struggle for the greater welfare of the poor. Its vision of how society might be organized was not clear. In a word, secular leftists looked for structural changes in Peru. Religious leftists sought empowerment.

To contest a common enemy, persons from these differing tendencies often continued to pull together effectively. "The great achievement of Peru's human rights movement was speaking with one voice. Peru exceeded most other countries in this regard," in Alexander Wilde's and other observers' judgments.[99]

That consensus was possible for more than ten years has been a hard swim against the tide; Peruvian society became increasingly fragmented and riven by political corruption and controversy. Traditional political parties would virtually disintegrate, none gaining even 4 percent of the vote in national elections in 1995.

Cultural preferences influence Peruvians supporting Fujimori's authoritarian measures. However, a remarkable consensus exists among human rights groups, domestic or international, not only in Peru but throughout most of Latin America. Both sets have emphasized the rule of law. One could argue that they see this as the cornerstone of democratic life and human rights activity.

NOTES

1. Among several accounts of Berenson is John H. Richardson, "The Revolutionary Girl Next Door," *New York* (February 19, 1996), pp. 26–35.

2. Peru's military is covered comprehensively by Daniel M. Masterson, *Militarism and Politics in Latin America: Peru from Sánchez Cerro to Sendero Luminoso* (Westport, Conn.: Greenwood, 1991). See also Masterson, "The Armed Forces and the Contemporary Crisis in Peru," in Billie Jean Isbell and Mary Jo Dudley, *Threats to Democracy in the Andean Region* (Ithaca, N.Y.: Cornell University Latin American Studies Program, 1993), pp. 111–119; Victor Villanueva Valencia, *Ejército peruano: Del caudillaje anárquico al militarismo reformista* (Lima: Mejía Baca, 1973); Philip Mauceri, *Militares: Insurgencia y democratización en El Perú* (Lima: Instituto de Estudios Peruanos, 1989); and David Scott Palmer and Kevin Jay Middlebrook, "Corporatist Participation under Military Rule in Peru," in David Chaplin, ed., *Peruvian Nationalism: A Corporatist Revolution* (New Brunswick, N.J.: Transaction Books, 1976), pp. 428–453.

3. Cuba is often ignored in analyses of Latin American reforms. William C. Thiesenhusen's assessment of agrarian reform in Latin America is in *Broken Promises: Agrarian Reform and the Latin American Campesino* (Boulder, Colo.: Westview, 1995), p. 87 and passim. David Scott Palmer believes the Peruvian agrarian land reform "effectively eliminated large private land holdings." See his edited *Shining Path of Peru*, 2d ed. (New York: St Martin's Press, 1994), p. 12. See also Peter Dorner's assessment in his *Latin Americam Land Reforms in Theory and Practice: A Retrospective Analysis* (Madison: University of Wisconsin Press, 1992), pp. 37–38 and passim. Among many commentaries, all of them dated, taking up agrarian reform in Peru, see Michael R. Carter and Elena Alvarez, "Changing Paths: The Decollectivization of Agrarian Reform Agriculture in Coastal Peru," in William C. Thiensenhusen, ed., *Searching for Agrarian Reform in Latin America* (Boston: Unwin Hyman, 1989), pp. 156–187; Elena Alvarez, *Política agraria y estancamiento de la agricultura* (Lima: Instituto de Estudios Peruanos, 1980); Howard Handelman, *Struggle in the Andes: Peasant Mobilization in Peru* (Austin: University of Texas Press, 1975); and Cynthia McClintock, "Velasco, Officers, and Stealth," in McClintock and Abraham Lowenthal, eds., *The Peruvian Experiment Reconsidered* (Princeton, N.J.: Princeton University Press, 1980), pp. 275–308.

4. Catherine M. Conaghan and James M. Malloy, *Unsettling Statecraft: Democracy and Neoliberalism in the Central Andes* (Pittbsurgh: University of Pittsburgh Press, 1994), p. 100.

5. Patricia Abozaglo Jara and Martín Vegas Torres, "Aportes para una pedagogia por la vida y por la paz," in n.e., *Educar en Derechos Humanos* (Lima, co-edition of Comisión Episcopal de Acción Social and other groups, 1991), p. 46.

6. Interviews, Lima, May 24–29, 1995.

7. For allegation of U.S. involvement, see Penny Lernoux, *Cry of the People* (Garden City, N.Y.: Doubleday, 1980), passim.

8. Centro de Información, Estudios y Documentación (CIED), *Dinámica de la luchas populares: Informe Peru 1977–78* (Lima: CIED, 1979), p. 7.

9. A full account of Sendero Luminoso has yet to be written. The second edition of David Scott Palmer's edited volume, *Shining Path*, serves as a good introduction. See also Carlos Iván De Gregori, *El surgimiento de Sendero Luminso: Ayacucho 1969–1979* (Lima: Instituto de Estudios Peruanos, 1990), and his "Shining Path and Counterinsurgency Strategy since the Capture of Abimael Guzmán," in Joseph S. Tulchin and Gary

Bland, eds., *Peru in Crisis: Dictatorship or Democracy* (Boulder, Colo.: Lynne Rienner, 1994), pp. 81–100; Gustavo Gorriti, *Sendero: Historia de la guerra milenaria del Perú*, vol. 1 (Lima: Apoyo Editores, 1990); Henri Favre, ''Sendero Luminoso: Horizontes oscuros,'' *Que Hacer* 31 (October 1984), pp. 25–34; and a journalistic account by Simon Strong, *Shining Path: Terror and Revolution in Peru* (New York: Times Books, 1992).

10. See Gordon H. McCormick's assessment of MRTA, *Sharp Dressed Men: Peru's Túpac Amaru Revolutionary Movement* (Santa Monica, Calif.: Rand, 1993).

11. Interview, February 5, 1996.

12. Michael L. Smith ''Talking the High Ground: Shining Path and the Andes,'' in Palmer, *Shining Path*, p. 38; David Scott Palmer, ''Introduction: History, Politics, and Shining Path in Peru,'' in Palmer, *Shining Path*; p. 20; and Henri Favre, ''Sentier Lumineux et Horizon Obscurs,'' *Problem D'Amerique Latine* 72, 2 (1984), pp. 23–28.

13. Ibid.

14. The majority of the rural population initally offered strong resistance to civil patrols. See De Gregori, ''Shining Path,'' in Tulchin and Bland, *Peru in Crisis*, p. 85.

15. Interview with Isbell, February 5, 1996; see her ''Shining Path and Peasant Responses in Rural Ayacucho,'' in Palmer, *Shining Path*, pp. 77–99; ''Time and Terror in Peru,'' in Isbell and Dudley, *Threats to Democracy*, pp. 139–154; *To Defend Ourselves: Ecology and Ritual in an Andean Village* (Austin: University of Texas Press, 1978); ''The Texts and Congress of Terror in Peru,'' paper prepared for research conference, ''Violence and Democracy in Colombia and Peru,'' Columbia University, November 30–December 1, 1990.

16. Centro de Información, Estudios y Documentación (CIED), *Dinámica*, pp. 206–207.

17. See a view of Andean statism in Conaghan and Malloy, *Unsettling Statecraft*, passim.

18. Hernando de Soto, *The Other Path: The Invisible Revolution in the Third World* (New York: Harper and Row, 1989). For commentaries on the informal sector, see esp. Conaghan and Malloy, *Unsettling Statecraft*, passim, and John Crabtree, *Peru under García: An Opportunity Lost* (Pittsburgh: University of Pittsburgh Press), esp. pp. 3–11.

19. See Susan E. Stokes, *Cultures in Conflict: Social Movements and the State in Peru* (Berkeley: University of California Press, 1995); and Felipe Zegarra, ''Derechos humanos y construcción de las paz,'' *Páginas* 130 (December 1994), p. 9. However, increased fragmentation and institutional disintegration occurred after the period which Stokes describes. See Fernando Rospigliosi, ''Democracy's Bleak Prospects'' (p. 54), and Francisco Sagasti and Max Hernández, ''The Crisis of Governance'' (pp. 29–31), in Tulchin and Bland, *Peru in Crisis*.

20. Interviews with directors and staff of human rights organizations, Lima, May 23–29, 1995. See also Hortensia Muñoz, ''Derechos humanos y construcción de referentes sociales'' (unpublished paper, n.d.), p. 6.

21. Interviews with directors and staff of human rights organizations, Lima, May 23–29, 1995. See also chronology of Hortensia Muñoz, ''Derechos humanos y construcción de referentes sociales'' (unpublished paper, n.d.).

22. James D. Rudolph, *Peru: The Evolution of a Crisis* (Westport, Conn.: Praeger, 1992), p. 88. See an early report by Americas Watch Committee, *Abdicating Democratic Authority: Human Rights in Peru* (New York: Americas Watch, 1994).

23. Susan C. Bourque and Kay B. Warren, ''Democracy without Peace: The Cultural Politics of Terror in Peru,'' *Latin American Research Review* 24, 1 (1989), p. 23.

24. Alfred Stepan, *Rethinking Military Politics: Brazil and the Southern Cone* (Princeton, N.J.: Princeton University Press, 1988), p. 134.

25. Ibid.

26. Amnesty International, *Peru: Human Rights in a Climate of Terror* (New York: Amnesty International, 1991), p. 91.

27. Amnesty International, *Peru: Human Rights in a State of Emergency* (New York: Amnesty International, 1989), pp. 31–35.

28. Javier Diez Canseco, *Democracia, miltarización y derechos humanos en El Perú 1980–84* (Lima; Asociación Pro Derechos Humanos, 1985).

29. Valle-Riestra, in Diez Canseco, *Democracia*, p. 10.

30. Milagros Peña discusses aspects, of the activist-intellectual networks in ch. 3 of her *Theologies and Liberation in Peru: The Role of Ideas in Social Movements* (Philadelphia Pa.: Temple University Press, 1995), pp. 86–119.

31. Abozaglo Jara and Vegas Torres, ''Aportes,'' p. 47.

32. One of the few histories of Peruvian human rights groups recounts at length internal struggles. See Darío A. López Rodríguez, ''Evangélicos y derechos humanos en El Peru 1980–1992: La experiencia social de paz y esperanza'' (Lima: mimeo, 1996).

33. Jeffrey Klaiber, ''The Church in Peru: Between Terrorism and Conservative Restraints,'' in Edward L. Cleary and Hannah Stewart-Gambino, eds., *Conflict and Competition: The Latin American Church in a Changing Environment* (Boulder, Colo.: Lynne Rienner, 1993), p. 101.

34. Louis M. Colonnese, ed., *Human Rights and the Liberation of Man in the Americas* (Notre Dame, Ind.: University of Notre Dame Press, 1970).

35. Anderson and Stansky, Introduction (p. 37); and Richard A. McCormick, ''Human Rights and the Mission of the Church,'' in Anderson and Stansky, *Mission Trends No. 4: Liberation Theologies* (New York: Paulist Press, 1979), pp. 37–50.

36. One of the clearest statements of opposition was made by Aloysius Pieris, S.J., for the 60th birthday celebration of Gustavo Gutiérrez, and published as ''Human Rights Language and Liberation Theology,'' in Marc H. Ellis and Otto Maduro, eds., *Expanding the Vision: Gustavo Gutiérrez and the Future of Liberation Theology* (Maryknoll, N.Y.: Orbis, 1990), pp. 157–170.

37. See, for example, Phillip Berryman, ''The Infinite Worth of the Poor: A Critical Vision of Human Rights,'' in his *Liberation Theology: The Essential Facts about the Revolutionary Movement in Latin America and Beyond* (New York: Pantheon Books, 1987), pp. 111–124.

38. See esp. David Hollenbach, *Claims in Conflict: Retrieving and Renewing the Catholic Human Rights Tradition* (New York: Paulist, 1979).

39. Hugo Assmann, ed., *Carter y la lógica del imperialismo*, 2 vols. (San José: Educa, 1978); and Elsa Tamez and Saúl Trinidad, eds., *Capitalismo, violencia y anti-vivda: La opresión de los mayorías y la domesticación de los Dioses*, 2 vols. (San José: Educa, 1978 and 1980).

40. One of the major centers for Catholic intellectuals is Centro de Estudios y Publicaciones (CEP) and its major journal, *Páginas*.

41. Klaiber, ''The Church in Peru,'' pp. 92–93.

42. Ismael García, *Justice in Latin American Theology of Liberation* (Atlanta: John Knox Press, 1987), p. 1.

43. See ''Human Rights, Evangelization, and Ideology,'' ch. 3 of Juan Luis Segundo, *Signs of the Times: Theological Reflections* (Maryknoll, N.Y.: Orbis, 1993), pp. 53–66.

44. See Aloysius Pieris, ''Human Rights,'' pp. 157–170. See also an earlier discussion by David Hollenbach, *Claims*.

45. Leonardo Boff, ''O Deus defensor dos direitos do pobre: O clamor do pobre e o Deus da vida,'' in José Aldunate, ed., *Direitos humanos, direitos dos pobres* (Petópolis: Vozes, 1991), pp. 91–107.

46. Instituto Peruano de Educación en Derechos Humanos y la Paz et al., *Educar en derechos humanos: Reflexiones a partir de la experiencia* (Lima: IPEDEHP et al., 1991), pp. 197–198.

47. In addition to *Educar en derechos humanos*, see also Elsa Rubín de Celis, *Educación peruana y derechos humanos: Los maestros opinan* (Lima: IPEDEHP, 1990); and Juan Ansión et al., *La escuela en tiempos de guerra* (Lima: CEAPAZ, TAREA, IPEDEHP, 1992). For statements by Gustavo Gutiérrez and associates in 1993, see Polo Coordinador de la Red Peruana de Educación en Derechos Humanos (Coordinating Group for Human Rights Education), *Pensando el Perú: Educación en derechos humanos y la propuesta nacional para la democracia, la paz y el desarrollo* (Lima: Polo Coordinador de la Red Peruana de Educación en Derechos Humanos, 1993).

48. Interviews with directors and staff members, human rights groups, Lima, May 24–29, 1995.

49. *Tercera Semana Interamericana de Acción Católica* (Lima and Chimbote: n.p., 1953); see also William J. Coleman, *Latin American Catholicism: A Self-Evaluation* (Maryknoll, N.Y.: Maryknoll Publications, 1958) and Helmut Gnadt Vitalis, *The Significance of Changes in Latin American Catholicism since Chimbote* (Cuernavaca: Centro Intercultural de Documentación, 1969).

50. Edward L. Cleary, *Crisis and Change: The Church in Latin America Today* (Maryknoll, N.Y.: Orbis, 1985), pp. 62–65 and passim.

51. William A. Gamson, *Talking Politics* (New York: Cambridge University Press, 1992).

52. Ibid., p. 32.

53. Interview, April 4, 1996.

54. See, for example, *Open Letter from Human Rights Watch to Abimael Guzmán* (n.p., 1991).

55. Masterson, *Militarism*, p. 271.

56. Americas Watch, *Peru: Abdicating Democratic Authority* (New York: Human Rights Watch, 1984).

57. Klaiber, ''The Church,'' p. 101.

58. See esp. annual reports, *Informe sobre la situación de los derechos humanos en el Peru* (Lima: various years).

59. Klaiber, ''The Church,'' p. 101.

60. Americas Watch, *Human Rights in Peru: After President García's First Year* (New York: Americas Watch, 1986), p. 86.

61. Hopes which many in the human rights movement had for repeal of the 1981 antiterrorist law, for holding military personnel responsible for human rights violations, and for other measures were dashed when the touted Peace Commission and its lengthy report were disregarded.

62. Core groups and individuals included: Coordinador Nacional de Derechos Humanos, Comisión Andina de Juristas, Comisión Episcopal de Acción Social, Centro de Estudios y Acción para La Paz, Asociación Pro-Derechos Humanos, Instituto de Defensa

Legal, Comisión de Derechos Humanos, Centro de Investigación y Promoción Amazónica, Father Hubert Lanssiers, and DESCO.

63. Appointments of Opus Dei and conservative Jesuit bishops, although a minority, changed the character of the national conference of bishops. See Klaiber, "The Church," passim.

64. De Gregori, "Shining Path," in Tulchin and Bland, *Peru in Crisis*, p. 84.

65. See analysis of army prerogatives in Enrique Obando, "The Power of Peru's Armed Forces," in Tulchin and Bland, *Peru in Crisis*, passim.

66. *Sí* weekly magazine in Lima reported on June 9, 1991 (p. 15) that the monthly pay of $U.S. 210 compared to $558 in Ecuador, $910 in Bolivia, $915 in Colombia, $1,115 in Chile, and $3,700 in Brazil; Masterson, in Isbell and Dudley, *Threats*, p. 114. Enrique Obando, a respected researcher at the Peruvian Center for International Studies (CEPEI), a general of a division receiving the equivalent of $U.S. 283.42 in 1993. Obando, "The Power of Peru's Military Forces," in Tulchin and Bland, *Peru*, fn. 28, p. 124.

67. Masterson, *Militarism*, p. 285.

68. De Gregori,"Shining Path," p. 84; see also Obando, "The Power of Peru's Armed Forces," p. 112, both in Tulchin and Bland, *Peru in Crisis.*

69. Masterson, *Militarism*, pp. 283–284.

70. See Amnesty International, *Peru* (1989), pp. 31–33.

71. Carlos Iván De Gregori, in Palmer, *Shining Path*, p. 92.

72. For 1989: Patricio Orellana and Elizabeth Quay Hutchinson, *El movimiento de derechos humanos en Chile, 1973–1990* (Santiago: Centro de Estudios Políticos Latinamericanos Simón Bolívar, 1991), p. 202; for 1994: *Human Rights Internet Reporter Masterlist* (Ottawa: Human Rights Internet, 1994), passim.

73. Published interview with Paco Muguiro, *Vida Nueva* No. 1,987 (April 1, 1995), pp. 8–10.

74. One of the principal figures of the Velasco era, retired General Edgardo Mercado Jarrín, publicly criticized policy in his *Un sistema de seguridad de defensa sudamérica* (Lima: Centro Peruano de Estudios Internationales, 1989). Masterson ("The Armed Forces," p. 115) cites several individual field commanders who saw the necessity of multidimensional policies.

75. David Scott Palmer, " 'Fujipopulism' and Peru's Progress," *Current History* (February 1996), p. 73. The estimate of deaths is one commonly cited. See also Calvin Sims, "Growls from the Barracks," *New York Times* (June 20, 1995).

76. Andean Commission of Jurists, *Boletín Informativo* (December 10, 1990).

77. By 1990, 87 provinces and 53 percent of the population were in emergency military zones.

78. Charles Humana, comp., *World Human Rights Guide*, 3d ed., passim.

79. See *Human Rights World Report 1996* (New York: Human Rights Watch, 1995), pp. 117–119.

80. Rosenberg, "Beyond Elections," pp. 77–78.

81. Interview, Isbell, February 5, 1996.

82. Rospigliosi, "Democracy's," esp. p. 55; and d'Ornellas, "Commentary," p. 69, both in Tulchin and Bland, *Peru in Crisis.*

83. Ibid.

84. See Catherine J. Allen's discussion of time in *The Hold Life Has* (Washington, D.C.: Smithsonian Institution Press, 1988).

85. Kay B. Warren, ''Interpreting *La Violencia* in Guatemala: Shapes of Mayan Silence and Resistence,'' in Warren, ed., *The Violence Within: Cultural and Political Opposition in Divided Nations* (Boulder, Colo.: Westview, 1993), p. 27.

86. Kirk, ''Good Enough,'' p. 12.

87. Warren, ''*Interpreting*,'' p. 33.

88. Ibid., p. 40.

89. Ibid., p. 32.

90. ''Public Secrets,'' paper presented at Latin American Studies Association International Congress, September 29, 1996, p. 1.

91. Summarized by Stoll from a talk given at the University of California, Berkeley, February 13, 1992. *Between Two Armies in the Ixil Towns of Guatemala* (New York: Columbia University Press, 1993), p. 302.

92. *Between Two Armies*, p. 302.

93. Warren, ''Interpreting,'' p. 49.

94. Paper presented at Latin American Studies Association International Congress, September 29, 1996.

95. *Anthropology Newsletter* (American Anthropological Association) (February 1996), p. 11.

96. Kirk, ''Good Enough,'' p. 9. See also Jorge Parodi and Wálter Twanama, ''Los pobladores, la ciudad y la política: Un estudio de actitudes,'' in Parodi, ed., *Los pobres, la ciudad y la política* (Lima: Cedys, 1993).

97. Interviews, Lima, May 23–29, 1995; Brian K. Goonan, phone conversation, October 24, 1995; John Gitlitz, February 5, 1996.

98. Interviews, Lima, May 23–29, 1995; and with John Gitlitz, February 5, 1996.

99. Interviews with Wilde, Santiago, March 13, 1995; and with directors of human rights organizations, Lima, May 23–29, 1995.

6

Transnational Networking for Human Rights Protection

The extremes to which the Chilean and other military governments were willing to go in international politics became evident when Chilean authorities imprisoned Sheila Cassidy. A medical doctor and English Catholic volunteer, Cassidy became the object of an international tug-of-war. Great Britain and Chile, traditional allies in many enterprises, found themselves pitted in a struggle both wished had not occurred. However, neither government backed away from conflict over the case.

Working in the slums of Santiago, Cassidy had witnessed the shroud of military control settling over the country. Cassidy began work during the early 1970s, heady days of grassroots activity in Allende's Chile. Nonpolitical, she kept busy with tending the sick poor at Posta 3, a primitive, immediate-care station on the outskirts of Santiago. Dr. Cassidy saw only glimpses of the grim tightening of the political environment. Her views began to change in September 1975. Little more than two years after the military coup, Dr. Cassidy was called to the examination room of her post. She had to examine for a forensic report the body of a young man with seven bullet holes. The incident opened her eyes: "This was no terrorist, no guerrilla, but a lad of seventeen who had made the mistake of being out only a few minutes after the curfew."[1] Soldiers drinking on duty shot him.

Cassidy had become friends with many religious and lay volunteers working in poor neighborhoods. In October a priest friend asked Dr. Cassidy if she would treat a wounded person who sought sanctuary in a North American sisters' residence. She and others believed that, if taken to a hospital, the injured person would then be transferred to prison and probably killed. Compelled by her understanding of her duties as a doctor, she treated the man twice in the sisters' home. The wounded man then found asylum at the Papal Nuncio's residence, before exile. Cassidy went back to her familiar routines.

A week later, while visiting a sick nun on the second floor of a sisters' home, Cassidy was startled. The lower floor of the home where she was attending the sick person was being machine-gunned. The bullets killed a maid. Of the three persons still alive in the house, Cassidy was the only one taken into custody. A secret policeman (DINA) struck her a sharp blow to the face. The DINA agents drove on to Casa Grimaldi, an interrogation center.

Although she was a medical doctor, British, and the daughter of an air vice-marshal, none of it stopped her arrest and subsequent treatment. One of her captors told her: "Our international image is so bad we do not care."[2] She was told to undress, was subjected to electric shock, and lived through hours of repeated torture.

EMERGENCY NETWORKING

One hallmark of the human rights era that was unfolding was the international emergency networks. Thousands of letters poured from Britain and other places petitioning Cassidy's release or expressing solidarity. The network, centered in Britain, operated quickly. The British then stood at the center of rudimentary international human rights defense.

Systematic practice of ordinary persons engaging in letter-writing campaigns only began in the 1960s. Previously, imprisonment of British subjects in authoritarian lands would have been left to consular officials to work out. This time Amnesty International's example of letter-writing campaigns fueled the solidarity campaign for Cassidy. To reinforce these efforts, Britain recalled its ambassador in a formal gesture of disapproval. Diplomatic relations between Britain and Chile remained closed for five subsequent years.

THEORETICAL FRAMEWORK

Until the mid-1990s, social scientists had not routinely analyzed transnational social movements. Few accounts of transnational collective action from a social movement perspective existed.[3] Margaret Keck and Kathryn Sikkink opened the door for wider transnational analysis through their explorations of the human rights and environmental networks.[4] Alison Brysk,[5] Ron Pagnucco and J. D. McCarthy,[6] and Ian Guest[7] made pioneering delineations of the transnational, nongovernmental organizations supporting the human rights movement in Argentina. Jackie Smith followed with her marking of the outlines of human rights as a transnationally organized social movement.[8]

A variety of organizational and individual actors have been acting in defense of human rights in world politics. They range from the Ford Foundation and John Paul II's journeys for human rights to the United Nations investigative commissions. Since it is difficult to speak of mobilizing resources when dealing with the Ford Foundation as though one were dealing with individuals at the grassroots level, adequate analysis needs a wider frame of reference than social movement theory. Network analysis provides such a view.[9]

Theories to explain transnational political activity are not fully developed. But explorations, guided by network analysis and social movement theory, reward those who follow with an intriguing view of world politics as it currently unfolds. These issue networks address human rights as a subset of international issues, characterized by principled ideas.

These networks contrast with other nets dealing with instrumental goals, such as banks, or emphasizing shared causal ideas, such as scientific communities. Actors, often nongovernmental, emphasize interpretations rather than just information. Strategic image-making becomes a central enterprise, as Amnesty International's efforts will show. In sum, issue nets "carry and reframe ideas, insert them into policy debates, pressure for human rights regime formation, and enforce existing international norms and rules."[10]

Here I employ issue networks[11] to describe the large phenomenon that has grown up around human rights protection transnationally. I explore the large set of actors working internationally on human rights protection. Shared values, common discourse, and dense exchange of information and services bind them together.[12] However, I focus on a smaller and tighter transnational social movement with the larger issue network.

Arguments about networks or movements concern academics. Human rights activists know from experience that something like a transnational social movement exists and it has become increasingly dense, technologically sophisticated, and moderately strong. When one investigates the accounts of activists and their networks, a more elaborate picture of international organizing emerges than previously presented. Beyond state-to-state relations, multiple pathways to transnational influence have come into being.

Further, this perspective opens for view what was done informally by persons who feared retaliation from security forces and death squads. At the time of the Chilean coup (1973) the Swedish ambassador, Harold Edelstam, took to the streets. He traveled around Santiago, contacting those in danger from the military regime. Edelstam went to the National Stadium (being used as a prison) and persuaded Major Iván Lavandero to release a group of Uruguayan prisoners. He arranged asylum at the Swedish embassy, and eventual escape. He thus saved hundreds of Chileans and other nationals from imprisonment and possible death. At the end of the year Edelstam was declared persona non grata and left Chile.[13]

Resistance and change in the U.S. State Department, murders in Washington's Sheridan Square, protests throughout the United States, plotting by exiles, and heroes like Peter Benenson make up the history of the emerging Age of Human Rights. When analyzed within a wider frame of network analysis, human rights finds global political significance.

The framing of a central part of this history within social movement perspective again benefits from Sidney Tarrow's landmark *Power in Movement.*

Tarrow makes clear the extension of social movement theory to the transnational sphere, using both the 1848 European revolutions and the movement that destroyed the Soviet "multistate empire in one blow."[14]

Effective international political action, within the movement perspective, is possible because of the universality of repertoire of collective action, the rapidity of global communication, and transnational cycles of protest. For Tarrow the archetypical case is militant, fundamentalist Islam. Islam does offer a dramatic example of a transnational movement. Nonetheless, Jackie Smith's survey of transnational movements shows: "The human rights issue has attracted the vast majority of organized transnational movement activity."[15]

Using the framework of social movement theory helps make sense of the transnational phenomenon that has grown up around human rights issues. Terms employed previously in national contexts, such as seizing opportunities, acting collectively, framing collective action, and mobilizing structures illuminate the transnational picture, as well. Context becomes particularly salient for analysis, the international often contrasting with domestic context.

The shift to the transnational also allows profound questioning, such as, why now? Why only after centuries of Western civilization is there now an Age of Human Rights? One may find this newness an exaggeration. After all, power is cumulative, building on practices and institutions of the past.[16] Nonetheless, one may argue that only now has a context arisen which sustains the current amount of national and international human rights organizations.

Donnelly believes: "The catalyst that made human rights an issue in world politics was the Holocaust."[17] However, genocide is not new. Systematic analysis demands accounting for the appropriate structural and spacial organization of the populations that facilitate human rights movements.

True, the Holocaust was a catalyst. However, the social context necessary for the birth (mobilization) of human rights movements occurred when democratic institutions spread widely in the latter third of this century.[18] Democracy has taken hold globally only in the last one hundred years.[19] The latest and largest wave of democratization to reach Latin America, Africa, and Asia is less 30 years old.[20] Smith argues: "The international community is committed to encouraging—with words, if not deeds—democratic participation."[21] Freedoms of association and speech contribute to a favorable environment. So, too, do technologies that speed information. For the first time in human history national boundaries have ceased being encapsulating barriers.

A further question remains: Why only recently the study of transnational movements? "The history and practice of democracy has focused until now on the idea of locality (the city-state, community, the nation)," says Held. He adds: "In the future it will be centered on the international or global domain."[22] Transnational social movements will thus receive increasing attention.

This chapter explores the central veins of the movement and marks off newer avenues as governmental nets. It leaves for future exploration the full range of transnational organizations, such as environmental and indigenous groups. Sections that follow examine nongovernmental, intergovernmental, and governmental organizations that form part of the transnational human rights networks tied to Latin America.

NONGOVERNMENTAL ORGANIZATIONS

The Cassidy and similar cases illustrate outstanding characteristics of modern international human rights activity. Two salient weapons stand out from these cases: information and leverage. Governments controlled information. Human rights advocates needed to provide reliable information to counter governmental misinformation or stonewalling. In Latin America military governments tended to issue curt communiques or fell back on a basic military tactic: silence (no information, no entrapment in debate with inferiors). Defenders of Cassidy had to counter the picture painted by the Pinochet regime that she was a "foreign extremist."

By leverage ordinary persons without political power convince a spokesperson more powerful than themselves to deal with authorities. Leverage is well understood in Latin America. There bosses (*patrones*) speak to bosses (*patrones*). Clients do not typically speak for themselves. An elaborate cultural system of brokers often enters in.

Institutionalization

In the unequal struggle of private individuals against the repressive power of the state, Peter Benenson stands out. The presumption of international politicians was that only states could deal with states. (The Vatican carefully maintains its status as a city-state.) Peter Benenson thrust the nongovernmental element forcefully into the mix of international politics. Benenson was a 40-year-old lawyer with invaluable connections because of his Eton and Oxford education. In 1959 he helped found a group of British lawyers dedicated to international observance of the United Nations Declaration on Human Rights. His wide field of vision came to rest the following year on an incident in Catholic Portugal. The government arrested and sentenced two students to seven years' imprisonment for raising glasses to toast freedom. For Benenson, a fellow Catholic given to toasting freedom, this was too much. He organized a bombardment of letters to the Salazar government. Only a person with a certain chutzpah could imagine mounting a challenge to a government by writing letters.[23]

Benenson went further. He was driven by a vision that would catch attention around the world. He pictured human rights victims in prison cells as "prisoners of conscience." Benenson had captured the angle needed to frame the issue: individual persons asserting their rights in heroic conflict with sovereign governments.

In the world of power, individuals and their convictions had to count for something. If personal experience was the basis of twentieth-century philosophy (and Pentecostal religion), if individualism was the hallmark of the age, if the heroes of film were Thomas More and Cool Hand Luke, Benenson had it exactly right: Human rights should be portrayed as the principled person sitting in a prison cell offering mute prophecy against power exercised without accountability.

Benenson's imagination quickly moved from two students sitting in a Portuguese prison to a much wider field. He and his colleagues designed a one-year worldwide campaign drawing attention to political and religious prisoners around the world. To kick off the campaign, the Sunday *Observer* printed a full-page article from the group.[24] *Le Monde* simultaneously carried the message to French-speaking readers.

The *Observer* article so captured what others were thinking that leading newspapers around the world reprinted it or carried sympathetic commentaries. Benenson targeted publication of the original piece for Trinity Sunday, May 28th, that year. The religious symbolism of three persons carried over to the strategy of ''A Three Network.'' Supporters would adopt three prisoners and work for their release. Each prisoner would be from three parts of the world: West, Communist-bloc, and Third World.

Benenson was credited with the forcefulness of the article to the extent that later supporters thought of him as a journalist. He focused on eight persons who were ''forgotten prisoners.'' They included an Angolan doctor, a Spanish lawyer, and an American minister jailed for civil rights activities in the South, and Catholic bishops in Budapest and Prague. Letters and money flooded in. Equally, great bits of information about thousands of similar prisoners came pouring in. This deluge brought great pressure to institutionalize and almost overwhelmed initiatives in years to come.

Resource Mobilization and Framing the Issues: Amnesty International

In 1961, Benenson and colleagues focused on channeling the flood they had caused. Amnesty International (AI) began putting its supporters in touch with other sympathizers living nearby. Schools and churches were encouraged to set up groups. These groups learned how to find forgotten prisoners. They nagged governments, supported prisoners' families, and attempted to get letters through to prisoners. Their shared belief was: Even one letter that reached a prisoner enhanced a sense of hope.

They realized hopes in Dr. Cassidy's case. International groups responded quickly because, by 1975, international groups had routinized support for her type of ordeal. Cassidy recalled that through the letters and cables the outside world began to take shape. ''Cables [came] from many different countries and there were messages of love from my own family. . . . It has given me a sense of being ransomed that I think I shall never lose.''[25]

As Jonathan Power comments: "This [Amnesty] idea, characteristically English—parochial, low-key, without much money, committed to working across ideological, religious, and racial boundaries—was amazingly effective."[26] By the end of 1961 the founders had established AI. They promoted a globally recognized symbol, a candle encircled by barbed wire. AI representatives lighted the first candle at Trafalgar Square during Human Rights Day in December.

International organizational efforts began at an informal gathering in Luxembourg, two months after the Benenson article. By the end of the year AI groups appeared in most North Atlantic countries. Despite almost fatal internal divisions, AI had grown to 550 groups by June 1968. Thousands of political prisoners had been released in part, it was believed, through AI pressure.

Other groups joined actively in the international human rights regime. The International Commission of Jurists, Freedom House (New York–based), the churches, and unions began to pull together. The human rights regime would come to be accepted as a set of principles, norms, rules, and decision-making procedures that international actors accept as binding for human rights protection.[27] At this less organized stage, Power believes that among these groups: "Amnesty symbolized the concern, provided much of the raw data on which other organizations based their efforts, and was a constant inspiration to individuals around the world . . . to set up their own watchdogs."[28]

AI was achieving modest strength in international politics. The human rights regime established a strong center. Instead of viewing human rights as meddling, many supporters of AI and similar groups saw human rights defense as a contemporary manner of building peace. The Nobel committee awarded its 1977 peace prize to AI. The award confirmed the value of the painstaking accuracy that the organization attempted. These efforts affected a global perception of human rights. Power summarizes: "Human rights, instead of being generally regarded as a problem marginal to the real affairs of state, became the issue which determined governments' images in the eyes of the world."[29] Power exaggerates a bit, but even Pinochet felt the sting of embarrassment from a fellow violator. In 1980, President Ferdinand Marcos canceled the planned state visit of Pinochet to the Philippines because of world perception of Chilean human rights abuses.

AI had grown to more than one million members by 1994. Its organizational structure—8,000 grassroots groups in 70 countries[30] and rapid communication along an international network—furnishes the strong backbone for the transnational human rights issue network.

Human Rights Watch (HRW) joined as an effective partner to AI's work. Its yearly *World Report* has become a standard guide for assessing human rights declines or advances, along with AI's yearly reports. HRW took its impetus from the Moscow Helsinki Group, a dissident group of intellectuals, which issued dozens of reports on a variety of human rights issues. It initiated discussion, published statements, appeals, and letters, often at great personal risk.

The Helsinki process served as a model for regional watch committees, including Americas Watch. HRW does not have the grassroots base of AI but operates as a select, elite enterprise.[31] While AI at times appears limited to a narrow range of issues, such as torture and unjust imprisonment, HRW ranges widely. Its creative activities have caught media attention, and its annual dinner in New York City has been attended by *The New Yorker*.[32]

Exile Groups: Mobilizations, Framing Issues, and Transformations

Both AI and HRW have added stability to the transnational human rights issue movement.[33] Among other groups in the movement, exile groups stand out for their effectiveness in shorter-term mobilizations. Argentines and Chileans especially were capable advocates.[34] Given the cosmopolitan outlooks and professional backgrounds of many of these exiles, they fit in quickly with human rights organizations or expatriates formed their own groups.

Argentine exiles especially sought refuge in France and Spain in Europe, Mexico and Venezuela in Latin America. They eagerly sought human rights information from Argentina (then a scarce commodity) and communicated it with enthusiasm. They organized marches and sit-ins. Fifteen thousand supporters marched in Paris. These activities were noted in the media; national and international coverage intensified efforts to frame the issue of repressive governments. Military governments were cast as violators of human rights.

Through the years, Latin American exiles often portrayed themselves as opposition parties or even governments in exile. This was the traditional frame. In the present era a major Argentine exile organization set itself as a human rights commission, *Comisión Argentina por los Derechos Humanos* (CADHU). It formed branches in Mexico City, Geneva, Rome, and Washington. Thus cast, CADHU members testified in the U.S. House and provided documentation on disappearances elsewhere.

The connections of exile groups and external forums became especially salient with Chile's deported. As many as 200,000 may have left Chile between 1973 and 1986.[35] A surprising number found their way into North Atlantic universities, such as the Sorbonne, Toronto, Duke, Minnesota, and Notre Dame. These moves quickly brought the repressive image of Chile before a wide audience of colleagues and students. Exiles added weight to human rights organizing within professional organizations like the Latin American Studies Association, in the United States, Canada, and Europe.

Expatriate human rights groups, in effect, functioned externally for the internal groups that could not function well under repression. In Guatemala repression was so acute that human rights organizations found it necessary to suspend operations in the early 1980s. Exile communities also provided direct financial support or petitioned foreign agencies for support of internal human rights activities. Exile groups became the glue between human rights groups in various nations, attempting to deal with the human rights crisis in Latin America.

Exile stimulated an extraordinary literary production dealing with exile and human rights.[36] Perhaps no country matched Chilean exiles' first-rate productions. Isabel Allende's *Of Love and Shadows* and *The House of the Spirits*, Ariel Dorfman's *Hard Rain* and *Death of a Maiden*, Fernando Alegría's *The Chilean Spring*, and Antonio Skármeta's *Burning Patience* all chronicled the repressive situation in Chile.

These elite creative efforts expressed mostly middle- and upper-class exiles' convictions. Transnational human rights groups enthusiastically supported their efforts. They amplified and helped frame the message of the movement. However, popular cultural efforts burst forth more directly from grassroots human rights organizing. Chileans and Argentines helped to foster a world popular music genre, *nueva canción*.[37] Chileans added a popular cultural expression in another medium, woven wall hangings, called *arpilleras*.

Nueva canción folk songs basically express desire for revolutionary change or opposition to authoritarian control. Victor Jara's painful death at the hands of the Chilean military enshrined his music. Violeta Parra (Chilean) and Mercedes Sosa (Argentine), among many others, continued the songs of protest. ''Inti-Illimani'' became the most prominent exile musical group. They carried the exile/human rights message throughout Italy and Europe.

Accompanied protest songs are an old cultural form. By contrast, Chilean women weavers created a new use of popular culture for human rights promotion. Women whose husbands or children had disappeared (some 3,000) or were imprisoned without charge (some 2,000) organized themselves with the help of the churches, as seen earlier.[38] Their weavings were purchased by the hundreds overseas. There the weavings were hung in human rights headquarters, university offices, and private homes. This human rights ''frame'' depicted ordinary women overwhelmed by repression but somehow protesting and hopeful for resolution of grievances.

Harassment and death from secret police and their networks greatly increased exiles' fears. Brazilian and Argentine military and police intelligence units aided DINA's efforts to terrorize and silence protesters. Right-wing extremists attacked not only Letelier in Washington but Bernardo Leighton and wife in Rome.

Human rights activity had a transformative effect, as well. Many political and intellectual expatriates from Chile went through personal changes. During the first years of the Pinochet dictatorship they worked as Ricardo Núñez did in East Berlin: ''We worked fourteen hours a day, maintaining contact with Chile, checking on the fate of prisoners, building links with human rights groups.''[39]

As dictatorship and exile continued, many leftist exiles had ample time to examine reasons for Allende's inability to gain the support of the majority of Chileans. Many expatriates went through a deeply reflective process. As Jeffrey Puryear remarks: The transformation ''did not begin with the question of democracy, focusing instead on more pressing issues such as human rights.''[40] The left's political sector had suffered disproportionately from authoritarianism. That insight led them, Puryear says: ''to see democracy in a different light—as guarantor of human rights.''[41]

Human rights activity forged a kind of conversion. From viewing democracy as a step toward socialism, democracy itself became an end.[42] The largely positive experience of living in democratic socialism in Europe helped this revision. So, too, did viewing, often at close hand, the deterioration of socialist societies of Central and Eastern Europe. This Soviet slide also carried Cuba, once an ally of Allende, to further decline.

The international network is now thick with nongovernmental organizations. Its size and shape can be glimpsed from the United States' side. In Washington alone, some 40 groups participate in the Latin America Working Group. Their meetings about every six weeks offer only surface evidence of dense and frequent interactions in Washington and around the world.

INTERGOVERNMENTAL ORGANIZATIONS

The United Nations (U.N.) and the Organization of American States (OAS) have been major players in speaking for human rights in Latin America. The U.S. government found the U.N. an unwieldy instrument for U.S. interests. (The U.S. largely lost dominance of the United Nations to Third World countries in 1967).[43] Not until 1992 did the U.S. Congress embrace one of the three basic rights agreements, the Covenant on Civil and Political Rights. The Congress, to the scandal of other countries, has not endorsed the Covenant on Economic Rights[44] nor documents on racism, rights of the child, and rights of women.

From weak or nonexistent strength in dealing with human rights, both the U.N. and OAS have carved out important political space. Even the U.N. Security Council that did its best to avoid human rights issues has increasingly involved itself with human rights within states.[45] An international consensus is growing that human rights denied cause wars and put at risk international security.[46]

Within the U.N. three entities especially have had an impact on Latin America. The U.N. Commission on Human Rights has set standards through elaboration of international human rights norms. For many Latin American countries, this commission and its norms provide an external mentor. Most Latin American societies lack an academic class devoted to the systematic study of law. Even the best of them have lawyers who lack juridical scholarship or who work as full-time politicians.[47]

At strategic moments—especially as societies turn to democracy and lack experience in what democracy implies—the U.N. Commission on Human Rights norms are the closest thing to international standards. Activists can employ these norms, ''off the rack.'' Through movements like the Streetchildren's Movement in Brazil the norms become national law. The internationally established norms at least save time. They furnish starting points for debates in societies without academic juridical experts.

After 1967 the U.N. Commission on Human Rights could publicize human rights violations within individual countries. This was a constricted mandate. Some Latin American countries have ignored requests for information, as Paraguay delayed scrutiny of genocidal massacres for nine years. Or, governments deflected criticism by pretending to ignore U.N. critiques. However, the U.N. Commission on Human Rights has had an effect. Donnelly believes: "Even vicious governments may care about their international reputation. Furthermore, publicity often helps at least a few of the more prominent victims of repression."[48]

The presence of human rights concerns at the U.N. has been upgraded through the establishment of an undersecretary-general for human rights. This greater emphasis also became clearer in the initiative for the World Conference on Human Rights (Vienna, 1993). Philip Alston, the Australian human rights leader, may be correct in believing that the U.N. system has made "immense progress."[49] In Latin America the U.N. has had unusual success, at least in El Salvador.

An Opening in El Salvador

The stand-off between systematically repressive government and frequently oppressive guerrilla forces made a political settlement appear unrealistic for El Salvador. Twelve years of civil war, nonetheless, ended by consent of both parties.[50] This consent also extended to allowing the U.N. to help make peace,[51] since terms of peace were so complex.[52] Ian Johnstone says: "The UN in effect became the junior partner in the process of creating a less militarized and more open society."[53]

El Salvador excelled in Latin America only in the depth of cleavages between competing parties and the ravages inflicted by violence. Key here as elsewhere was human rights. Johnstone believes of El Salvador: "Human rights were central to the process because, by tackling that problem head on, it was possible to root out some of the political, social, and institutional conditions that gave rise to the conflict in the first place."[54]

Of all the tasks Salvadorans asked of the U.N., the telling of truth about past rights violations appeared the most difficult. The murderous atmosphere had left the country with virtually no human rights groups or individuals capable of investigations of often hidden events. Nor were there, by that time, sufficient professionally trained legal experts, trusted by all sides.

In a most unusual strategy for Latin America, the truth commission was externally appointed. The U.N. Secretary-General named three foreigners as commissioners and fifteen staff and several administrators, none of them Salvadorans. The stature of the commissioners made criticism difficult: Belisario Betancur, ex-president of Colombia; Thomas Buergenthal, former president of the Inter-American Court; and Reinaldo Figueredo, Venezuela's former minister of foreign relations.

Under such constraints, expectations for the truth commission were low. The commission published its report as *From Madness to Hope.* The Report,[55] strongly worded, and naming over 40 persons believed to be responsible for human rights crimes. Five days later, as demanded by the military, the legislature passed an amnesty law. A measure of truth had been spoken. Peace has held.[56] Mark Ensalaco believes that the U.N. made an "appreciable contribution."[57] Alexander Wilde, for years desperate for a solution in El Salvador while director of WOLA, calls the U.N.'s work "a major and unusual achievement."[58]

At a higher level at the United Nations, the General Assembly has had a political bias by which it condemns only some countries. The Assembly passes over other countries, equally violators of human rights, in silence. However, it repeatedly passed human rights resolutions about El Salvador and Guatemala. Donnelly has found an evolution within the Assembly: "An increasing number of states have begun to accept the idea of more or less nonpartisan international monitoring of at least some rights, in a growing number of particular countries."[59]

A third level at the United Nations includes the Committee on Human Rights of the Economic and Social Council, which provides what Donnelly calls "a substantial degree of independent international monitoring."[60] Investigations brought a measure of justice that might not have prevailed. From 1986 to 1989 final verdicts of the Committee on Human Rights went against six Latin American countries: Bolivia, Colombia, Dominican Republic, Ecuador, Peru, and Uruguay.

Further, within the U.N. Commission on Human Rights a major single-issue regime has emerged in recent years. The Commission created a special rapporteur on torture in 1985. This post was created to carry out the Convention against Torture and Other, Cruel, Inhuman or Degrading Treatment or Punishment. This Convention followed the establishment of the U.N. Voluntary Fund for Torture Victims in 1981 and was opened for signature in 1984.

Here the long-suffering work of AI at the United Nations and within many countries becomes clearer. For example, AI lobbied and provided information for ten years at the U.N. This effort contributed mightily to establishing the convention against torture and the human rights rapporteur.[61]

The crowning achievement for AI has been the granting of observer status by the U.N. This allows AI staff members easy access to nation-members and presentation of key information in relevant committee meetings. Delegations, especially those of smaller countries, rightly or wrongly, use AI as if it were the countries' own research staff.

AI's presence at the U.N. bonds the nongovernmental sector to intergovernmental in a relatively secure structural embrace. Its presence at the U.N. provides a much needed service. As Louis Henkin says: "The fact is that the condition of human rights leaves much to be desired in many countries, including many that are party to international covenants. Much of the task of enforcing international standards has fallen to nongovernmental organizations. . . . International nongovernmental organizations often act to fill a void left by inadequate governmental and intergovernmental institutions.''[62]

Inter-American Intergovernmental Organizations

The OAS is not the United Nations on a smaller scale, having a distinct history. Cynical observers judged the OAS as a puppet organization for carrying out U.S. anti-Communist strategies. The OAS's value for improvement of human rights in Latin America, however, demands separate assessment.

While the Inter-American Court's actions have yet to prove more than episodic value,[63] the Inter-American Commission on Human Rights (IACHR) is another story. It has carried on sustained, strong promotion of human rights. The IACHR did not suffer fully the constraints of the parliamentary system of the OAS. The IACHR headquarters was far enough removed from OAS headquarters in Washington to have a measure of life of its own.

Through key members, IACHR picked up the spirit of Oscar Romero, Oscar Arias, and Central American colleagues. Committee members prepared reports on human rights situations, a novelty in the OAS. They received individual complaints. In a few crucial cases IACHR conducted notable on-site investigations of human rights questions. Reports and words seemed weak in the face of military repression. However, they were all Romero and many Central Americans had to defend themselves. If Central American human rights advocates lacked the sophistication of Argentine or Chilean legal experts, they also lacked the fatalism of persons from these more developed Latin American countries.

The IACHR replaced internal human rights groups where those were lacking in a country, reinforced weak voices of groups within countries that had human rights organizations, and countered either the silence or the misinformation emanating from repressive regimes. The IACHR also served as the single place where citizens in some countries could go with complaints; it also stood in contradiction, on important occasions, to creative fictions found in the country reports of the U.S. State Department.

The IACHR has conducted studies and issued reports for twenty countries. Its on-site investigation of Argentina in 1979 was a major accomplishment. In a two-week visit, it interviewed a vast range of political and other leaders and ordinary citizens in four cities. It received 5,000 complaints. Human rights practice seemed to have improved in Argentina after that. IACHR members could note with satisfaction that by 1992 Argentina was regarded as having the third best record in Latin America.[64]

Tom J. Farer believes Western hemispheric collective actions in defense of human rights for the last twenty years have been problematic. The one exception in his view has been IACHR. As the 1970s rolled on, he judged: ''The Commission moved slowly at first, then with gathering speed to exercise its authority to expose and publicize the full gamut of human rights delinquencies.''[65]

The Costa Rican ethos of having no standing military and of a spirit of conciliation fueled part of the initiative for the unusual and highly effective Inter-American Institute of Human Rights (IIHR). With headquarters in San José, Costa Rica, IIHR is an independent academic and research institute. It functions as an intergovernmental organization, aiding both governments and NGOs. Helping to establish structures for open elections has been a major activity; this is probably its most visible activity.

The IIHR is especially nimble and creative at a critical juncture. One by one, Latin American governments have been creating offices within their governments to deal with human rights. These offices came about for mixed motives, such as to satisfy the demands of national human rights movements, to defuse human rights efforts, or to train security forces in the rule of law. Often persons appointed to head or to staff human rights offices had insufficient training to carry out their tasks. IIHR staff act as teachers and brokers, bringing in Latin Americans and others more experienced in human rights practices.

Roberto Cuéllar heads the office on Civil Society at IIHR. He is well practiced on fitting into the needs of other countries. In El Salvador Cuéllar was a principal proponent of human rights through the famed office of Socorro Jurídico. Asked if he works in the spirit of Oscar Romero, Cuéllar draws from his wallet a piece of the alb Romero wore when murdered. During exile in Mexico, Cuéllar co-founded Centro Vitoria. Since then he has acted as consultant to many Latin American countries.

GOVERNMENTAL STRUCTURES FOR TRANSNATIONAL HUMAN RIGHTS ISSUES

Another dense network within the transnational human rights issue net is governmental. Growth in this area is recent and exceptionally large. The difference between the eras before 1964 and after is largely that of episodic and systematic reporting.

The reporting on human rights situations has become a noteworthy function of some diplomatic missions. Two important cases, the Vatican and the United States, illuminate the change. The Vatican is anchored in international diplomacy through nunciatures.[66] In the 1960s a *plecu* (diplomatic pouch) went regularly by air from Latin American nunciatures to Rome. From about 1968 these weekly pouches increasingly contained reports of systematic human rights violations in many Latin American countries.[67] Often church personnel were involved as victims or as defenders of human rights.

This reporting brought the Vatican secretariat of state mounting evidence and increased clarity about the repressive environment. Faced with these systematic challenges the Vatican needed more than ad hoc responses. It created an institutional mechanism that would, as Lowell W. Livezey reports, ''apply the human rights commitments of Vatican II to the post-Vietnam world.''[68] The Pontifical Commission for International Justice and Peace thus began in 1967. The commission was well placed as a vanguard organizational reform from Vatican Council II, completed two years previously. International justice and peace issues emerged as a major focus for the church in the Vatican Council's final session. This was expressed in the final document, *Gaudium et Spes* (Church in the Modern World). The Pontifical Commission for International Justice and Peace represented the continuation of that impulse. Both conservatives and progressives agreed on the emphasis.

What the commission provided was especially the theoretical and organizational framework for human rights advocacy. More was involved here than passing on information; rather, the value of the commission came from its *interpreting* the meaning of repressive events reported. Paul VI and John Paul II then expressed these interpretations through hundreds of human rights pleas in various countries.

Creating the structure of the Pontifical Commission for International Justice and Peace was extraordinarily fortunate for Latin America, occurring just as human rights was becoming an acute regional issue. Latin American bishops a year later forged a strong theoretical link by the Medellín Conference (1968). This conference, as Livezey affirms, will ''undergird engagement by Roman Catholics in the human rights issue.''[69]

A major function of Vatican diplomacy is obtaining secure conditions for work of its personnel.[70] This is an especially delicate task when personnel are missionaries, that is, foreign persons working outside their countries. (In the 1960s about half of priests in Chile were foreign-born; about 40 percent in Brazil.)[71] Governments used participation in protests as the basis for exiling missionaries or for curtailing activities of personnel who are citizens. In the first two years after the coup the Chilean military junta forced 380 priests, 318 of them foreigners, into exile.[72]

However, the scope of activity for the nunciatures was far wider than protecting church personnel. Throughout Latin America papal nuncios and their assistants spent long hours in private audiences and phone conversations attempting to stave off exile or imprisonment for citizens, elite and ordinary. Archbishop Angelo Sodano attempted to persuade Pinochet not to exile Andrés Zaldivar, president of Chile's Christian Democrats.[73] This was but one of thousands of interactions between nunciatures and repressive governments.

Vivid insight into how this network operated came in Chile. As noted, Latin Americans responded slowly to violations in most countries, but Chileans were an exception (Table 4.2). Vatican response to the Chilean crisis was equally swift. Within days of the coup Paul VI expressed deep regret over the ''tragic drama'' occurring in Chile.[74] Three weeks later the pope spoke publicly of ''violent oppression in Chile'' which caused him ''profound concern.''[75] In April 1974, just before a national bishops' meeting, the pope sent them a message to reinforce their commitment to ''those most in need.''[76]

These comments were reinforced by international politics. Paul VI made a rousing statement on human rights in December 1973, using the 25th anniversary of the U.N.'s Declaration of Human Rights.[77] The Pontifical Commission for International Justice and Peace and the Synod of Bishops followed with reinforcing statements for Paul VI's positions.[78]

Another branch of the church network spread the alarm about Chilean repression in the United States. The administrative board of the U.S. Catholic Conference (USCC) issued "Human Rights Violations in Chile" in early 1974.[79] The Office of International Justice and Peace of the USCC joined with the Human Rights Office of the National Council of Churches and the Washington Office on Latin America in a broad-scoped program. They supported politically and economically the efforts of the Vicariate of Solidarity and similar groups in Chile.

Further, many national-level or grassroots organizations in North America and Europe pressured their governments or church boards to respond to the human rights crisis in Chile. These efforts thus brought mobilization at all major levels of the transnational Catholic and mainline Protestant churches.

This mobilization impressed observers, enraged Pinochet, and empowered gargantuan efforts at human rights protection and humanitarian aid to victims and their families. Within six years (1973–1979), the governments of the United States and West Germany contributed over $20 million to church-sponsored programs in Chile.[80] In the same period Catholic organizations in the United States sent almost $34 million, Catholic organizations in West Germany almost $25 million, and those of other Western European countries $7.3 million.[81] Protestant agencies sent about $10 million through the World Council of Churches alone.[82]

Major Protestant groups acted through the mainline Protestant interchurch organization, the World Council of Churches (WCC), or on their own. The WCC was exceptional in the creativity and magnitude of its response to human rights organizing within Latin America. Pinochet complained about the $2 million that WCC sent annually to Chile, much of it to the Vicariate of Solidarity of the Catholic Church.[83] The WCC carried on huge assistance programs to support human rights and humanitarian projects in Brazil, Argentina, and other countries. Human rights organizing within Latin American countries could not succeed without this larger transnational support.

Governmental Counterattacks and Transnational Responses

Within countries, Vatican representatives typically opened their residences for asylum for hundreds of persons running from secret police or army agents.[84] To constrict this flow, plain-clothed security forces closely watched nunciatures and other embassy residencies. It was thus that government agents saw Sheila Cassidy exiting the nunciature in Santiago and followed her to the residence where she was entrapped.

Military rulers and church officials had been sparring for two years after the military coup. A major confrontation occurred in late 1975. The DINA used the Sheila Cassidy incident to cast a wide net for anyone who may have sheltered dissidents. Secret police summarily brought five priests to Los Capuchinos, a political prison. Government officials held incommunicado Gerald Whalen and Fermín Donoso (Holy Cross priests), Fernando Salas and Patricio Cariola (Jesuits), and Monsignor Rafael Maroto (diocesan vicar for Santiago's central zone). They were swept up in an indiscriminate search.[85]

The Pinochet government wished to use this incident to put a stop to the churches' Committee for Peace.[86] The DINA struck while the major figure of opposition, Cardinal Raúl Silva Henríquez, was out of the country. Constable and Valenzuela explain: "[Colonel Manuel] Conteras, who viewed the cardinal as his one true rival for power, worked to undermine Silva and to tar church human rights activities as Marxist infiltrated."[87]

At first, prison officials held Whalen and the others in solitary confinement. Then government agents transferred them to Tres Alamos, a common prison. An emergency network had gone to work in Chile, the United States, and Rome. Within days, William Lewers, an international lawyer and provincial superior of the Holy Cross priests, traveled to Santiago. He worked with the Jesuit provincial to establish a strategy for prisoners' release in Chile, not in exile. (Whelan was born in the United States but possessed Chilean citizenship.) Both provincials also talked urgently with their congregational superiors in Rome.

After Cardinal Silva arrived from Rome, he and the two provincials acted forcefully. Silva assured government officials he had the backing of Paul VI. The years of expressing the human rights situation through diplomatic reports laid a groundwork for this support. (Silva was also on close terms with Paul VI.) The government released Whelan and other priests in time for Christmas at home in Santiago.

Sanctuary and diplomatic brokerage by church officials were familiar forms of action. John Paul II introduced an entirely new Vatican governmental way to open political space for human rights advocacy. No pope has made journeys an integral part of his diplomacy, as has John Paul II. Mass media made his visits events and recorded verbal messages and other gestures. When David Hollenbach reviewed the pope's themes on his journeys, he found: "The central place which human rights have come to hold in Catholic social thought is evident even from a cursory reading of the numerous addresses of Pope John Paul II during his world travels. Whether in Poland or Brazil . . . the most consistent and forceful theme of the pope's message has been the appeal for the protection of human rights and the denunciation of patterns of human rights violations."[88]

This emphasis became acutely evident in John Paul's visit to Chile in April 1987. By then conservative advisers such as Archbishop Angelo Sodano and Bishop Jorge Medina were attempting to pull the pope into a more conciliatory stance with Pinochet. What would the pope do (gestures being remembered better than words)? John Paul embraced Carmen Quintana, whom government agents had badly burned. He made a point of visiting areas especially affected by repression.[89]

His words about human rights made the front page of major newspapers. Robert Suro wrote in the *New York Times* that when asked on his trip if he expected to bring democracy to Chile, John Paul replied: "Yes, yes [although] I am not the evangelizer of democracy, [for] I am the evangelizer of the Gospel. To the Gospel message of course belongs [*sic*] all the problems of human rights, and if democracy means human rights it also belongs to the message of the church."[90]

U.S. Governmental Structures

The continuing Chilean situation was a major motive for the U.S. Congress's institutionalizing human rights concerns. A major step was accomplished when the State Department responded to pressures by creating the Office (later Bureau) of the Coordinator for Human Rights and Humanitarian Affairs. More, the law stipulated that the State Department had to make annual reports on human rights in all countries receiving aid. Congress made this first step in June 1976, before Jimmy Carter's election. Carter upgraded the directorship of the Bureau of Human Rights to assistant secretaryship. Then the State Department was required to make reports on human rights in all countries of the world.

Important influences within the State Department resisted the human rights lobby. They did not approve of making human rights a prominent part of diplomacy, nor were many embassy personnel trained in human rights law or reporting. Some State Department reports showed this reluctance and were poor, inadequate, or misleading.[91] With time, though, State Department reports have notably improved. Embassy and Washington staffers became more adept and professional in their handling of human rights issues. Some personnel devoted themselves, at least part-time, to the issues. The State Department also hired graduates of Columbia University's human rights and humanitarian affairs or similar university programs.

Now State Department reports more faithfully reflect the situations in foreign countries. These reports offer a mirror to offending nations who attempt to deny or ignore the negative views of themselves pictured by AI or the U.N. The same mirror is available to groups in Washington testifying against human rights abuses overseas.

The public side of human rights reporting by the State Department allowed human rights groups a double-barreled opportunity. They could criticize State Department reports and U.S. policies. Second, they had a yearly occasion to mount protests against human rights violators, such as Guatemala or Haiti.

The Lawyers Committee for Human Rights offered the most effective counterweight to State Department's sometimes arbitrary depictions of human rights situations. The members of this committee enjoyed status as respected professionals, with long experience in international law and contacts overseas. This gave it an unusual cachet. Many ambassadors come from the same backgrounds. (Of the eight Georgetown University alumnae who were active as ambassadors in 1995, five were from Washington law firms.)[92]

The Lawyers Committee for Human Rights began offering yearly a *Critique: Review of the Department of State's Country Reports on Human Rights Practices.*[93] By 1991 they had published twelve critiques. In their 1991 critique they judged: "Reports on the whole continue to improve and accurately reflect 1990's tumultuous events affecting human rights."[94] They went on to note the stronger or weaker country reports.

However, the Lawyers Committee for Human Rights made two telling criticisms. First, reports often had uneven treatments. For example, for Brazil, reports fail to mention threats and attacks on lawyers and key human rights monitors. Then, reports frequently mistake law or statements of intent for actual practice. This became increasingly evident for Mexico.

Other weaknesses showed up in the critiques. However, a remarkable change has taken place within the State Department because of human rights advocacy. Paul Sigmund notes the shift by the mid-1980s: "Within the bureaucracy, even in a conservative administration, there was an institutionalized pressure group for a more vigorous policy for support of democracy—the State Department Bureau of Human Rights and Humanitarian Affairs."[95]

Other Governmental Networks

At the time of the Chilean coup (1973) no one asked for asylum at the U.S. embassy.[96] In contrast, the Swedish ambassador, Harold Edelstam, as noted, acted heroically. Nunciatures and embassies of various countries offered sanctuaries for dissidents. These foreign residences became intermediate stops on the way to exile. Both sanctuary and exile are salient aspects of the human rights story of Latin America. Although sanctuary was presumed to be a neutral, humanitarian effort, taking in persons on the way to exile was also seen as criticism of the repression that was taking place.

Embassies most active in these activities tended to be those of North Atlantic countries. The embassies acted not only as safe havens but as conduits to a life in contrast to Geisel's Brazil or Pinochet's Chile. These embassies were links, too, to human rights activities back home. In Great Britain, Sweden, and elsewhere, domestic groups prepared residences and sought employment for exiles, published critiques of military repression, and mobilized for foreign policy measures against Latin American military governments. Caring for exiles became a human rights frame, an energetic political comment.

Foreign governmental human rights activities had a substantial reinforcing effect for domestic groups. When Jacob Timerman, the famed Argentine eyewitness to human rights abuses,[97] visited Chile in 1986, he uncovered strong foreign governmental support for the Vicariate of Solidarity. When Vicariate members had "need for shelter or escape, or seek special information through confidential channels, there are diplomatic missions in Santiago that act as watchdogs over the regime—the embassies of France, Italy, Canada, West Germany, Sweden, Spain, the United States, Argentina, and Holland.''[98]

CONCLUSION

Thus national, exile, and governmental groups and agencies seized political opportunities, mobilized protest, and framed images of human rights violations, melding into a transnational movement.

Highly organized transnational human rights collective action has taken place only in the last third of this century. If the Holocaust was the catalyst, democracy the context, improved technologies became the indispensable tool for making transnational human rights challenges. Judith Adler Hellman concludes: ''Human rights as a transnational concern in which domestic and foreign activists work together to influence international public opinion is not only new in its conception but also . . . relies on a network of international communication that has become feasible only in the computer age.''[99]

Wireless technologies eliminate dependence on government-controlled lines of communication. These technologies offer small groups in remote areas a degree of access to the international community that had been reserved to much greater power-holders. Equally important are the international receptors and bystanders impressed with the message. Local and national activists are thus able to conceptualize human rights protests more comprehensively and strongly when joined with transnational actors.

This advance follows not only from a turn to a democratic context but from a notable widening of personal vision. Emilio Mignone, the Argentine human rights advocate, was asked why a person would be interested in defense of human rights in another country. He responded simply: ''The defense of human dignity knows no boundaries.''[100]

NOTES

1. Sheila Cassidy, *Audacity to Believe* (Cleveland, Ohio: Collins World, 1978), pp. 137–139.

2. Ibid., p. 173 (trans. mine).

3. Early attempts at suggesting international linkages include: Chadwick Alger and Saul Mendlovitz, ''Grass-roots Initiatives: The Challenges of Linkages,'' pp. 333–362, and Richard Falk, ''The Promise of Social Movements: Explorations at the Edge of Time,'' pp. 363–386, both in Saul Mendlovitz and R.B.J. Walker, eds., *Towards a Just World Peace: Perspectives from Social Movements* (London: Butterworths, 1987).

4. Margaret Keck and Kathryn Sikkink, ''Transnational Issue Networks in International Politics,'' paper for Latin American Studies Association (LASA) International Congress, September 1995.

5. Alison Brysk, ''From Above and from Below: Social Movements, the International System, and Human Rights in Argentina,'' *Comparative Political Studies* 26, 3 (October 1993), pp. 259–285.

6. Ron Pagnucco and J. D. McCarthy, ''Advocating Non-Violent Direct Action in Latin America: The Antecedents and Emergence of Serpaj,'' in B. Misztal and Anson Shupe, eds., *Religion and Politics in Comparative Perspective* (New York: Praeger, 1992), pp. 125–147.

7. Ian Guest, *Behind the Disappearances: Argentina's Dirty War Against Human Rights and the United Nations* (Philadelphia: University of Pennsylvania Press, 1990).

8. Smith, ''Transnational Political Processes and the Human Rights Movement,'' in Michael Dobkowski et al., *Research in Social Movements, Conflicts, and Change* (Greenwich, Conn.: JAI Press, 1995), pp. 185–219.

9. In addition to Keck and Sikkink, see Thomas Risse-Kappen, ''Structures of Government and Transnational Relations: What Have We Learned?'', in Thomas Risse-Kappen, ed., *Bringing Transnational Relations Back In: Non-State Actors, Domestic Structures, and International Institutions* (New York: Cambridge University Press, 1995), p. 286 and passim.

10. Keck and Sikkink, ''Transnational,'' p. 26.

11. A more suitable term, ''advocacy networks,'' may supplement the usage of issue networks in Keck and Sikkink's analysis. Interview with Keck, January 25, 1996.

12. Definition adapted from Keck and Sikkink, ''Transnational,'' p. 2.

13. He is remembered as a latter-day Raoul Wallenberg. See Paul Sigmund, *The United States and Democracy in Chile* (Baltimore: Johns Hopkins University Press, 1993), p. 90; Mary Helen Spooner, *Soldiers in a Narrow Land: The Pinochet Regime in Chile* (Berkeley: University of California Press, 1994), pp. 98–99; and Pamela Constable and Arturo Valenzuela, *A Nation of Enemies: Chile under Pinochet* (New York: Norton, 1991), p. 54.

14. Sidney Tarrow, *Power in Movement: Social Movements, Collective Action and Politics* (New York: Cambridge University Press, 1994), p. 193.

15. Jackie Smith, ''Movement and Organization: Change in the Post-1945 Transnational Social Movement Sector,'' in C. Chatfield et al., eds., *Solidarity Beyond the State: The Dynamics of Transnational Social Movements* (Syracuse, N.Y.: Syracuse University Press, forthcoming).

16. Tarrow, *Power*, p. 191. Ian Herman Burgers, the influential Dutch diplomat, argues that the idea of human rights in our time is a revival of a movement begun in the early seventeenth century. ''The Road to San Francisco: The Revival of the Human Rights Idea in the Twentieth Century,'' *Human Rights Quarterly* 14, 4 (November 1992), pp. 447–477.

17. Jack Donnelly, *International Human Rights* (Boulder, Colo.: Westview, 1993), p. 6.

18. See Smith, ''Transnational Political Processes,'' esp. pp. 192–196.

19. David Held, ''Democracy,'' in Joel Krieger, ed., *The Oxford Companion to the Politics of the World* (New York: Oxford University Press, 1993), p. 220.

20. See, for example, Samuel P. Huntington, *The Third Wave: Democratization in the Late Twentieth Century* (Norman: University of Oklahoma Press, 1991), p. 3 and passim.

21. Smith, ''Transnational Political,'' p. 193.

22. Held, ''Democracy,'' p. 224.

23. Martin Ennals, later secretary-general of AI, still found this tactic "an amazing contention." Quoted in Jonathan Power, *Amnesty International: The Human Rights Story* (New York: McGraw-Hill, 1981), p. 10.

24. *The Observer* (May 28, 1961), p. 21.

25. Cassidy, *Audacity*, p. 224.

26. Power, *Amnesty*, p. 11–12.

27. Definition is taken from Jack Donnelly, *Universal Human Rights in Theory and Practice* (Ithaca, N.Y.: Cornell University Press, 1989), p. 205.

28. Power, *Amnesty*, p. 19.

29. Ibid., pp. 18–19.

30. Interview, Amnesty International, London, January 3, 1995 and AI External Bulletin ORG 10/04/93.

31. Human Rights Watch took its impetus from the Moscow Helsinki Group which issued dozens of reports on a variety of human rights issues. It initiated discussion, published statements, appeals, and letters, often at great personal risk. The Helsinki process served as a model for regional watch committees, including Americas Watch.

32. *The New Yorker* 69, 45 (January 10, 1994), p. 70.

33. For a sense of the human rights international groups taking part in the movement, see organizations consulted by Lawyers Committee for Human Rights for their annual critiques (New York: Lawyers Committee for Human Rights); and also consultors to Charles Humana's reports (New York: Oxford University Press, various editions).

34. The magnitude of their education and professional experience was much greater than many other exile groups, such as those from Guatemala.

35. Constable and Valenzuela, *A Nation*, p. 336.

36. The richness of the literary output can be seen in Jason Wilson, *Traveller's Literary Companion: South and Central America* (Lincolnwood, Ill.: Passport Books, 1995), passim.

37. See "Nueva Canción," in Simon Broughton et al., eds., *World Music: The Rough Guide* (London: Rough Guides, 1994), pp. 569–577.

38. See Chapter 3 of this volume.

39. Constable and Valenzuela, *A Nation*, p. 149.

40. Puryear, *Thinking*, p. 61.

41. Ibid.

42. See Tomás Moulian, *Democracia y socialismo en Chile* (Santiago: Facultad Latinoamericana de Ciencias Sociales, 1983); Ignacio Walker, *Socialismo, democracia: Chile y Europa in perspectiva comparada* (Santiago: CIEPLAN-Hachette, 1990); and Antonio Manuel Garretón, "La oposición partidaria en el regimen militar chileno. Un proceso de aprendizaje para la transición," in Marcelo Cavarozzi and Garretón, eds., *Muerte y resurreción: Los partidos polititcos en al autoritarismo y las transiciones del Cono Sur* (Santiago: FLACSO, 1989).

43. Donnelly, *International*, p. 61.

44. See J. Kenneth Blackwell, book review, *Human Rights Quarterly* 14, 4 (November 1992), esp. pp. 498–501.

45. Sydney D. Bailey, *The U.N. Security Council and Human Rights* (New York: St. Martin's Press, 1994), pp. x–xiii.

46. Ibid., pp. x and 125. See also Sydney D. Bailey, *How Wars End* (Oxford: Clarendon Press, 1982), vol. 1, p. 10.

47. See Jorge Correa Sutil, ed., *Situación y políticas judiciales en América Latina* (Santiago: Escuela de Derecho, Universidad Diego Portales, 1993), esp. Carlos Peña González, "Informe sobre Chile," pp. 285–423.

48. Donnelly, *International*, p. 60.

49. Philip Alston, "The UN's Human Rights Record: From San Francisco and to Vienna and Beyond," *Human Rights Quarterly* 16, 2 (May 1994), p. 378. See also the lengthy assessment of one year by Joe W. Pitts and David Weissbrodt, "Major Developments at the UN Commission on Human Rights in 1992," *Human Rights Quarterly* 15, 1 (February 1993), pp. 122–196.

50. Among many works providing background for the conflict or its settlement are: Joseph Tulchin, ed., *Is There a Transition to Democracy in Salvador?* (Boulder, Colo.: Lynne Rienner, 1992); Tommie Sue Montgomery, *Revolution in El Salvador: From Civil Strife to Civil Peace* (Boulder, Colo.: Westview, 1995); George Vickers, "Keeping the Peace: The History and Challenge of the Accords," *Harvard International Review* 17, 2 (Spring 1995), pp. 8–11 and 56–58; Americas Watch, *El Salvador: Decade of Terror* (New Haven: Yale University Press, 1991); Anjali Sundaram and George Gelber, eds., *A Decade of War: El Salvador Confronts the Future*; and Liisa North, *Bitter Grounds: Roots of Revolution in El Salvador* (Westport, Conn.: Lawrence Hill, 1985).

51. U.N. activity would only be successful by building on work already done within El Salvador to make new political spaces. See Mario Lungo Uclés, "Redefining Democracy in El Salvador: New Spaces and New Practices for the 1990s," in Suzanne Jonas and Edward J. McCaughan, eds., *Latin America Faces the Twenty-First Century: Reconstructing a Social Justice Agenda* (Boulder, Colo.: Westview, 1994), pp. 142–157.

52. See Ian Johnstone, *Rights and Reconciliation: UN Strategies in El Salvador* (Boulder, Colo.: Lynne Rienner, 1995); Ensalaco, "Truth Commissions"; Priscilla B. Hayner, "Fifteen Truth Commissions," *Human Rights Quarterly* 16, 4 (November 1994), pp. 597–655; and Nomi Bar-Yaacov, "Diplomacy and Human Rights: The Role of Human Rights in Conflict Resolution in El Salvador and Haiti," *The Fletcher Forum* 19, 2 (Summer/Fall 1995), pp. 47–63.

53. Johnstone, *Rights*, p. 86

54. Ibid.

55. UN Security Council, *From Madness to Hope, The 12-Year War in El Salvador: Report of the Commission on the Truth for El Salvador* (New York: UN, 1993)

56. For assessment of situation and future prospects, see Richard Stahler-Sholk, "El Salvador's Negotiated Transition: From Low-Intensity Conflict to Low-Intensity Democracy," *Journal Of Interamerican Studies* 36, 4 (Winter 1994), pp. 1–59.

57. Ensalaco, "Truth Commissions," p. 674.

58. Interview, Santiago, March 13, 1995. The *New York Times* (May 5, 1995), in an editorial, called the work of the U.N. a "heartening success." A *New York Times* front-page story (April 29, 1995) by Larry Rohter was also laudatory.

59. Donnelly, *International*, p. 64.

60. Ibid., p. 66.

61. Centers for dealing with victims of torture which exist in Denmark, Canada, Norway, and other countries also made substantial contributions.

62. Louis Henkin, *The Age of Rights* (New York: Oxford University Press, 1990), p. 24.

63. By 1992, the court had heard seven contentious cases. For a view of the court from the judges' perspectives, see Lynda A. Frost, "The Evolution of the Inter-American

Court of Human Rights: Reflections of Present and Former Judges,'' *Human Rights Quarterly* 14, 2 (May 1992), pp. 171–205.

64. Humana, *World Human Rights*, see comparisons, pp. xvi–xix.

65. Tom J. Farer, ''Collectively Defending Democracy in a World of Sovereign States: The Western Hemisphere's Prospect,'' *Human Rights Quarterly* 15, 4 (November 1993), p. 728.

66. One of the first treatments of the Catholic Church as transnational actor is Ivan Vallier, ''The Roman Catholic Church: A Transnational Actor,'' in Robert O. Keohane and Joseph S. Nye, eds., *Transnational Relations and International Politics* (Cambridge, Mass.: Harvard University Press, 1972), pp. 129–152. See also Stephen D. Krasner, ''Power Politics, Institutions, and Transnational Relations,'' in Thomas Risse-Kappen, ed., *Bringing Transnational Relations Back In* (New York: Cambridge University Press, 1995), esp. pp. 262–263. The Vatican has chosen not to be a member of the United Nations, as has Switzerland, but maintains an active presence through its observer mission status at the U.N.

67. The following is based on service as English secretary at the nunciature in La Paz, Bolivia, 1963–1964, and regular interviews with Monsignor Giovanni Gravelli and nunciature staff in La Paz in 1968–1971. Also interview with Gravelli, Santo Domingo, February 1981.

68. Lowell W. Livezey, ''U.S. Religious Organizations and the International Human Rights Movement,'' *Human Rights Quarterly* 11, 1 (February 1989), p. 15.

69. Ibid.

70. See Vallier, ''The Roman Catholic,'' p. 131.

71. *Foreign Priests in Latin America*, Special Note (Brussels: Pro Mundi Vita Institute, 1970), p. 3.

72. In 1973 there were 2,491 priests in Chile. See Smith, *The Church*, pp. 329–333.

73. Spooner, *Soldiers*, pp. 156–157.

74. *L'Osservatore Romano* (September 17–18, 1973).

75. *L'Osservatore Romano* (October 8–9, 1973).

76. Cable quoted in *Chile-America* 4 (January–February 1976), p. 50.

77. ''Message on the XXV Anniversary of Human Rights Declaration,'' *L'Osservatore Romano* (December 20, 1973).

78. Pontifical Commission of International Justice and Peace, ''The Church and Human Rights'' (1975), pp. 344–393; Synod of Bishops, Fourth General Assembly, ''Evangelización y derechos humanos,'' pp. 591–592.

79. USCC (February 13, 1974), p. 19.

80. U.S., $13.3 million and West Germany, $7.6 million. See Smith, *The Church*, p. 326.

81. Ibid.

82. Considerable financial assistance came from Protestant agencies in Europe and North America. Published and exact figures are not known. See Smith, *The Church*, p. 325, n. 100.

83. Ibid., p. 328.

84. In the controverted case of then Archbishop Pio Laghi in Buenos Aires, see *The Tablet* (London) (July 1, 1995), pp. 829–830.

85. Interviews with Whalen, March 1992 and March 1994; Cariola, March 1994; and Lewers, November 1995.

86. See Chapter 1 of this volume.

87. Constable and Valenzuela, *A Nation*, p. 93.

88. David Hollenbach, "Both Bread and Freedom: The Interconnection of Economic and Political Rights in Recent Catholic Thought," in Arthur J. Dyck, ed., *Human Rights and Global Mission of the Church* (Cambridge, Mass.: Boston Theological Institute, 1985), p. 31. John Paul's comments on human rights during his journeys fill two volumes thus far. See *Juan Pablo II y los derechos humanos (1978–1981)* (Pamplona: Ediciones Universidad de Navarra, 1982); and *Juan Pablo II y los derechos humanos (1981–1992)* (Pamplona: Ediciones Universidad de Navarra, 1993).

89. Pinochet managed to partially dilute the effects of these gestures by having photographs of the pope blessing himself and his wife at the presidential chapel.

90. *New York Times* (April 1, 1987), p. 1.

91. By 1990 improvements had been made but, for example, the 1990 report on Guatemala does not convey the severity of human rights violations and minimizes attacks on politicians. See Lawyers Committee for Human Rights, *Critique Review of the Department of State's Country Reports for Human Rights Practices for 1990* (New York: Lawyers Committee for Human Rights, 1991), pp. 92–99.

92. *Georgetown Magazine* (Fall 1995), pp. 21–25.

93. (New York: Lawyers for Human Rights, yearly).

94. Ibid., p. 1.

95. Sigmund, *The United States*, p. 152.

96. Ibid., p. 90.

97. See Jacob Timerman, *Prisoner Without a Name, Cell Without a Number* (New York: Random House, 1981).

98. Timerman, *Chile: Death in the South* (New York: Knopf, 1987), p. 115.

99. Judith Adler Hellman, "The Riddle of the Social Movements: Who They Are and What They Do," in Sandor Halebsky and Richard L. Harris, eds., *Capital, Power, and Inequality in Latin America* (Boulder, Colo.: Westview, 1995), p. 174.

100. Alison Brysk, interview with Mignone, "From Above," p. 281.

7

Response in the United States: Challenging Foreign Policy

As Brazil's military government turned from authoritarian to hard-line dictatorship, Washington and New York offices received emergency warnings in late 1968. Virtually all political space had been squeezed shut in Brazil. In December, General Artur da Costa e Silva conferred dictatorial powers on himself and presidential successors.

''A brutal military hand reached out to snuff out the last flickering flame of liberty in Brazil,'' wrote E. Bradford Burns.[1] The U.S. government hardly noticed, except to applaud.[2] However, Thomas Quigley and William Wipfler began reacting with increasing urgency. They perceived a new evil growing in Latin America. Reports from Brazil and elsewhere of torture, disappearance, and arbitrary imprisonment came in small bits. Quigley and Wipfler tried to piece together patterns and causes.

RESPONSE IN THE UNITED STATES TO HUMAN RIGHTS VIOLATIONS IN LATIN AMERICA

Informal Organizing

Quigley sorted through what was happening in Brazil from his office at the United States Catholic Conference's former headquarters in Washington, D.C. Quigley was assistant director of the Division for Latin America. In New York, at the Latin American desk at the National Council of Churches, William Wipfler had similar puzzlements. Wipfler, an Episcopal priest, had worked in Latin America. A stream of Latin American visitors brought them urgent and confidential messages of torture, death, and widespread fear.

What Quigley and Wipfler heard was new to Latin America. By 1969 they detected a pattern of systematic torture by Brazilian police and military. It was spreading to Bolivia. Staff members at the Methodist, Presbyterian, and other church headquarters, along with Quigley and Wipfler, became alarmed. They sought explanations from the State Department. U.S. officials excused human rights violations by Brazilian security forces as necessary to maintain order. After all, the U.S. ambassador to Brazil had been kidnapped by guerrillas in late 1969. Brazilian military rulers needed to control the threat of tiny bands of insurgents. Quigley, Wipfler, and other staff members were not satisfied with these explanations. They formed an informal Latin American Strategy Committee (LASC) to pool their information. They also coordinated their informal efforts to alleviate the situation in Brazil and elsewhere. Quigley, Wipfler, and a small group of Brazilian scholars published 10,000 copies of *Terror in Brazil: A Dossier*. The group urgently wanted to send warnings to wider circles. They relayed their information to the Inter-American Commission on Human Rights.

A wedge was being driven between U.S. foreign policy and its presumptive supporters. Bishops and church administrators at higher levels of administration than Quigley and Wipfler found it difficult then to be skeptical of U.S. official versions. Even less, they could not imagine taking an adversarial position with the U.S. State Department.

The close ties between North American and Latin American churches built up over the years now became crucial. In the Catholic Church the two distant cultures drew closer together at mid-century. The four-year process of Vatican Council II (1962–1965) played a major role in this bonding. So too did extraordinary numbers of Canadian and U.S. men and women who went to missionary work in Latin America. Many Catholics and Protestants in Canada and the United States found themselves thinking about Latin America for the first time. Religious leaders in the United States and Canada became informed of the growing repression by Brazilian bishops and by missionaries from the United States and Canada. Most of their visits, letters, and phone calls contradicted the official U.S. State Department story.

More than public defense of military dictators by U. S. officials was involved; invasive agents were also working. Father Michael Colonnese, executive director of the Catholic bishops' Division for Latin America, believed his and other offices were bugged and mail intercepted by U.S. secret agencies. For visitors from Latin America, Colonnese produced an electronic device from a desk drawer. "See," he said, "this shows what channel they're using."[3] Colleagues considered Colonnese's concerns extreme until months later.[4]

The Latin American Strategy Committee (LASC) continued meeting informally for three years. The Uruguayan and Chilean military coups in 1973 greatly increased awareness that more systematic responses than LASC's were needed.[5] Uruguay and Chile had enjoyed reputations for stability and democratic traditions. Their dramatic political changes shocked observers. LASC members met as quickly as they could, two days after the Chilean coup. That coup, reportedly with strong support of the U.S. government, pushed committee members to press for greater human rights protection for Latin America. Members now saw the need for a "permanent presence on Latin America in Washington."[6] They began a search for funding.

Founding of Washington Office on Latin America

Diane Le Voy attended LASC meetings, representing the Friends' Committee on National Legislation. A service branch of Quaker churches, this committee followed the traditions of peace churches and of American populist roots.[7] Le Voy was thus deeply committed to nonviolence as an essential element of mounting protest. She was also profoundly convinced of being able to influence government policy. While waiting to be admitted to graduate school, she assumed the first directorship of the Washington Office on Latin America (WOLA).

Some months later, with a budget of $400 a month, WOLA began operations. In Le Voy's mind: "There was a real social energy in the country. We wanted to pick up some of that energy and channel it in a positive way." Le Voy believed that WOLA was set up "not to be an emergency group but an ongoing source of reliable information" for Congress and the State Department.[8]

In 1974, WOLA was one of the first private groups to attempt to participate in the formulation of foreign policy decisions. WOLA was especially concerned with human rights in Latin America, anticipating later efforts by Jimmy Carter. In Le Voy's view, WOLA was "a red, white, and blue organization" speaking to Congress for American values.[9]

A wide spectrum of mainline Protestant churches and Catholic religious orders supported WOLA.[10] Many groups had ties to missionaries in Latin America. The impulse for WOLA was fundamentally an expression of missionary concerns[11] about repression in Latin America and about the conduct of U.S. foreign policy.

The WOLA took shape more as a social movement than an organization. It brought together interests of national Protestant denominations and provinces (regional jurisdictions) of Catholic religious orders. Its base of support widened quickly. From the mid-1980s onward, less than a quarter of its income has come from church bodies. The remainder continues to come from foundations and individuals.

The WOLA operates with a degree of autonomy. Governing board members offer oversight and public accountability. However, WOLA staffers also believe they represent the interests of Latin Americans. George Rogers expressed WOLA's understanding of its mission and accountability: "We try to represent the people in Latin America. We do not speak for the people who give us funding."[12]

Looking to the persons represented is a movement perspective. This contrasts with organizational analysis that would impose hierarchical analysis, and left

Allen Hertzke puzzled. He found WOLA unusually successful in dealing with Congress, but he concludes: "What is curious about this effectiveness is that [the Washington Offices on Latin America and Africa] operated with the least accountability to anything other than the vision of the staff."[13]

The WOLA became increasingly institutionalized. A long-term director for WOLA was found in late 1974 when Le Voy departed for graduate school. Reverend Joseph Eldridge, a Methodist missionary, had fled Chile. He worked for the next twelve years as WOLA's director or co-director, and brought singular energy and vision to the post.

The Methodist Church paid Eldridge's salary. The church also made room for WOLA's offices in the well-situated Methodist Building, next to the Supreme Court building. The WOLA was poised for an exceptional role as a broker in foreign affairs.

From Closed to Open Foreign Policy. Before the early 1970s a broad elite consensus existed on foreign policy. Several persons in the executive and congressional branches[14] formulated policy toward Latin America.[15] They depended on specialists within the State Department, embassy reports,[16] and, from time to time, spokespersons from more powerful U.S. corporations. For the most part, this process was unchallenged politically.

The circle of decision makers and embassy advisers was fairly closed, elite, and unaccustomed to public scrutiny. Ordinary citizens who would raise questions about Latin American policy decisions often found members of the circle unresponsive, secretive, and arrogant.

Mobilization from Latin America. A major cleavage was occurring in Latin America between some Catholic and Protestant missionaries and the U.S. embassy, USAID, and armed forces personnel in Latin America. In the 1950s and 1960s they shared Thanksgiving meals, played on one another's softball teams, and cooperated in hundreds of assistance projects. An almost universal determination to combat Latin American Marxism increased this bonding of Americans on a common mission. Fidel Castro's wholesale exiling of priests and sisters in 1961 tightened the bond. This close cooperation began changing in the late 1960s. Acutely attuned to Latin American views of the U.S. as interventionist, some missionaries began to distrust U.S. involvement in Vietnam. Older missionaries were also aware of U.S. history of interfering in many Latin American countries.[17] Many new missionaries came to Latin America with strong reservations about U.S. policies overseas.

In the early 1970s, activist mission personnel, veteran and rookie, found themselves side by side at meetings of Iglesia y Sociedad en América Latina (ISAL), Oficina Nacional de Información Social (ONIS), and many other clergy groups in Latin America then.[18] They began raising questions in public about U.S. policies. In embassy staffers' eyes this critical stance broke mutual understandings. Embassies had routinely sent invitations to missionaries for Fourth of July embassy garden parties and for receptions for visiting Southern Command generals. Invitations were no longer sent. Requests for USAID assistance, U.S.

Army civic-action highway, and other assistance projects were carefully screened based on loyalty to the official line.[19]

As missionaries witnessed the turn toward military repression in Latin America, they also heard Latin American interpretations for human rights violations. Prominent theologian José Comblin in Brazil and Chile pointed to the flawed vision of the Doctrine of National Security.[20] Latin American military academies and war colleges widely taught this doctrine.

The United States was accused as having a strong hand in helping to formulate the national security doctrine and in military repression sweeping through Latin America. Penny Lernoux captured this in the title of her widely read book, *Cry of the People: United States Involvement in the Rise of Fascism, Torture, and Murder and the Persecution of the Catholic Church in Latin America.*[21]

Lernoux's and Comblin's views may have exaggerated U.S. influence. They implied that military men universally believed and internalized the doctrine. Military secrecy and covert actions made this understandable. Latin American military doctrine was increasingly troubling to many in Latin America. Latin American bishops expressed strong opposition to the doctrine, especially in their Puebla Conference (1979).[22]

Respected Latin Americans, such as Hernán Montealegre, reflected a common view: "A new doctrine, that of national security . . . includes the disavowal and violations of fundamental human rights as one of its basic characteristics."[23] Some missionaries thus saw the militarization of Latin America as essentially flawed. For the first time they began using human rights as the frame within which they cast their challenges.

Mounting a Challenge. Defense of human rights became a major political challenge in the United States as well as in Latin America. Missionaries who went to Latin America on a crusade[24] would help to spark one at home. The impasse of activist missionaries and embassy staff, increasingly defensive of foreign policy implementation, found no resolution in Latin America. As a last gesture, missionaries attempted to explain themselves in Washington to Catholic Church contacts at the State Department.[25] Unsatisfied with lack of change there, they returned to Colonnese's, Quigley's, and other offices.

Missionary discontents were thus funneled to the United States. A final spark was struck in Chile. The participation of the United States in the overthrow of the elected Chilean government was ardently believed or sufficiently proved to warrant sustained and organized action to change U.S. foreign policy.[26]

Institutional church leadership could not provide the platform necessary for such an effort. Latin American crises called for flexibility, speed, and independence. Creators of the human rights movement clearly had the civil rights movement in mind. As Eldridge recalls: "The church groups that took on the cause of human rights in the 1970s were aglow from the victories of the civil rights battles of the 1960s, anti-Vietnam struggles, and the Watergate corruption scandals."[27]

These challenges and events provided a climate for change in Washington. The civil rights movement offered a repertoire of actions to replicate. The human rights movement learned two lessons from impressive civil rights victories. More than street actions were needed. They had to mount protests but the ultimate target was congressional action. Second, the country needed more than temporary change of foreign policy. Activists sought structural change through legislation. Instruments for human rights protection had to be built into governmental structures.

How could Latin America have an impact on U.S. foreign policy? After all, as Frederick Turner says, the North American public had little interest in Latin America then.[28] The human rights movement owes much to fortunate circumstances. Before 1973 Congress was apathetic about human rights in foreign affairs.[29] By contrast, vanguard organizations like WOLA burned with a desire to change policy toward Latin America,[30] especially human rights protection. WOLA began its campaign, as Virginia Bouvier says, just as a groundswell of skepticism grew in the American public about U.S. government agencies. Shifts within the U.S. Congress itself created a receptivity for listening to groups such as WOLA.[31] The movement needed a political opening.

CONGRESS: POLITICAL OPPORTUNITIES

Within Congress obscure congressmen were taking first steps toward change in foreign policy orientation. They were becoming active in 1973, a year before WOLA was fully organized. Representative Donald M. Fraser (D-Minnesota) chaired hearings on Republican foreign policy in the little known Subcommittee on International Organizations and Movements. Crucial for the human rights movement, Fraser framed his criticism of U.S. foreign policy in terms of human rights protection.[32]

Fraser and associates were thus positioned to pose challenges to the State Department. After the Chilean coup that year, speakers on the Senate and House floors soon expressed distrust of the State Department about what was occurring in Latin America. Ten days after the coup, senators quizzed Henry Kissinger about CIA involvement in Chile, during Kissinger's confirmation hearings. Assistant Secretary of State Jack Kubisch followed him to Capitol Hill three days later. Three weeks later, CIA Director William Colby made a similar trek. Sharp interchanges between aggressive questioners and these witnesses in Congress failed to produce full disclosure. Congressman Michael Harrington flew to Chile in late October to see for himself.

In November 1973, Richard Fagen, in the *New York Times*, wrote of "Lies, contradictions, and ineptness" of the American consul in Chile, Frank Purdy.[33] Also, in November the Senate called the Ambassador to Chile, Nathaniel Davis, to testify especially about the Charles Horman case. Davis failed to reduce concern about the disappearance and possible death of Horman.

In the Senate, Edward M. Kennedy, using his position as chair of the Refugee

Subcommittee, helped carry on debate about Chile. Paul Sigmund reported that a key informant, Mark Schneider, encouraged and briefed Kennedy. Schneider, "a former Peace Corps member . . . had returned from Latin America convinced that human rights should be at the core of U.S. foreign policy."[34]

Kennedy opened a campaign against Chile shortly after the coup and kept up the effort for years after that. Within days of the coup he and Donald Fraser proposed a sense of Congress resolution on human rights in Chile. Chile's coup thus touched nerves in the United States and intensified a human rights effort in the United States almost as quickly as it had in Chile itself.

Framing Issues. Contentious relations between Congress and the executive branch increased with the revelations of Seymour Hirsch in the *New York Times.* In several articles in December 1973, Hirsch revealed that the CIA (contrary to its charter) had carried on extensive domestic spy operations. Members of Congress, to their chagrin, found that they had been included in the surveillance. (Colonnese, now departed from the D.C. scene, felt vindicated.)

Hirsch's reporting was a small part of the media's role in framing issues of human rights and foreign policy.[35] Television and major newspapers carried conflicting images and interpretations to the American public. William Gamson may be correct when he says: "Media often obstructs and only rarely and unevenly contributes to the development of collective action frames."[36] Further, the media were, on occasion, manipulated.[37] At times, though, WOLA staff proved masters in getting out their message expressed through many outlets, including Bill Moyers, Jack Anderson, and *60 Minutes*.[38]

Films added considerable weight to framing foreign policy issues in human rights terms. The Horman case was manipulated by Constantin Costa-Gavras and Donald Stewart into the film *Missing* (1982), with Jack Lemmon and Sissy Spacek.[39] Although deficient in the presentation of historical evidence, the film had an unusually strong impact. Long-term observer of foreign policy Paul Sigmund believes the film "was a major factor in making the defense of human rights a major aim of American foreign policy."[40]

Other films helped to frame the human rights issues of Latin America for a wide public. Costa-Gavras's earlier work, *State of Siege* (1973), was based on political assassination in Uruguay and portrayed CIA involvement in security force training.[41] Hector Barbenco's *Kiss of the Spider Woman* (1985) and Luis Puenzo's *Official Story* (1985) showed Latin American views of the cost of repression. Two films made for television also had a strong impact: *Roses in December*, recounting the death of Jean Donovan and three nuns in El Salvador, and *Romero*, Raul Julia's portrayal of the Salvadoran archbishop. These films had wide circulation as class and family room videos.

Enhancement of Challenge (1973–1976)

The confluence of these further events enhanced the possibility of mounting a challenge to foreign policymaking. In sum, after decades of largely deferring to the executive branch, the Congress entered into struggle for control of foreign policy.[42] At the same time, political space was opening for small, nongovernmental organizations to pose demands for change in foreign policy.[43] From an elite enterprise, the policymaking process became more like a bazaar with many groups competing for attention.[44]

For the NGOs and some members of Congress, human rights became the central issue for changing policy.[45] As David Forsythe says of Congress: ''Human rights lay at the center of its renewed concern, a more durable and troublesome concern than many anticipated.''[46]

Fraser's subcommittee progressed in systematic hearings. They concluded with a final report, a first of its kind in congressional views of foreign policy: *Human Rights in the World Community: A Call for U.S. Leadership*.[47] The distancing of the legislative from the executive increased the need for independent and reliable information about the political situation in Latin America. The WOLA was well positioned to supply the need.

In 1974, WOLA was just beginning its advocacy in Congress and found a ready audience among 75 new Democrats elected to the House. The new representatives helped reform the seniority system and managed to unseat three senior chairs. Bouvier believes: ''The redistribution of power allowed nongovernmental organizations proportionately greater access to policy makers.''[48]

Human rights movement members established long-term ties with younger members of the House and Senate. These included Tom Harkin, Toby Moffett, George Miller, Paul Simon, and Christopher Dodd. Their interactions continued as these men moved into leadership positions. Two persons from the movement, Eldridge from WOLA and Ed Synder from the Friends Committee for National Legislation, contributed text for the Harkin's crucial Amendments. They included language calling for the United States to oppose multilateral development bank loans to governments that show a pattern of gross and consistent violations of human rights.[49]

Movement members performed two major functions: They furnished intellectual leadership (understanding of human rights and legal definitions) and information. Since human rights was a new term,[50] movement activists asserted competency in developing the idea and its implications. Their church ties and legal expertise gave movement activists a measure of moral and professional credibility. Their unmatched sources of information enhanced their usefulness.

The movement also served other important functions, especially on an episodic basis: representing interests of others (as ''voice of the voiceless'') and as program monitors or watchdogs. As a result, Forsythe says: ''Nonprofits in the human rights area were almost universally regarded as legitimate participants in policy making—especially from a congressional viewpoint.''[51]

The human rights movement waxed and waned. Like all social movements, it has gone through cycles of protest. Here the focus is not on success or failure but mounting challenges or retreating to inertia. The periodization of the movement in the United States lacks full analysis, but one may point to several peaks and valleys. Four periods of protest will be characterized.

The initial period from 1973 to 1976, already described, marked a determination to move from ad hoc, episodic activities to full-time interest group activities, especially with Congress. The challenge mounted largely was, some said, to the Imperial Presidency.[52]

Major Legislation and Decline (1976–1981)

The second period (1976–1981) was one of consolidation, anxiety, and waning in terms of movement challenges. Congress passed fundamental pieces of human rights legislation. These served as the framework for including human rights considerations in foreign policy. They were not a full body of law, were often ignored in practice during the Reagan period, frequently did not flow clearly from philosophical or moral convictions, but they were legal instruments. They remained laws and became more important in the 1990s, once the assaults of the Reagan years subsided.

Three pieces of legislation became major elements for foreign policy debates. The Fraser initiatives of 1974 had a payoff in 1978. Congress forbade security assistance "to any country the government which engages in a consistent pattern of gross violations of internationally recognized human rights violations."[53] (This became known as the Section 502B amendment.)

The following year Congress made funding of foreign assistance partly dependent on human rights performance. The so-called Harkin Amendment was itself revised but, as Forsythe says, "its intent was clear. Where there was a consistent pattern of gross violations of human rights, the United States should not encourage or reinforce such violations by economic assistance promoting economic growth that would benefit the repressive regime."[54]

A third major congressional initiative passed in 1977. International Financial Assistance required that U.S. directors working with World Bank and other international financial institutions vote for or against assistance based on human rights performance. For the first time Congress had a way to exercise oversight on human rights observance. To these three, Congress added others.[55] Prominent from time to time, Refugee Law was changed in 1980 to allow into the United States persons about whom there is a well-founded fear of being persecuted.

Carter and Ambiguous Leadership

The president began to share in leadership for human rights promotion. Jimmy Carter exceeded some movement participants' goals of seeking only specific legislation. Carter wanted to make human rights a major element of long-range foreign policy. Human rights activists at the time were directing their efforts to Brazil and the Southern Cone countries in Latin America. Carter accepted activists' critique of policy for this region. Carter, Secretary Cyrus Vance, and other officials emphasized human rights violations in the area. They joined with Congress in reducing aid, and helped to obtain the release of many political prisoners, including Jacob Timerman and Adolfo Pérez Esquivel. No head of state from that area found a ready welcome in Washington. With Carter's leadership, human rights activists made modest gains in access to the State Departments and to American embassies.

However, the Carter administration did not know how complicated a human rights orientation would turn out to be. For Central America Carter made only selective efforts at improving human rights.[56] However, he also managed to stir important public opposition (perhaps the first of its size). More than one hundred members of Congress signed a full-page ad in the *New York Times*: "Please Mr. President, Not Another Cuba."[57] Nor did Carter achieve a coherent human rights policy during his presidency.[58] The ineptness of his aides in dealing with Congress and Carter's failure to consult influential persons in policy networks made Carter's leadership (then) a liability.

CONFLICT: THE MOVEMENT EXPANDS (1981–1988)

The third period (1981–1988) brought the kinds of targets movement leaders find useful. More, it brought, for the first time, widespread grassroots support. A prolonged conflict between human rights activists and the executive branch followed.

Ronald W. Reagan entered office and continued for some time with a clearly stated Latin American agenda. This program adversely affected the lives of many Latin Americans and was deeply felt in the United States. Not only did extensive grassroots support for the Latin American human rights movements come forward but also involvement meant strong personal investment. Participants invested time and money and put reputations, even lives, at risk.

Ronald Reagan came to the White House determined to reverse foreign policy. Mr. Carter, he believed, had weakened the United States. In part Carter had done that by overemphasizing human rights especially in friendly authoritarian nations. Reagan raised Jeanne Kirkpatrick from academic obscurity to spokesperson for his views. First in *Commentary* and then at the U.N., Kirkpatrick attempted to show that Carter brought down the Somoza regime because of human rights violations. Then he would see it replaced by "a Marxist-Leninist dictatorship."[59]

The Reagan administration took steps first to address the Chilean situation. Reagan took office in January 1981. By February his administration began sending off several signals. His administration would allow Chile to conduct joint exercises with the U.S. military. The Export-Import Bank could conclude a technical agreement with Chile in preparation for loans. The U.S. delegation in

Geneva voted against further U.N. investigations of human rights violations in Chile. Kirkpatrick called for the normalization of relations with Chile.[60]

Movement activists quickly mounted protests, directed to the House where countering actions could be effective. House Democrats responded in March, calling public hearings to criticize Reagan's intended policy changes. Eventually, under intense pressure from the president, Congress first gave the president what he wanted in repealing the ban on military assistance to Chile. Then Congress took it all back with hindering legislation.[61]

The Reagan government would notably amend its position toward Chile in its second term.[62] His administration would criticize Chile for continuing human rights violations, now in a context of increasing world democratization. The human rights movement and the U.N. reports on Chile had made whitewashing a much more difficult enterprise.

Reagan and Central America

The main focus of Reagan's Latin American policy shifted to Central America. "No U.S. government has ever devoted as much of its political capital and the nation's resources to Central America as did the Reagan administration," concluded John Coatsworth in his history of Central American policy.[63] Similarly, human rights activity in the United States became focused on Central America. From April 1981 to 1988 the Reagan administration waged a sustained campaign against Nicaragua.[64] First, the government stopped economic aid, despite Nicaragua's need to rebuild after a devastating earthquake and civil war. A few months later the CIA began supporting a rebel force, called the Contras. The Reagan administration defied Western European and Latin American countries who wished to mediate the internal Nicaraguan disputes. The administration, in public and in secret, employed a full range of resources to assault Nicaragua. Officials deployed troops to neighboring Honduras, studied direct military intervention, and mined harbors. Funds were illegally employed and Congress lied to under oath. In the end, some 40,000 Nicaraguans died in rebel fighting and 250,000 were displaced. Food production declined by one-fourth. Inflation was at 31,000 percent. By 1989, when Reagan left office, the Nicaraguan economy was devastated.

Reagan also made aid to El Salvador a priority. El Salvador, a small country dominated by a military force with an appalling human rights record, received about $4 billion in aid during the 1980s. Paramilitary squads killed with impunity, including those best remembered by North Americans, Archbishop Oscar Romero, Jean Donovan, and three nuns. Civilian death toll would reach some 40,000.

After years of congressional apathy and then a brief period of assertiveness for foreign policymaking, the executive staked a dramatically tough claim for foreign policy control. Ordinary North Americans watched in some amazement at the hyperactivity aimed at Central America. President Reagan was much liked by many North Americans. Even his supporters found his Central American initiatives unusual. A majority of North Americans opposed aid to the Contras.[65]

Central America and Human Rights Movements

Nothing concerning Latin America affected Americans as much as this cause. The movement that swelled over Central America contained groups and individuals disturbed over what was happening to Central Americans. Human rights organizations gave backbone to the larger movement. Moreover, human rights issues framed much of the debate and furnished much of the motivation of the Central American peace movement.[66]

Central America furnished the spark for the movement to challenge U.S. foreign policy for several reasons. Legislators, Robert Pastor believes, "feel an emotional attachment [for Latin America] that is not manifested for other regions."[67] Presumably, the same attachment was true for many North Americans. The magnitude of death and disappearance in Guatemala and El Salvador approached Holocaust proportions. Internal wars with religious colorings were being waged in which many decent persons were dying.[68] Prominent victims, such as Archbishop Oscar Romero, gave a face to the issue.

Again movement leaders made Congress and proposed legislation their objectives. David Dent conducted a careful survey of interest groups and U.S. policy toward Latin America. Dent concludes: "Once Central America became the focus of attention during the Reagan era, the human rights lobby grew larger, often monitoring human rights legislation, foreign assistance programming, and democratization efforts in the region."[69] Within this lobby, "four human rights interest groups—Amnesty International, Americas Watch Committee, the Lawyers' Committee for Human Rights, and the Washington Office on Latin America—dominated the congressional debate over U.S. Central American policy during the Reagan and Bush administrations."[70]

The Catholic bishops and Protestant church leaders were among the first to respond to the aggressive administration's assault on Central America. Church leaders testified in Congress and spoke about Central America for national audiences. The Catholic bishops made strong and clear their convictions. "Outside military assistance from any source or party is not a useful contribution, but simply intensifies the cycle of violence," they wrote in November 1981. They also urged that Nicaragua be aided in its reconstruction.[71] Almost all mainline Protestant denominations took similar public positions. The Catholic bishops based their stands on well-grounded information. Archbishop Hickey of Washington, for one, had made many visits to priests in El Salvador.[72] Through the years, bishops from the United States met often with Latin American bishops on human rights and development issues.[73] The U.S. Catholic Conference had long-standing ties and ready communication with bishops in Latin America.[74] Mainline Protestants had a presence in Central America and other countries for almost a hundred years.

Mobilization of Resources

Reagan policy planning for Central America intensified. Stealth increased. Right-wing think tanks increased their efforts for foreign policy justification.[75] The Institute for Religion and Democracy attempted to counter church leadership.[76] National and more intense efforts to contest Reagan's Central American policy were called for. Hundreds of groups began forming at the grassroots level in all states to form challenges to Reagan initiatives.[77] The organizations ranged widely in their activities but generally managed a central focus, often coming together for specific actions.[78] Catholic justice and peace centers existed in some 90 locations, mostly in central cities of Catholic dioceses with members throughout the surrounding areas. Charles Dahm and seven full-time members worked at Chicago's Eighth Day Center. Dahm, a Dominican priest, had worked in Bolivia, where he had protested the intended return to Bolivia of billionaire Luis Patiño. He also continued to discuss issues with directors of Citibank and Bank of America. Returning to the United States, he reflected on his experience in Latin America while finishing a Ph.D. in political science and Latin American Studies at the University of Wisconsin-Madison.

Dahm and others at the Chicago Center found themselves drawn into a flurry of activity about Central America. They made direct arguments for Latin American policy revisions with Senators Everett Dirksen and Charles Percy and Illinois congressmen in their home offices, went on fact-finding (and dangerous) trips to Guatemala and elsewhere in Central America, used national corporate meetings to successfully challenge Coca-Cola practices in Guatemala, and helped establish the Chicago Task Force for Central America.

The range and sophistication of technical instruments and political repertoire were impressive. Hundreds of other centers joined in. They mobilized members quickly.[79] In many ways Eighth Day and other centers functioned as counterweight to U.S. media. The centers grimaced as CBS correspondents like Leslie Stahl reported that Reagan had his mind on Marxist Nicaragua. They countered with trustworthy information and historically based analysis. Among many activities Eighth Day never lost its focus: influencing legislative action.[80]

Parallel Protestant organizations, especially among progressive wings of Protestant churches, joined in.[81] Ministers, using bases in Madison, Wisconsin, and Pleasantville, New York, dedicated most of their time to educating congregations about Central American issues.[82]

Great conflicts began brewing within some Protestant churches. Bill Moyers caught this battle in "God and Politics: The Kingdom Divided," produced for Public Television.[83] One part deals with the United Methodist Church, with many of its predominantly middle-middle class, white members taking positions for and against involvement in Central America. By the time of the filming, Eldridge had left WOLA and was working in Central America. As an assigned Methodist missionary in Honduras he could show television viewers of the Moyers program the destruction wrought by Reagan policies in Central America.

To lesser degrees than churches, colleges and universities became instruments of education for some students who grew up after the Vietnam debate. Moderately conservative Calvin College set aside faculty and students for a year to educate themselves, the college, the Reformed Church, and a national audience on the issues involved.[84] Connecticut College had 15 percent of its students enrolled in courses on Central America. Ohio University and many other campuses came alive with courses on Nicaragua or El Salvador and with assistance projects.

Some groups were continuations of organizations formed in protest to the Vietnam War. Most organized specifically with demands about Central America in mind. Parallels existed with Vietnam. (El Salvador and Nicaragua, with their subtropical backgrounds, even looked like Vietnam on television.) However, as Gary MacEion wrote, mobilization was taking place especially among middle-class and lower-class Catholics and Protestants.[85] Recruitment was not primarily among young draft-age students, nor the liberal lobby, nor leftist political groups.

Further, many persons came into the movement through personal contact with Central American refugees or directly in Central America. Immigrants from Central America had not been numerous in the United States. Now they flooded into most major cities in the United States. Many found their way to churches. Some 300 church and religious houses even took the extreme (and costly) step of declaring themselves part of the Sanctuary movement.[86]

A pivotal group in the movement provided direct contact with Central America. Witness for Peace drew deeply from missionary experience in Latin America.[87] Catholic and Protestant missionaries, returning home in the 1970s and 1980s, became advocates for democracy and human rights.[88] Early risers among groups in the movement believed that ordinary Americans needed to see Central America for themselves. These groups conducted intense phone organizing. They sent twenty delegates from all over the United States and from almost a dozen denominations to meet in Philadelphia in 1983. There the delegates drew up guiding principles for Witness for Peace. Using nonviolent protest they would "mobilize public opinion and help change U.S. foreign policy."[89]

Witness for Peace took cues from the civil rights movement but played out their actions on a grander scale. Key to their effort was taking ordinary persons to see for themselves what was going on in Central America. Gail Phares, a former Maryknoll missionary, accompanied the first group. They went from a North Carolina church to the border of Nicaragua and Honduras. They lived with the people and saw for themselves the damage and turbulence caused by Contra forces. For the next eight years Witness for Peace took 4,500 persons from the United States to talk with Nicaraguans, high and low, pro and Contra.

Most Witness for Peace participants returned home burning with convictions that U.S. Central American policy had to change. At stake for them was what constructed story[90] Americans should believe: Reagan and his operatives' myth of America under threat or what most Witness for Peace participants saw, an undeclared and illegal war. As Ed Griffin-Nolan said: "They did what no member of Congress has done in the course of the Contra war—spend a week or two under the thatched roofs of campesinos who live in the path of this mortal threat."[91]

Their convictions were such that participants typically funded trips to Central America from their own pockets. Back home, they attempted to tell their story locally, speaking at Methodist, Presbyterian, Catholic, and other churches in thousands of engagements. Participants in Witness for Peace were determined that no American would be ignorant of what was taking place in Nicaragua. They then extended their vision to other Central American countries. They thus added extensive and vocal grassroots support to what movement leaders reported to denominational leadership and to what movement lobbyists were saying in Washington.

By 1985, activists had formed some 850 national and local groups.[92] The struggle against the war brought steady conflict over Contra aid in Congress. Men and women experienced in using the media surrounded Reagan. At home, in Europe, and in Latin America they used what Eldon Kenworthy calls a "panoply of methods" many deemed "inappropriate for use within the United States."[93]

To combat disinformation, leaders within Witness for Peace saw that the movement needed more than short-term visits. They began recruiting a long-term team of Spanish-speaking volunteers. At times numbering 40, these volunteers moved around Nicaragua. They collected information on Contra attacks. They challenged versions of ambushes, bombings, and kidnappings, versions given by the U.S. embassy or printed in the *New York Times*. They publicized the CIA's manual for terror.

A communications net developed from Nicaragua to Washington and to almost 1,000 activists nationwide. Movement spokespersons quickly conveyed information to local press and television and local offices of senators and house members. Tens of thousands took to the streets to protest Reagan's Central American policies.[94] Witness for Peace and many other groups succeeded in their aim of rousing thousands of ordinary Americans to move from inertia to concern about Central America.

Conflict intensified throughout Central America. The search grew for causes and explanations other than the constructed stories of the Reagan administration.[95] Phillip Berryman had served as a missionary in Panama. In 1976 he and his wife Angela went to Central America as representatives of the American Friends Service Committee (AFSC). This posting was fortunate for the Central American movement as their reports to AFSC resulted in Philip Berryman's widely read and highly regarded *Religious Roots of Rebellion*.[96] He then published *Inside Central America: The Essential Facts*.[97]

Assessment of Central American Movement

Through the eight years of Reagan's administration thousands of Americans stepped forward in the Central American movement. What did this massive effort, with the human rights movement at its core, achieve? Viewed from the grassroots religious groups who mounted challenges to Central American policy, historian Edward Brett believes the groups failed to achieve their primary goal: "They were unable to alter the basic direction of U.S. policy toward Central America."[98]

Viewed from Reagan's perspective, another historian, John Coatsworth, concludes: "The Reagan administration achieved none of its goals in Central America, though it mobilized vast resources and invested a great deal of political capital in pursuing them."[99] Coatsworth writes: No president "left office with so little control over events in the region."[100] The Sandinistas still controlled Nicaraguan government. The FMLN guerrillas were strongly contesting El Salvador's armed forces. Guatemala's first civilian president in years could not control either his army or dissidents. Manuel Noreiga dug in deeply to maintain himself in Panama against U.S. wishes.

Many persons active in the Central American movement satisfied themselves that their efforts had been worthwhile. They believed they forestalled a probable invasion of Nicaragua by North American military. They had vowed that another Vietnam would not occur. At least the Reagan government never took that step.

The urgency felt by many Central American movement participants faded quickly as Reagan left office. What happens to ex-participants? This is one of the least studied areas of research in social movements. Patterns described by Tarrow can be found among participants in the Central American movement.[101] Some experienced disillusionment, others bitterness (confirming for them and others why Americans hate politics[102]). A large number returned to political inertia. However, thousands emerged empowered.

HUMAN RIGHTS MOVEMENT: ACCOMPLISHMENTS AND FAILURES

This volume focuses primarily on organizing to protect human rights in Latin America. Within this narrower focus, how effective has the movement been? To assess the nonprofit human rights lobby groups, David Forsythe interviewed staff members or officials of nonprofits, Congress, and the State Department. He did this over six and a half years, from September 1979 to March 1987. He first attempted to assess factors that influenced change of policy. The most important were the temper of the times and the type of government official responding to the climate. Second in influence were the nongovernmental groups: "Their leadership, their quality of information, their image of legitimacy."[103]

What effect did the groups have? Forsythe judges this as "major change in American foreign policy on human rights between 1973 and 1979."[104] Overall, it may have been the temper of the times that explains positive acceptance of human rights. However, human rights activists capitalized on political opportunities. Experienced students of movements know that opportunity is key to movements, not conviction of grievance or depth of resources.

Nonprofits contributed in several ways. They collected information and painstakingly checked the authenticity of their accounts. Forsythe judges: They "knew well the legislative calendar and congressional personnel, and that leadership apparently recognized that the monitoring of executive agencies with the opportunity to criticize reports and embarrass officials—generated considerable influence."[105]

Nonprofit human rights organizations opened a way to change in national politics. The human rights lobbying groups were evidence of a new middle-class politics. This, as Forsythe says, is "based on affluence and leisure time, interest in reform, distrust of established traditions and procedures, and a focus on single-issue areas. Human rights lobbying was thus part of a larger phenomenon in American politics that led to new activity by previously weak groups which demanded new legislation and new agencies to represent their interests."[106] Thus some observers in Washington saw "the network of nonprofit agencies as "often a decisive factor propelling recent U.S. promotion of human rights."[107] In sum, the human rights groups furnished "much new information and many new ideas."[108]

The human rights movement primarily accomplished moderate but lasting structural reforms[109] of U.S. foreign policy (not just Latin American policy). A small movement, it has had an influence beyond its numbers. It focused well, not overemphasizing frequent and flashy demonstrations, but rather, change in laws and structures. Movement leaders wisely chose Congress as a target because new opportunities for influence occurred primarily there, and not in the executive branch.

Congress passed three major pieces of human rights legislation: linking human rights performance to security assistance, economic aid, and U.S. voting in international financial institutions. The larger Central American movement protected these laws and institutions in contested times.[110] The Reagan and Bush administrations could ignore but not do away with new legal structures.

In addition, requirements for information on the rights situations led to structural changes in the State Department. A new organizational branch and new positions appeared within the State Department: the Bureau of Human Rights and Humanitarian Affairs and an assistant secretary of state for human rights and humanitarian affairs.

With the passage of time, State Department reporting on human rights has become more professional and accurate. National security and national interest will weigh more in foreign policy decisions than human rights considerations. But a major shift in strategic thinking emerged from congressional debates, linking rights with security. Both sides acknowledged that extreme human rights abuses destabilize regimes practicing them.[111] Human rights are now a central issue in world politics.

Another major gain has been allowing Central Americans to work out a peace (and human rights) plan for themselves. Coatsworth, in his historical study of Central America policy, found: "Perhaps the greatest obstacle, which no one in the administration took seriously at first, turned out to be the Central Americans themselves."[112]

The human rights and Central American movements in the United States acted to support and to promote Latin American initiatives. The movements contested changes in the U.S. congressional or executive branches ultimately to encourage basic equality and the establishment of law in Latin America. It was a solidarity movement. (Some in the United States even believed this was weakness: Human rights and Central American solidarity groups represented foreign interests, not American ones.[113])

Which organization attempting to influence foreign policy in recent times was judged most effective by observers? Investigators found it to be WOLA.[114] Victory or defeat, the underpaid and hardworking staffers felt, were less important than the conviction of having to struggle. A poster in the WOLA explains: "Human rights violations cause the righteous anger that put fire in the belly and iron in the soul."[115]

Renewed Vigor (1989–Present)

Many former activists were exhausted by efforts to influence the course of U.S. actions in Central America. Others saw new political opportunities emerging in Latin America, ones worth working to enhance. Their efforts are central to the fourth period of the human rights movement (1989 to present). The dissolution of the Soviet Union in 1991 opened further opportunities for human rights organizing. Energy from the Central American movement flowed into renewed activity for human rights protection in Washington.

Political opportunities are still to be seized. In looking forward in 1992, Jonathan Hartlyn, Lars Schoultz, and Augusto Varas believed that many nongovernmental interest groups, public opinion polls, grassroots organizations, and organized lobbies would continue to influence policy formation and implementation.[116]

Further, the number of groups coordinating activities in Washington has grown larger, more technically sophisticated, and legally adept. The work never abated. Colombia, Haiti, Mexico, and Peru replaced El Salvador and Nicaragua as central concerns. Guatemala never ceased being a country of special interest. Turmoil in Chiapas received broad attention, because of trade, treaty, indigenous, and diplomatic concerns. In most Latin American countries human rights movements were growing, this time in response to democratic openings.

Amnesty International (with 1.1 million members, many of them in the United States), Human Rights Watch, and the Lawyers Committee on Human Rights stand with WOLA. They have strengthened their financial and organizational resources. Groups such as Maryknoll's Justice and Peace Office have opened offices in Washington. Altogether some 60 groups meet regularly as the Latin America Working Group in Washington to coordinate human rights activities.

Also, in the Washington area, the 10,000-member American Anthropological Association (AAA) made human rights an integral part of its institutional priorities in 1994. This empowered Thomas Greaves and the AAA Human Rights Committee to pursue oversight of Brazil's indigenous groups' rights and similar concerns. A strength of AAA is the vast networks anthropologists have with their overseas contacts. Abundant information about local and national situations passes frequently and almost simultaneously on e-mail and the Internet.

North American groups dedicated to human rights in Latin America cluster as well in New York. The Franciscan Network for Human Rights and Ecology maintains a formal liaison with the United Nations.[117] The man who coordinates these efforts at the U.N. is Ignatius Harding, a Franciscan missionary. He absorbed a sense of the struggle for human rights from grassroots activities in Cochabamba, Bolivia. Other nongovernmental groups have followed similar paths to First Avenue, New York.

Elsewhere in the United States, the Central America Resource Center has become the Human Rights Documentation Exchange. From its center in Austin, Texas, Tom Barry and associates have published many volumes on Latin American countries and rights issues. Although small in staff, Carter Center in Atlanta has become a major player in diplomatic negotiations, especially with a view to human rights. The Guatemalan Scholars Network presses on with refugee and indigenous rights concerns. These and many other parts of the movement continue energetically.

Many groups, such as the Latin American Studies Association (LASA) with some 8,000 members, have thrown themselves into the foundational activity of safeguarding electoral rights. One of the first major achievements took place in Nicaragua when notably free elections were held in 1990. Since then thousands of Americans have gone with LASA and other teams to guarantee fair elections in Central America, Peru, and Mexico.[118]

The bonding of North and Latin Americans through movement activity has been one of the best products of the movements. The experience of having to take a stand with Latin Americans forged for hundreds of thousands of North Americans an empathy they would not have had. The number of North American volunteers willing to monitor clean elections in remote areas of Peru, Mexico, and elsewhere impresses older observers who remember apathy and not involvement by middle-class North Americans.

If Latin Americans owed a debt to the United States and Canada for sending aid and missionaries, Latin Americans have now repaid the favor with a greater sense of shared humanity and human rights. This became clear when rebellion broke out in Chiapas on January 1, 1994. Human rights violations occurred at the hands of security forces. Within days, dozens of human rights organizations, Mexican and international, were present. Violations diminished greatly.

Legal experts from Minnesota Advocates, forensic physicians from Boston acted as if they belonged in Chiapas.[119] E-mail, fax, and phone messages transmitted within hours brought messages of alarm. In the early 1970s, when Brazil's military systematized human rights violations, the response in the United States was slow and sporadic. In the 1990s no lag exists between alarm and response.

The tightening of bonds brought an unusual step in November 1996. U.S. Ambassador James R. Jones pressed Mexican authorities to investigate death threats against members of the Miguel Agustín Pro Center for Human Rights. Víctor Bienes, a lawyer working for the group said: "It's never happened before and it wasn't something we were seeking."[120] This show of support showed further how strongly human rights have tied North and Latin Americans together.

NOTES

1. E. Bradford Burns, *A History of Brazil*, 3d ed. (New York: Columbia University Press, 1993), p. 461.
2. Ibid.
3. Interview, Washington, D.C., March 26, 1970.
4. Some members of LASC did take precautions to protect their sources of information. Some informants were at risk of imprisonment or death in Brazil. A key informant, Jaime Wright of the Presbyterian Church in Brazil, suffered the disappearance and death of his brother, Paulo. Many other Latin American informants were imprisoned or threatened.
5. The following account is based on Virginia Bouvier, "The Seeds Bear Fruit: Origins of the Washington Office on Latin America" (unpublished paper), and numerous interviews, 1970–present, by Cleary, especially with Thomas Quigley, Bouvier, Joseph Eldridge, Arthur Sist, Alexander Wilde, and current staff members.
6. Bouvier, "The Seeds" (p. 3), from interview with Thomas Quigley.
7. Quaker influence on transnational human rights movement is noted by Jackie Smith et al., "Transnational Social Movement Organisations in the Global Political Arena," *Voluntas* 5, 2, p. 130.
8. Bouvier, "The Seeds," p. 4.
9. Ibid.
10. Contributions came from United Presbyterian Church, United Methodist Church, Church World Service, Disciples of Christ, American Baptists, United Church of Christ, Lutheran Church of America (N.Y.), Episcopalian Church, Church of the Brethren, Mennonite Central Committee, U.S. Catholic Conference, Maryknoll, Capuchins, Jesuits Missions, Dominicans, and others. Maryknoll and the Methodists were exceptional in their support. Contributions through service included Wipfler, Quigley, and others on the board of directors. (The original LASC board continued for some time.)
11. Within the precursor group which gave birth to WOLA, members had worked in thirteen Latin American countries.
12. Interview with Allen D. Hertzke, in *Representing God in Washington: The Role of Religious Lobbies in the American Polity* (Knoxville: University of Tennessee Press, 1988), p. 86.

13. Ibid., pp. 86–87.

14. Jonathan Hartlyn, Lars Schoultz, and Augusto Varas believe that before World War II: ''No more than two dozen men, and on most issues the number of policymakers was less than half that size'' (in the Introduction to their edited work *The United States and Latin America in the 1990s: Beyond the Cold War* [Chapel Hill: University of North Carolina Press, 1992], p. 6).

15. The academic literature on the characteristics of U.S.–Latin American policymaking is not well developed. But key scholars and volumes furnish a valuable introduction. These include: Hartlyn, Schoultz, and Varas, eds., *The United States*; and David W. Dent, ''Introduction: U.S.–Latin American Policymaking'' and Harold Molineu, ''Making Policy for Latin America: Process and Explanation,'' both in Dent, ed., *U.S.–Latin American Policymaking: A Reference Handbook* (Westport, Conn.: Greenwood, 1995), pp. xiii–xxxi and pp. 221–247, respectively.

16. The sometimes strong, often ignored role of U.S. ambassadors is covered by Cole Blasier, *The Hovering Giant: U.S. Responses to Revolutionary Change in Latin America*, 2d ed. (Pittsburgh, Pa.: University of Pittsburgh Press, 1985); and C. Neale Ronning and Albert P. Vannucci, eds., *Ambassadors in Foreign Policy: The Influence of Individuals on U.S.–Latin American Policy* (New York: Praeger, 1987).

17. John J. Considine, *New Horizons in Latin America* (New York: Dodd, Mead, 1958) p. vii.

18. These included Sacerdotes para el Tercer Mundo (Argentina) and the Chilean Ochenta (later, Los Doscientos and then, Cristianos para El Socialismo).

19. Author interviews in Peru, Bolivia, and Washington, D.C., 1969–1971.

20. José Comblin lectured widely. His written views in English translation are in his *The Church and the National Security State* (Maryknoll, N.Y.: Orbis, 1979).

21. Penny Lernoux, *Cry of the People: United States Involvement in the Rise of Fascism, Torture, and Murder and the Persecution of the Catholic Church in Latin America* (Garden City, N.Y.: Doubleday, 1980).

22. See brief history of this opposition in Edward L. Cleary, *Crisis and Change: The Church in Latin America Today* (Maryknoll, N.Y.: Orbis, 1985), esp. pp. 157–159.

23. Hernán Montealegre, ''The Security of the State and Human Rights,'' in Alfred Hennelly and John Langan, eds., *Human Rights in the Americas: The Struggle for a Consensus* (Washington, D.C.: Georgetown University Press, 1982), p. 190.

24. Gerald Costello, *Mission to Latin America: The Successes and Failures of a Twentieth-Century Crusade* (Maryknoll, N.Y.: Orbis, 1979).

25. The author, as president of the Bolivian Institute of Social Study and Action, attempted to relate a point of view of social scientists, including some from the United States working in Bolivia, to George Lister and others in Washington.

26. See Paul Sigmund's careful review of events in Chile and the United States in *The United States and Democracy in Chile* (Baltimore: Johns Hopkins University Press, 1993), esp. pp. 81–84.

27. Quoted by Dent, ''Introduction,'' p. 6.

28. ''Public Opinion,'' in Dent, *U.S.–Latin American*, p. 207.

29. Philip L. Ray, Jr., and J. Sherrod Taylor, ''The Role of Nongovernmental Organizations in Implementing Human Rights in Latin America,'' *Georgia Journal of International and Comparative Law*. Supplement to vol. 7 (Summer 1977), p. 497, cited by Dent, ''Interest Groups and U.S. Policy toward Latin America,'' paper presented at International Congress of Latin American Studies Association 1994, n. 25.

30. While examination of U.S. foreign policy has been exhaustively carried out, policy toward Latin America has not. See Harold Molineau, ''Making Policy for Latin America: Process and Explanation,'' in Dent, *U.S.–Latin American*, pp. 221–247.

31. Bouvier, ''The Seeds,'' esp. pp. 19–22.

32. Fraser and his assistant, John Salzberg, have written extensively about foreign policy and human rights. See references in David P. Forsythe, *Human Rights and U.S. Foreign Policy: Congress Reconsidered* (Gainesville: University of Florida Press, 1988), p. 187, n. 1.

33. November 19, 1973.

34. Sigmund, *The United States*, pp. 88–89.

35. John Spicer Nichols provides a preliminary survey in ''The U.S. Media,'' in Dent, *U.S.–Latin American*, pp. 163–189.

36. William Gamson, ''Constructing Social Protest,'' in Hank Johnston and Bert Klandermans, eds., *Social Movements and Culture* (Minneapolis: University of Minnesota Press, 1995), p. 104.

37. Simon Serfaty, ed., *The Media and Foreign Policy* (New York: St. Martin's Press, 1991); Patrick O'Heffernan, *Mass Media and American Foreign Policy: Insider Perspectives on Global Journalism and the Foreign Policy Process* (Norwood, N.J.: Ablex, 1991); and Freedom Forum Media Studies Center, *The Media and Foreign Policy in the Post–Cold War World* (New York: Freedom Forum Media Studies Center, 1993).

38. Interviews in Washington with WOLA staff, esp. Art Sist, 1981–1983.

39. Leonard Maltin characterized the film as ''a carefully manipulated drama that works,'' in *Leonard Maltin's TV Movies and Video Guide* (New York: North American Library, 1989), p. 694.

40. Sigmund, *The United States*, p. 81.

41. Maltin, *Leonard Maltin's*, p. 1005, assessed the film as ''way too one-sided to be truly effective,'' but gave the film three (of four possible) stars.

42. See, for example, Cynthia J. Aronson, *Crossroads: Congress, the President, and Central America 1976–1993*, 2d ed. (University Park, Pa.: Pennsylvania State University Press, 1993).

43. David W. Dent provides an especially useful introduction in ''Interest Groups,'' in Dent, *U.S.–Latin American*, pp. 139–161.

44. This wide field is covered by Hartlyn, Schoultz, and Varas in their introduction to *The United States*; by Dent et al., in Dent, *U.S.–Latin American*; and Michael J. Kryzanek, *U.S.–Latin American Relations*, 2d ed. (New York: Praeger, 1990).

45. See esp. Elizabeth Cohen, ''Human Rights,'' in Dent, *U.S.–Latin American*, pp. 424–456; Jack Donnelly, *International*, pp. 99–132; David P. Forsythe, *Human Rights and World Politics*, 2d ed. (Lincoln: University of Nebraska Press, 1989), pp. 127–159. See also Forsythe, *Human Rights and U.S.* The pioneering and masterful study is Lars Schoultz's *Human Rights and United States Policy toward Latin America* (Princeton, N.J.: Princeton University Press, 1981).

46. Forsythe, *Human Rights and U.S.*, p. 2.

47. House Committee on Foreign Affairs, Subcommittee on International Organizations and Movements, report, 93rd Congress, 2nd sess., 1974.

48. Bouvier, ''The Washington Office on Latin America: Charting a New Path in U.S.–Latin American Relations'' (unpublished paper), p. 7.

49. Bouvier, ''The Seeds,'' p. 9.

50. "Most Americans think first of constitutional rights," says Donnelly. See his view of American perception of rights in *International Human Rights*, pp. 100–103. Eldridge claimed not to have heard the term in common usage before the 1973 Chilean coup.

51. Forsythe, *Human Rights and World*, p. 135.

52. Forsythe believes that 1974 may have been the peak of congressional assertiveness in foreign policy (*Human Rights and U.S.*, p. 12). But Forsythe's formal analysis ends in 1984 before Reagan's "Ad campaign" and congressional response in 1986. (See Eldon Kenworthy, *America/Américas* [University Park, Pa.: Penn State Press, 1995].)

53. Text of Section 502B is found in Forsythe, *Human Rights and U.S.*, pp. 175–179.

54. Forsythe, *Human Rights and U.S.*, p. 10.

55. Ibid., pp. 6–7.

56. See esp. Donnelly, *International*, pp. 112–114.

57. June 18, 1979. The ad supported Somoza. Within Carter's administration National Security Adviser Zbigniew Brzezinski opposed the Nicaraguan Sandinista takeover of government.

58. Forsythe, *Human Rights and World*, p. 110.

59. Jeanne Kirkpatrick "Dictatorships and Double Standards," *Commentary* 68, 5 (November 1979), pp. 34–35; and "U.S. Security and Latin America," *Commentary* 71, 1 (January 1981), pp. 29–40.

60. Other signals were sent as well. In March one of the Chilean junta members, Air Force General Fernando Matthei, was invited to visit the United States. Also in March, General Vernon Walters testified about the value of normal U.S.–Chile relations. See Sigmund, *The United States*, pp. 134–135.

61. For details, see Forsythe, *Human Rights and U.S.*, p. 104.

62. For a short view, see Forsythe, *Human Rights and U.S.*, pp. 105–106. For a comprehensive view, see Sigmund, *The United States*, pp. 132–178.

63. John Coatsworth, *Central America and the United States: The Clients and the Colossus* (New York: Twayne, 1994), p. 203.

64. Coatsworth divides the Reagan offensive against Nicaragua into four definable periods. See his *Central America*, pp. 176–206.

65. Opinion polls, as a general trend, showed only 30 percent favoring aid. See Kenworthy, *America*, pp. 102–103.

66. See Cynthia J. Aronson, *Crossroads*, esp. pp. 11–12.

67. Quoted by Dent, "Introduction," p. xxiv.

68. See, for example, Anna L. Peterson, *Martyrdom and the Politics of Religion* (Albany: State University of New York Press, forthcoming); and Victor Perera who sees the potential for "little Belfasts" (p. 331), in his *Unfinished Conquest: The Guatemalan Tragedy* (Berkeley: University of California Press, 1993).

69. Dent, "Interest Groups," p. 11.

70. Ibid.

71. Quoted by Philip Berryman, *Stubborn Hope: Religion, Politics, and Revolution in Central America* (Maryknoll, N.Y.: Orbis, 1994), p. 221.

72. Hickey had been bishop of Cleveland diocese which has staffed and supported parishes in El Salvador for some years.

73. When Archbishop John Quinn reported to the U.S. bishops at their semiannual meeting on his two-week attendance at the Latin American Bishops Conference at Puebla (1979), he received a standing ovation.

74. Catholic bishops were exemplary to the degree that Ronald T. Libby wrote in *Foreign Policy*; "Listen to the Bishops," *Foreign Policy* 52 (Fall 1983), pp. 78–95.

75. Howard J. Wiarda provides a view in "Think Tanks," in Dent, *U.S.–Latin American*, pp. 96–128.

76. See brief comments by Hertzke, *Representing God*, pp. 87, 110. For a controversial view of the IRD and the Christian Right see Sara Diamond, *Spiritual Warfare: The Politics of the Christian Right* (Boston: South End Press, 1989). The institute gained special attention in Latin America through the works of Ana María Ezcurra.

77. Edward T. Brett provides a vivid insight into their activities in "The Attempts of Grassroots," pp. 773–794. Christian Smith provides a masterful account of three largely Protestant groups within the Central American Movement in *Resisting Reagan: The U.S. Central America Peace Movement* (Chicago: University of Chicago Press, 1996).

78. Some of the groups, such as Network in Solidarity with the People of Nicaragua (1979) and Committee in Solidarity with the People of El Salvador (1980) were formed before the Reagan initiatives toward Central America. See chronology provided by Philip Berryman in *Stubborn Hope*, pp. 222–224.

79. Many Catholic groups coordinated efforts through the Religious Task Force on Central America in Washington. For a description of this group see Brett, "Attempts," pp. 782–783.

80. Its frequent mailings to thousands on its lists highlighted "Legislative Action," suggesting ways to influence senators and congressional representatives.

81. Interreligious Task Force on Central America, in New York, helped to coordinate activities of many of these groups.

82. Interviews, Dubuque, Iowa; Madison, Wis.; Columbus, Ohio; and Pleasantville, N.Y., 1977–1987.

83. Produced by Elena Mannes and Bill Moyers for Public Affairs Television and distributed by WNET, New York, 1987.

84. See the volume which resulted from their year-long reflections: Gordon Spykman et al., *Let My People Live: Faith and Struggle in Central America* (Grand Rapids, Mich.: Eerdmans, 1988).

85. Quoted by Berryman, *Stubborn Hope*, p. 224.

86. Brett, "The Attempts," p. 784. See also Ann Crittenden, *Sanctuary: A Story of American Conscience and Law in Collision* (New York: Weidenfeld and Nicolson, 1988); Renny Golden and Michael McConnell, *Sanctuary: The New Underground Railroad* (Maryknoll, N.Y.: Orbis, 1986); and Susan Bibler Coutin, *The Culture of Protest: Religious Activism and the U.S. Sanctuary Movement* (Boulder, Colo.: Westview, 1993).

87. Ed Griffin-Nolan, "Witness for Peace," unpublished paper, p. 2. See also his *Witness for Peace: A Story of Resistance* (Louisville, Ky.: Westminster/John Knox Press, 1991).

88. Griffin-Nolan, "Witness," p. 3.

89. Ibid., p. 7.

90. For views of construction and distortion see Eldon Kenworthy, *America/Américas*; and Nichols, "U.S. Media."

91. Griffin-Nolan, "Witness," p. 5.

92. Their variety can be seen in *Directory of Central American Organizations* (Austin, Tex.: Central America Resource Center, 1985).

93. Kenworthy, *America/Américas*, p. 87.

94. For striking examples see Brett, ''The Attempts,'' pp. 773–775.

95. For constructed myths, see Kenworthy, *America/Américas*, passim.

96. Philip Berryman, *Religious Roots of Rebellion* (Maryknoll, N.Y.: Orbis, 1984). A follow-up work is Berryman's *Stubborn Hope*.

97. Full title: *Inside Central America: The Essential Facts Past and Present on El Salvador, Nicaragua, Honduras, Guatemala, and Costa Rica* (New York: Pantheon, 1990).

98. Brett, ''The Attempts,'' p. 793.

99. Coatsworth, *Central America*, p. 165.

100. Ibid., p. 203.

101. Tarrow, *Movement*, esp. pp. 172–177.

102. See E. J. Dionne, Jr., *Why Americans Hate Politics* (New York: Simon and Schuster, 1991).

103. Forsythe, *Human Rights and World*, p. 156. Largely similar assessments are found in Abraham Lowenthal, ''Changing U.S. Interests and Policies in a New World,'' in Hartlyn, Schoultz, and Varas, eds., *The United States*, p. 77; and Schoultz, *Human Rights and United States Policy toward Latin America* (Princeton, N.J.: Princeton University Press, 1981), passim.

104. Forsythe, *Human Rights and World*, p. 156.

105. Ibid., p. 157.

106. Ibid.

107. Ibid.

108. Ibid., p. 159.

109. The focus in this chapter has been on structural reforms and furnishing information and interpretations. Others have made evaluations of human rights activity on foreign aid. See Steven Poe, Suzanne Pilatovsky, Brian Miller, and Ayo Ogundele, ''Human Rights and U.S. Foreign Aid Revisited: The Latin American Region,'' *Human Rights Quarterly* 16, 3 (August 1994), pp. 539–558.

110. The Reagan administration not only attacked outside human rights activists but cut short the State Department careers of employees.

111. Aronson, *Crossroards*, p. 11.

112. Coatsworth, *Central America*, p. 166.

113. Dent says: ''They often promote unpopular foreign causes,'' in ''Interest,'' p. 11.

114. Forsythe, *Human Rights and World*, 137; and Hertzke, *Representing God*, p. 86; Hertzke also cites Michael J. Englehardt, ''The Foreign Policy Constituencies of House Members,'' Ph.D. diss., University of Wisconsin, 1984.

115. Interview, Washington Office on Latin America, January 4, 1994.

116. Quoted by Dent, ''Introduction,'' p. xxv.

117. Human rights concerns are now intermingled in Latin America with environmental concerns.

118. The Carter Center and Global Exchange have been especially prominent in recruiting for and monitoring elections.

119. A number of foreign and national NGOs were already in Chiapas, working routinely on human rights and similar issues.

120. Victor Bienes, *Boston Globe* (November 29, 1996).

Bibliographical Essay

The readings and videos that follow have been tested with undergraduate and adult audiences for three years. Two indispensable resources ground the understanding of the human rights situation in Latin America. The first set includes the yearly and special reports of Amnesty International (AI) and Human Rights Watch (HRW). These external reports typically reflect internal, nongovernmental human rights groups' views. Note that *Human Rights Watch World Report* (New York: Human Rights Watch [yearly]) only reports on the Latin American and Caribbean countries that have more than average human rights issues. In its 1995 World Report, HRW did not deal with Argentina, Nicaragua, and many other counties. *Amnesty International Report* (New York: Amnesty International [yearly]) covers all Western Hemisphere countries, including the United States, but not the smaller Caribbean ones. AI and HRW (called Americas Watch when dealing with Western Hemisphere countries) also publish special country or issue reports from time to time.

Many human rights experts regard ranking countries based on human rights abuses or observance as an impossible (or purposeless) enterprise. Nonetheless, Charles Humana and associates furnish an approximate sense of how countries and regions compare in *World Human Rights Guide* (New York: Oxford University Press). The third edition was published in 1992.

A number of centers in the United States or Latin America deal only with individual countries or subregions. Among small groups that issue reports, Minnesota Advocates' publications, especially on Mexico, stand out. External groups dealing with Guatemala were for some time the only reliable sources of information.

As government repression has eased, national human rights groups have collected and published annual reports. Here are but a sampling: Centro de Estudios Legales in Argentina, Coordinadora Nacional de Derechos Humanos in Peru, Oficina Arquidiocesana de Derechos Humanos in Guatemala City, and Centro de Derechos Humanos Fray Francisco de Vitoria in Mexico City. Some Latin American governments have formed their own agencies and publications about the human rights situation. Two more systematic organizations are Mexico's Comisión Nacional de Derechos Humanos and Argentina's Subsecretaría de Derechos Humanos y Sociales, Ministerio del Interior.

The second set of indispensable resources for grounding one's understanding are the vividly described lives of persons touched by violations. Readers have found the following accounts compelling: Mark Danner, *The Massacre at Mozote* (New York: Vintage Books, 1993); Lawrence Weschler, *A Miracle, A Universe: Settling Accounts with Torturers* (New York: Penguin, 1990); Marjorie Agosín, ed., *Surviving Beyond Fear: Women, Children, and Human Rights in Latin America* (Fredonia, N.Y.: White Pine Press, 1993); Gilberto Dimenstein, *Brazil: War on Children* (London: Latin America Bureau, 1991); various works about Oscar Romero; and Ricardo Falla, *Massacres in the Jungle: Ixcán, Guatemala, 1975–1982* (Boulder, Colo.: Westview, 1994).

Selections from these resources could serve as basic readings for a college-level course. The present volume's seven chapters divided in fourteen weekly segments provide a didactic framework. To supplement this, Jack Donnelly's *International Human Rights* (Boulder, Colo.: Westview, 1993), is useful. He looks at human rights from a wide perspective. His chapters 1, 2, 4, and 5 are especially illuminating. Alexander Wilde and Coletta Youngers, "Latin America: The Challenge of the 90s" (*Peace Review* 2, 1 [Winter 1990], pp. 25–28) and Manuel Antonio Garretón "Human Rights in the Processes of Democratization" (*Journal of Latin American Studies* 26, 1 [February 1994], pp. 221–234) introduce readers to the contemporary situation in Latin America.

Elizabeth Jelin serves as a guide to issues from the past, such as settling accounts with torturers, in "The Politics of Memory: The Human Rights Movement and the Construction of Democracy in Argentina" (*Latin American Perspectives* 21, 2 [Spring 1994], pp. 38–58). To read the record of military repression directly, the University of Notre Dame Press has published in English the Rettig Commission Report on Chile. Joan Dassin, ed., *Torture in Brazil: A Report* (New York: Vintage Books, 1986) is the English version of the Brazilian heroic documentation effort.

Donnelly's *International Human Rights* serves well to explain the multilateral character of human rights protection. So, too, do Margaret Keck and Kathryn Sikkink in "International Issue Networks in the Environment and Human Rights" (paper for Latin American Studies International Congress, 1995).

When dealing with the evolution of human rights as an element in U.S. foreign policy, David Dent and colleagues provide a short and encyclopedic approach in specialized chapters, in *U.S. and Latin America Policymaking: A Reference Handbook* (Westport, Conn.: Greenwood, 1995). Older works, such as, Donnelly's "Human Rights in Foreign Policy," in *International Human Rights*, read along with David P. Forsythe's *Human Rights and U.S. Foreign Policy: Congress Reconsidered* (Gainesville: University of Florida Press, 1988) and Lars Schoultz's *Human Rights and the United States Policy toward Latin America* (Princeton, N.J.: Princeton University Press, 1981), help one to understand changes in making foreign policy.

But the personal motivations and the struggles of movement participants challenging U.S. foreign policy need to be seen in detail. Edward T. Brett's "Attempts of Grassroots Religious Groups to Change U.S. Foreign Policy: Methods, Successes, and Failures" (*Journal of Church and State* 36, 4 [Autumn 1994]), pp. 773–794 and Christian Smith's *Resisting Reagan: The U.S. Central America Peace Movement* (Chicago: University of Chicago Press, 1996) are well-written accounts of groups that vigorously participated in the movement.

Sidney Tarrow's *Power in Movement* (New York: Cambridge University Press, 1994) and similar works provide useful introductions to the theoretical framing of the human rights movement. Tarrow's work was hailed as a masterly synthesis. Other works in this rapidly developing field include: Thomas Risse-Kappen, ed., *Bringing Transnational Relations Back In* (New York: Cambridge University Press, 1995) and Doug McAdam, John D. McCarthy, and Mayer N. Zeld, eds., *Comparative Perspectives on Social Movements* (New York: Cambridge University Press, 1996).

Videos convey better than many books a sense of urgency about human rights protection. Care is sometimes required not to unduly focus on the sensational quality of the reporting but on persons who respond to violations. One could, for example, emphasize the cheapness of murder in Brazil or the dedicated human rights attorneys who appear in "Getting Away with Murder" (CBS, *60 Minutes*, December 1, 1991). Segments of this video have unfailingly drawn viewers into major human rights issues. Other salient *60 Minutes* videos include "Subcomandante Marcos" (December 31, 1995), "Jennifer Harbury" (November 6, 1994), and "Tales from a Dirty War" (April 2, 1995).

"Americas" (Annenberg/CPB Collection) contains ten hours of priceless footage which one may extract as appropriate. So, too, does the hour-long "The Houses Are Full of Smoke. Vol. 2: Guatemala" (Mystic Fire Video). Many documentaries from the 1980s strike viewers as dated and one-sided. However, the "Dance of Hope" (First Run Features) about the women of Chile still impresses audiences. Critics and teachers consider as standards three films: *Missing, The Official Story* (both available through Facets Multi-Media), and *Romero* (Vidmark Entertainment). These could be the basis of any educational experience dealing with human rights in Latin America.

Index

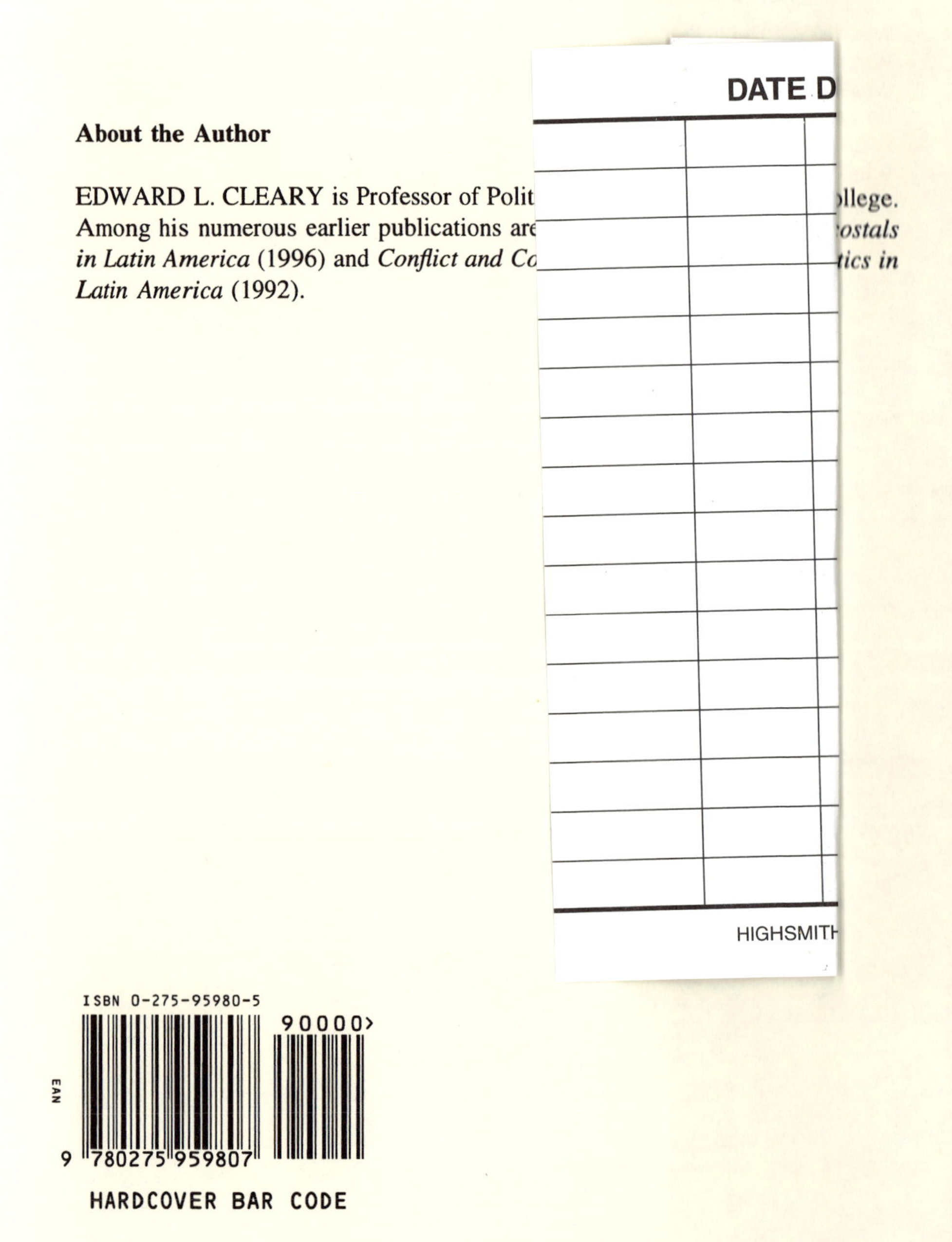

About the Author

EDWARD L. CLEARY is Professor of Polit ... llege. Among his numerous earlier publications are ... ostals *in Latin America* (1996) and *Conflict and Co* ... *tics in Latin America* (1992).

ISBN 0-275-95980-5

90000>

EAN

9 780275 959807

HARDCOVER BAR CODE